Changing Face of Women in Literature

The Flaming Spirit

Changing Face of Women in Literature

The Flaming Spirit

K.V. Dominic

GNOSIS

Nurturing the Aspirations

Worldwide Circulation through Authorspress Global Network
First Published in 2012
by
GNOSIS
(An Imprint of Authorspress)

Editorial
Q-2A Hauz Khas Enclave
New Delhi-110 016

Marketing
E-35/103, Jawahar Park
Laxmi Nagar, Delhi-110 092

e-mails: authorspress@rediffmail.com; authorspress@hotmail.com
Website: www.authorspressbooks.com

Changing Face of Women in Literature
The Flaming Spirit

ISBN 978-93-81030-34-9

Printed in India at Tarun Offset, Delhi.

Dedicated to

Sudarshan Kcherry

the motivating power behind the book

Preface

I have brought out several edited books on different genres of English literature—poetry, fiction including short stories—as well as on women writers, Diaspora literature, Canadian literature etc. But this edited book, unlike the earlier ones, is something special and unique. I haven't come across any such book focused on daring or brave women characters in English literature. The female protagonists in most of the novels, plays and short stories in Indian literature—both vernacular and English—are characteristic, representative Indian women—passive, submissive, slavish preys of patriarchy. Their plight in Indian society is very pathetic and hence it is the duty of the entire people—the rulers and the ruled—to bring women forward into the mainstream of the society including homes. As we Indians have the tendency to copy and imitate the West—very much needed in this multicultural, umbrella world—Indian women should rise above and overcome patriarchy as the Western women have done.

Though there are many feminist writers in India, it is a pity that there are only a few writers who have created immortal, ideal heroines who can inspire the society. Even though the actual scenario of women in India is the opposite, the writers should create an ideality by which the readers can long for or aspire for such women in the society. This book in fact is a search for such ideal women characters in novels, plays and short stories.

There are 28 research articles in this book. All except one are written by university/college professors, teachers and research scholars. There are three articles on African literature, one on *Lear's Daughters* by Women's Theatre Group (London), and rest 24 on Indian Literature in English, including Diaspora.

The chief motivator of this book is my own bosom friend, Sudarshan Kcherry, the publisher of Authorspress/Gnosis/Access to whom this book is dedicated. He has been the source of inspiration for hundreds of writers, editors and publishers. I don't think that there is any other publisher in the world who so matches with his talents and qualities. He is such a unique gem. Inexpressible is my mind to profusely offer my gratitude to him. Let the Almighty continue to give him strength and enlightenment to inspire more and more writers to exalted works. Before winding up my brief preface I extend my gratitude to all the contributors of this book who have made this book a reality. Wishing all the readers a real mental feast.

Dr. K.V. Dominic

List of Contributors

P.C.K. Prem, (IAS Rtd.) Trilingual poet, critic, novelist, short story writer. Palampur, Kangra, Himachal Pradesh.

G. Dominic Savio, Associate Professor of English, The American College, Madurai.

S.J. Kala, Assistant Professor of English, Fatima College, Madurai.

K.V. Dominic (Rtd. Professor of English), English poet, critic, short story writer, editor. Secretary, Guild of Indian English Writers, Editors and Critics (GIEWEC), Kannappilly, Thodupuzha East, Kerala

Aju Mukhopadhyay, Bilingual poet, critic, short story writer, novelist, essayist. Pondicherry.

Aleyamma John, Associate Professor and Head of the Department of English, Christian College, Kattakada, Kerala.

Asha Susan Jacob, Associate Professor, Department of English, St. Thomas College, Kozhencherry, Kerala.

Avis Joseph, Lecturer in English, Ibra College of Technology, Sultanate of Oman.

Bhaskar Roy Barman, Bilingual poet, critic, short story writer. Agartala, West Tripura.

Eliza Joseph, Associate Professor of English, Government College Thrissur, Kerala, India.

Kavitha Gopalakrishnan, Assistant Professor of English, Viswajyoti College of Engineering and Technology, Vazhakulam, Muvattupuzha, Kerala.

Grishma Khobragade, Assistant Professor of English, Birla College of Arts, Science & Commerce Kalyan, Dist: Thane- 421301, Maharshtra.

Kiran Thakur, Lecturer in Communication Skills. NIT, Hamirpur, Himachal Pradesh.

Lata Mishra, English Critic, Poet, Editor, Associate Professor of English, Govt. KRG (Autonomous) PG College, Gwalior, Madhya Pradesh.

Manoj Kumar, Lecturer, Dept. of English, Indira Kala Sangit Vishwavidyalaya, Khairagarh, Chhattisgarh.

Prameela K.P., Lecturer in Hindi as well as Coordinator, Centre for Translation Studies, SSUS, Kalady, Kerala.

H.S. Komalesha, Assistant Professor of English, Department of Humanities and Social Sciences, Indian Institute of Technology Kharagpur.

Priyanka Tripathi, Senior Lecturer in English, ITS Engineering College, Greater Noida, Uttar Pradesh.

V. Ramesh, Senior Lecturer in English, Thiagarajar Polytechnic College, Salem, Tamil Nadu.

Sangeeta Sharma, Associate Professor of English, Birla College, Kalyan, Maharashtra.

Satendra Kumar, Head of the Department of English, Government P.G. College, Lansdowne, Pauri Garhwal, Uttarakhand.

Sr. Sophy Pereppadan, Associate Professor, Department of English, Prajyoti Niketan College, Pudukad, Kerala.

Sujarani Mathew, Assistant Professor of English, K.E. College, Mannanam, Kerala.

Joydeep Banerjee, Associate Professor of English, Department of Humanities and Social Sciences, National Institute of Technology, Durgapur.

Taniya Chakraborty, Institute Research Scholar, Department of Humanities and Social Sciences, National Institute of Technology, Durgapur.

Trayee Sinha, PhD Research Scholar, Women's Studies Research Centre, University of Calcutta, Kolkata.

Contents

1

A Woman's Struggle for Identity with Special Reference to Anita Desai's *Where Shall We Go This Summer*

P.C.K. Prem

Born in June 1937, Anita Desai has a German mother and an Indian father. She grew up during World War II which had left a deep impact in her life and sensibilities as it was a collective conscience of two countries. Germany was a vastly devastated country and so she realized the pains of a rootless mother. The mother of four children, she had time for literary pursuits where emotions play a significant role.

As a teacher, Anita had always been a source of inspiration for many writers. Her education had been in Delhi and the family being quite unconventional in attitude towards life and relationships, these characteristics find ample expression in various creative works. Most of the women characters are constantly fighting within to emerge out as individuals of independence, one finds. At times, they are triumphant but most of the time disappointment dampens the spirits of life.

A widely read novelist, short story and children's author, so far her novels include: *Cry, The Peacock* (1963), *Voices in the City* (1965), *Where Shall We Go This Summer?* (1975), *Fire on the Mountain* (1977), *Games at Twilight and Other Stories, The Peacock Garden* (1979), *Clear Light of Day* (1980), *The Village by the Sea* (1982), *In Custody* (1984), *Baumgartner's Bombay*

(1987), *Journey to Ithaca* (1995), *Fasting, Feasting* (2000), *Diamond Dust and Other Stories* (2000) and *The Zig Zag Way* (2004).

Desai has a distinctive style, and the characters she creates remain original throughout and suffer a normal man's agonies with equanimity. She is realistic and highly personalized in the depiction of characters and scenarios of life. She does not stick to a theme but changes quite often, and so there is variety and freshness. Experience of life, interlinking of relations and creeping strains do a lot to build up a stable basis for a novel. At times, one finds, there is an attempt to deal with whatever is the best and the worst in the Eastern and the Western cultures, and traditions, and thus a conflict is constructed. She is a serious creative writer and in each novel, one can easily discern her anxiety about truth and reality. She is an author profoundly worried about the essential qualities of virtue and vice found in human beings who rarely contemplate on life beyond death or before birth. It is very much a living in flesh and blood.

When one studies *Where Shall We Go This Summ*er? one undertakes a journey into the psychological areas of a woman's heart. Here, the tale revolves around Sita, a suffering wife. These areas are beleaguered and partially devastated by the callousness of man—a husband. A hurt psyche travels to encompass the entire life and ultimately lands up nowhere. A woman confronts materialistic and emotional problems, and naturally, she looks up at her man for consolation. These are initial reactions. However, the situation at home worsens where financial and social security play a significant role. She feels stressed and consequently revolting feelings begin to erupt. In a fierce inner struggle, there is an ardent desire to get rid of the shackles of man's barriers. The woman fights out; gets hurt within. Here, outer incidents and inconveniences that a wife faces while going out with children and baby in the womb to another place to spend some time, get appropriate depiction in terms of sufferings of the heart. Sita had not been keeping amiable relationship with Raman, her husband. She gets no emotional security from him. It is a cold love affair with plenty of children. It is pleasure, it is pain and it is disgust saturated with pleasure. A common woman's inner feelings these are when she finds an apathetic man around. She observes:

> She had had four children with pride, with pleasure-sensual, emotional, Freudian, every kind of pleasure-with all the placid serenity that supposedly goes with pregnancy and parturition. Her husband was puzzled; therefore, when the firth time she told him she was pregnant, she did so with a quite paranoiac show of rage, fear, and revolt.
>
> (*Where Shall We Go This Summer*? 31-32)

This is Sita's understanding. It is unfortunate that she does not recognize the participation she had in this creativity. One is surprised at the insensitivity, which remains mystic. A woman at her age, if she finds fault with the man, there is something drastically wrong. That it fills her with anger and resentment and consequent feeling of rebellion against the social set-up, is not understandable. A man's reaction is equally despicable but natural, it appears.

> He stared at her with a distaste that told here it did not become her –a a woman now in her forties, graying, aging, to behave with such a total lack of control.
>
> (*Where Shall We Go This Summer*? 32)

At this stage, signs of revolt surface with slightly changed contours. Sita's desire for independence is evident when she decides to spend some time in a distant place, an island–Manori—her father had purchased long back. She is in search of love and affection. She also wants freedom but husband Raman is occupied. He does not speak much, observes mystifying silence or perhaps, it is more reasonable to say that he does not know what to talk when he has nothing to talk. For, he does not know that when one has nothing to talk, it is talk of love and love which fills the gap of an otherwise empty and vacant marital life, which is the consequence of living together without sharing the real feelings of love excepting the exciting physical relationship that lengthens out to drabness and boredom, quite killing. Here, loneliness stares in the face of a married woman when her man is busy elsewhere, either in business or in extra jaunts with another woman. This background of Sita's married life is essential to know the tensions she carries without any let-up.

The seeds of a disharmonious married life are sown in the beginning. The marriage with Raman is not an exciting affair. She dislikes the relation. She thanks this relation forced on her. Raman spares little time to spend with the family. He is more interested in material things of life. Though he tries to meet the requirement of the family yet there emerges emotional an vacuum difficult to fill. She thinks it is mercy and generosity, which gives birth to an unpleasant relationship. Incongruity of emotions and thoughts chill her, and life becomes a burden on her. Agonies inexplicable results in relations unwanted. When passions and love evaporates, she feels emptiness and recalls the days spent with her father in the island. Therefore, in order to run away from relations sans infatuation, she decides to go to the Manori Island, which becomes a symbol of insurgence within.

At that time, she has been nursing feelings of revolt and vengeance and leaves two children with Raman. She decides to spend time in the island with Menaka and Karan. The names of children create legendary feelings but undoubtedly dampen the enthusiasm as one remembers those figures. One gives birth to a child and deserts the baby on the river bank and the other lives an extremely tragic life. The very action to go to the island indicates rebellious spirits but later on the determination fizzles out.

As observed elsewhere, Sita is in search of a freedom but something restricts. She strikes at the root of traditions but, not quite obviously, withdraws. The surroundings increase sufferings when one observes the market of Marve. The teastall and the noise, the hustle and bustle around, raw and abusive language and the filth and dirt along the path appear gloomy, assailing Sita's sensitive mind, clamouring for autonomy. Tiny details of the bazaar with shops selling different goods from cigarettes to tears to liquor saturated with dirty pranks disturb her since these offer an authentic inner explanation of a woman tortured by the vagaries of marital life, and in the process, seek liberty. At another level, when a person suffers without fighting out or if struggling to achieve a semblance of a triumph, exits brusquely surrendering to traditional ways of life, it looks quite disastrous.

Sita observes Ali, Joseph, Miriam, Moses and Jamila. Their hilarious and at times, uncivil way of interface, appear intimate. She tries to identify inner pains with the lives of those who come into contact. At the psychological level, it is an escape to freedom with a determination to fight for personal liberty. Here, her attitude and mental areas speak of women who in hours of sufferings, because of the listless behaviour of their men, try to invent ways of fighting out against tyranny undesired, or manipulate situations to their advantage in a deadly manner.

A prolonged standoff between Raman and Sita has turned her into a stubborn woman. Now, passions are dead, warmth is icy and she is crude and harsh.

The rebel in Sita finds the world quite disorganized. Raman has been cruel. She is unwilling to give birth to the fifth child much against the wishes of Raman. However, she does not find it so easy. Here, she not only holds Raman responsible for a discriminatory treatment but thinks society is also equally guilty if she lives a lonely life. It appears the mystic powers and influences of her father are the cause of rebellion. To seek glory in the present is impossible, and going back to a loaned prestige and honour of a dead father adds to the already heightened sense of revolt, and then the consequent pessimism. One characteristic remains alive. It is the spirit of breaking the chains invisible and this drives her to frenzied approach and cerebral collapse. Perhaps, she wanted a husband who fulfilled her innate desires of stateliness but the lack of it only ignites feelings of revolt and disgust with life.

The inner antipathy is clear when Sita looks around. It appears to carry the burden of the past she has lived with Raman. It is past and she has no idea to go back, and an attitude of revolt is apparent in the inner space.

> . . . It was at once an inspiring and frightening sensation —and the passengers of the cart seemed to crouch and droop, clinging to the shifting planks, almost afraid of the gorgeousness they were disturbing. They stared and watched as those depthless fields drank and swallowed, drank and swallowed the liquid shades of gold, of sunlight, till all at once it was all gone. The sky and the water both turned to a toneless shade of pearl, then grey and then darkness.
>
> (*Where Shall We Go This Summer?* 24)

As observed at another place, "an outer portrayal eventually takes one to the mindscape of Sita exploring intensity of conflicts and agonies. When Sita stands in the veranda, the outwards swinging doors expose "the crowded darkness inside." The past makes her sad, a kind of delusion overtakes and she thought of "what had become of the house in twenty years of absence – a waste of ashes she saw, the cold remains of the bonfire her father had lit here to a blaze. Ashes, white, and waste. Dust lay as casually as sand on a beach; spider webs spanned the corners of the unfurnished rooms like skeletal palm leaves" (Ibid. 28). This, again, described metaphorically the mental state of Sita. When the children "sat in silence, hollow-eyed in the quavering shadows cast by the lantern like a pair of owls, watching Sita drag the bags from one room to another pulls the two string beds together, unpack and tidy" (*Where Shall We Go This Summer?* 30) these, actually appear an unveiling of the psychological woes and pains of a woman who deliberately chose to live independently while fighting a battle for survival amidst dark and dangerous forces of despondency working against her strong willpower. A faint light of hope, heavy bags of responsibility and shaky life of paucity in the house challenge Sita.

Sita, as observed earlier, is filled with repugnance and abhorrence at the thought of the fifth child she never wished, and she begins to hate Raman whose unbecoming attitude disillusions Sita. And a rebellion takes place within but rarely opens up. Sita is certainly "frightened" and childbirth is "unbearable" to her, as the husband remains lukewarm and lethargic. If it is disgusting for a woman, it is impossible for a man to determine the pains inherent. If looked at from another point of view, childbirth for a woman is awful but also an enjoyable moment and at that time, she is almost filled with hatred for a man responsible for the burden. The world goes on, but there comes a time, when burden and languid passion repel a woman from her man, and thus she becomes rebellious.

Again for a woman, coming of a child, forces her to a truce. "What I'm doing is trying to escape from the madness here, escape to a place where it might be possible to be sane again." It is middle class mindset, which loves to live with hatred and love alternately. When, little wishes appear fulfilled, it is joy and when there are obstructions, there is agony and revolt. This attitude is obvious in Sita with a little variation. Dr. Atma Ram's observes rightly when he says that the author "tries to penetrate the self-deception and hollow sophistication of the middle class life in her bid to find a meaning in life. Sita, the protagonist, is fed up with a dull, meaningless existence: 'I should have given my life a meaning.'...The novel dramatizes a powerful conflict in Sita's mind, the conflict that in parts is a palpable structure to the narrative." (*Indian Poetry & Fiction in English 40*)

Another revealing aspect of Sita's life is the cold-shouldering of Raman. She is mentally distressed, vexed and wounded. She suffers within and faces deprivations without emotional refuge. She needs emotional shield and requires comforts and support at the earthly level. A matter-of-fact man, Raman is unable to satisfy and so a rebel is born. Love, when it is plenty, Sita enjoys but when apathy and chill enter, it is appalling. She has become a machine of producing children. This concept of procreation is bereft of sanctity. In modern life, relations in most of the cases are interpreted in terms of physical needs and material gains, otherwise revolt and desperation torture, and this is exactly what happens to Sita in spite of a repulsive stance.

Sita's hurt ego drives her to impudence, and thus originates a furious feeling of revolt and disgust. Raman is reasonable but then he lacks the capacity to love Sita. He fails at the emotional level. These little inadequacies in marital relations as said earlier do not contribute to the happiness, and thus they refuse to shoulder responsibilities. If she holds Raman responsible for the outrageous and rebellious behaviour, she is a bit unreasonable. To clamour for liberty without the sharing of life's burden does not make sense. Here, many things are left unsaid. There is lack of understanding and so Sita's fight for independence and freedom leaves many fissures in the armoury required to fight against a man's prejudices. To infuse warmth in relations depends upon both.

A struggle for an identity among women has been the theme of many contemporary authors but still the outcome is not so obvious. Jean-Paul Sartre says pertinently:

> . . . there are many women who are not positively aware of their oppression, who find it natural to do all the domestic work themselves, to care for their children almost completely on their own. What do you think about the problem that members of the Women's Liberation Movement confront when they deal with working class women who are exploited not only in the factories where they work, but also at home by their husbands? Do you think their eyes should be opened to domestic oppression?
>
> (*Sartre in The Seventies—Interviews and Essays* 101)

Little incidents, like fight between the crow and an eagle, fondling of Karan and Menaka by Miriam and a callous attitude towards paintings fill Sita with revulsion. A sense of distaste results in revolt. When she thinks of past incidents, these do not give happiness. Even if there is anything pleasant in earlier life that too, now appears garish and monstrous. She gives birth to four children. One is constrained to imagine a situation in a married life where children are produced with a strange and disgusting regularity. It is difficult to say what kind of liberty she needs. Is it running away from the obligations of rearing up children simply by advancing reasons that the husband is lukewarm? A man in Indian society largely is entrusted with the duties to take care of his family. That makes it a unit. If after such a long period of love, passion and family life, the main protagonist feels that injustice is done, it needs an indepth study. Again, it is a gift of her father and not a satisfactory achievement of her husband, which creates comparisons. She begins to find the ability of her father in a husband who is cold now, it appears, when she carries the fifth child in the womb. One needs to go into this psyche to measure the gravity of reasons. He sincerely tries to dissuade her from going to an island and he also explained the reasons but she had "hurled slippers, papers, and nightgowns." At another level, it is observed:

> He had not read the Vedas or the Mahabharata, nothing more than scattered verses from the Bhagvad Gita – still, he was born a Hindu. Family planning was all very well, but not . . . .What did he mean? What did she mean? In that snarled moment of silence, time was a scummy sea, telling nothing.
>
> (*Where Shall We Go This Summer*? 34-35)

A feeble justification it is. It imparts terrible meanings to feelings, style of living and thoughts. A rottenness within appears insufferable. She is acutely cognizant of the happenings around and begins to relate every movement and word to her inner state of mind. It creates an upheaval in a hurt psyche. It also touches those sensitive emotional areas of women where they go back to past, to childhood, to the care of mothers and fathers and in moments of sadness or cynicism in marital relations, they are fed up with the family structure and crave for freedom - an illusive thought not clearly defined. This leads to thoughts of freedom and ambiguities about freedom.

Interestingly, Sita thought that giving birth was an act of violence - awesome and destructive. She understands that, "The line between the creative and the destructive grew so thin, so hazy and un-definable that, gazing at it, she seemed to see it vanish altogether" *(Where Shall We Go This Summer* 56). Perhaps giving birth to a fifth child appears appalling, she thinks, and so creation is uncalled-for. This adds to feelings of antagonism and protest, and so she wants to live alone and concretize feelings of rebellion while the thought of arrival of the fifth child is tortured. If thinking of spending sometime in Manori occurred, it is an escape from the realities of life. For Sita, a journey to the island symbolically is a voyage to rediscover the self, the individual choking within.

The tragic irony is that she refuses to see reality and yet claims she understands. It is an island of escape when she thinks of Manori. It puzzles and disturbs and she reflects:

> The mainland - the very word implied solidity, security: the solidity of streets, the security of houses. She had not realized then that living there would teach her only that was a crust of dull tedium, of hopeless disappointment – but a thin crust, a flimsy crust that, at every second or third step, broke apart so that she tumbled in, with the most awful sensation, in to a crashed pile of debris. She had no longer the nerve or the optimism to continue.
>
> (*Where Shall We Go This Summer*? 58)

In lonely moments when she is sadly filled with revolting feelings, the scent of the sand, sea, fruit, trees and green coconuts fill her with fresh energy. She remembers how her father used to get relief from hectic political activities. She also feels happiness when she is with him. But now after marriage, those dreary chores of a household, and lusty pranks and acts of her husband on the bed and then suddenly his icy demeanour repell Sita. Her father was a great man who was loved and admired. She remembers how everybody around wanted to boast of a relationship with her father. Those were times, she is inclined to claim, as great. To claim proximity to her father, people felt a kind of heightened glory. The memories are vivid but now it was disgusting.

Alone away from a passionless and loveless husband, she decays in the island and then simmers up with a revolting spirit, which also gives pain and mental torture. In these hours of inner crisis, she is tormented by the mysterious relations, which her sister and father had. Then, the prayers, a sad father offered. Again, it bewilders her when she observed that father was so much engaged in social service. If these inspired her, the scene of shadows of father and sister in the dimly lit room stun her even in memories giving hints of incestuous bonds. Carrying these mental conditions to future is not a happy experience. Whenever questions of a smooth relationship with Raman arise, there creeps in irritations, which lead to consequent rebellious temperament. She want to find a kind of profound satisfaction in relations but now everything is gone. Sita, at times, it looks, moves between two extremes of social and personal relationship and reaches nowhere. It is not her fault but a mechanism of social surroundings which makes her think, the way she wants to think. She lives a social and psychological life at the same time but is satisfied with none.

Anita Desai made certain valid remarks elsewhere in an interview which can be related to most of the women characters of her novels. In an interview to Dr Atma Ram, she observed, "I should hesitate to collect all of women's experience through history under the blanket word 'subjugation.' This would leave out the many variations, subtleties and complexities which are what really interest me as a novelist" (*Morality in Tess and other Essays* 96). These words contain a gist of women's life in totality. There are many areas in the lives of women which need careful scrutiny and understanding and one can find the real meaning. In fact, the word subjugation has an enlarged meaning when realistic picture is required to be painted with varied colours of thoughts and emotions. At another place, she says, "Marriage is not a profession for a woman any more than it is for a man: I think it is a mistake to take what is basically a biological state or institution as a full-time profession or vocation, and consider or judge it as one" (*Morality in Tess and other Essays* 96). If these words are read together they make the meaning clear, though certain debatable issues remain alive. In truth, it is difficult to find a cogent elucidation of what precisely the words 'subjugation' and 'marriage' mean in the context of a man and a woman relationship. Inner contradictions and inherent ambiguities stay on without ever becoming clear, for; here one meaning and interpretation leads to another volley of confusion.

She is not able to cut off herself from the past even while she struggles hard to get out of the present. Deteriorating health casts a gloom on the cheerful lives in the island, and she has to submit to father's wishes and so marries Raman. She is filled with antipathy when Rekha appeares cynical about her father's death. Raman, it dawns upon, marries Sita, "out of pity, out of lust, out of sudden will for adventure, and because it was inevitable-married her" (*Where Shall We Go This Summer?* 99) "to close the theatrical era of her life." Whatever illusions of warm relations she has been trying to cultivate with Raman, has disappeared. But the lonely life of the island proves inconvenient. If there are occasions of cheers, there is also the anguish of isolation from the active life which is, depressing. It is a wrong perception of life with not a reasoned-out sense of revolt. This life of escape and rebellion compels her to say in total helplessness when she tells Menaka, "you can coolly go ahead and burn me," "when on death bed." "I am unable to snatch a cigar."

A thought of 'Funerals' is a metaphor of persistent assault of negative feelings with a thin layer of uprising but the 'rain-drops' indicate failure of insurgent thoughts within and thus Sita loves to stay in a continuous struggle within. She wants to hitout but suddenly withdraws. Again, the surroundings instils hatred and she is very angry. She reflects on Menaka and it disturbs her. Efforts to figure out the unruly behaviour of brood, particularly Menaka, alarms her and she unconsciously tries to find parallels. Ironically, she establishes a relationship with nature and the surroundings outside, and relates it to her inner life of isolation, hatred, jealousy hazily defined, and then this inner pain goes back to the past and there rises up the monster of hate and animosity. Those moments destroy her internally and externally, it appears.

Unexpectedly, a sense of loneliness haunts and torments her, and issues of security to life and future trouble. Thoughts of rebellion disappear and she feels that a man is the body and soul of a woman, so they are inseparable. Now, Raman appears affectionate, loving and sensible. Killing thoughts of irritation and revolt, she craves for a sound reconciliation. If she is rebellious, perhaps Raman has also harboured similar feelings. The solitary life of the island changes, and thereafter, smoothens the uneven contours of Sita's feelings and philosophy of life. If, in thoughts of liberty and independence, a woman rediscovers her identity, in isolation she also invents new philosophy of life where living together in a spirit of understanding could open up vistas of a meaningful life. Here is hidden the meaning of revolt, of conciliation and of a true life, which can be beneficial to the family and society. To live in illusions and realities of life and to enjoy in the facts, truths and dreams of life while a search for ideal relations continues, encourages a man and a woman to redraft a distinct philosophy. One is pained to observe the following words:

> Her husband, with a greater capacity for accommodation than most had –even in a society with a truly remarkable capacity for accommodation, as long as it made for comfort, for security, continuity and safety from change or scandal —had grown, over the years, immune to the shocks and suspicions she contrived to create. Yet now, having been separated from her for such a stretch, he was startled again by her appearance –she saw it on his face and was once again, maliciously amused.
>
> (*Where Shall We Go This Summer?* 130)

As mentioned elsewhere in another critique, I find, "In the beginning, Sita appears a strong woman, slowly trying to establish her identity and individuality but finally she turns into a traditional woman possibly realizing that real life exists in the family. A feminist in Sita gets a burial so to say. Desai probably could not find better life for Sita and it is unfortunate. It appears a manipulated sad defeat and end of a well structured characterization. Hindu Philosophy equates a woman with nature as both create, preserve and destroy like Lord Shiva. It is in the act of creation and nursing, they are superb." Traditional views about women annoy.

One is tempted to observe that the change in Sita's attitude shocks. Initially, she presents the picture of a woman who wanted to create a separate niche but the eventually spirit of rebellion dies down. She is a woman of conventions at last, with all the chasing shortcomings and hiccups. The protagonist is never clear. One knows about the hazy ideas she nurses with regard to liberalism, independence and women's role in an emerging new world. To put a finger on the real definition of liberty escapes. In fact, it is still an enigma as to what liberty for a woman means. Is it social, economical, political, physical, psychological, philosophical, religious or spiritual? In wider perspectives, one must understand the intricacies of relations among men and women, where physical attraction is inseparable. From here, if any thought of independence and liberty is born, it could be authentic and viable. Later on, possibly acceptable to the society but the debate will remain inconclusive. To this extent, Anita Desai has not been able to defend the protagonist of liberty in a forcefully reasonable characterization, for past memories continue to haunt when Sita suffers and then decides to go back to years of peace and marital bliss. Here, she becomes weak. She wants to live with traditions and still a tinge of disgust and revolt chase her. It is indecisiveness, which tortures.

Images are clear and she often goes to nature to find relation with events, men and women walking on earth. It is also a search to find identity and consolation in objects of nature, animals and birds by identifying and correlating personal pains and joys. In the process, there is decay and lifelessness quite evident in the movement and feelings of the characters. If one wishes to find certain striking features in the characters, one finds a disappointing flow of greatness amidst shallowness visiting the minds and acts of nearly all the characters. They do not speak of great heights but want to live on earth like ordinary people. They are men of the family and not of society. It is a world of four walls and not beyond. Therefore; one witnesses a depressing isolation, a passivity where the will to move exists but it does not breathe. Moreover, in defeat and failure these characters find victory, a world of make-believe happiness.

Many a time, a feeling emerges while reading this novel that the author is very near the soil of India, its smell, colour and touch, and then suddenly she gets distracted. The going out to an island is an escape without consolation. Living there does not lessen sufferings while protests of Sita merely appear as drumbeats. There are subtle efforts to maintain identity and individual freedom but living separately from husband does not provide the satisfaction she needed, while not wanting the child she had been carrying in her womb. Through the protagonist, the author tries to explore the inner lives of her characters. Not very strongly built but these characters do give glimpses of future rebellion. It is a peep into the ailing society being troubled by traditions and outdated ideas with least respect for change. Therefore, a woman suffers. It is an effort to find life and meaning in overt oppression or at times quite visible assaults on personal freedom. There is an attempt to find peace and harmony among relations. The quest continues for enrichment and filling the vacuum in life bereft of warmth and emotions.

One is tempted to observe that in Sita a will to fight continues amidst failures, and that is perhaps an optimistic attitude. Perhaps, sometime in future, a strong Sita emerges and fights out, not a battle but a war to win. Sarah of *Bye-Bye Blackbird*, Maya of *Cry, the Peacock* and Sita of *Where Shall We Go This Summer?* are strong women who want to live assertively a life of meaning, one feels. There is a secret wish among women to live a comfortable nuptial existence despite weaknesses which could be ethical also but ultimately a conciliatory approach makes a life worthliving. Man knows it and a woman understands but still an inherent desire to fight and exist with grace continues but alas, happiness is the casualty.

I find it is always defeat in victory, and victory in defeat, when one evaluates relationships among men and women from the perspective of struggle for identity and survival. At another level, women characters of Mallikarjun, Reddy, P.C.K. Prem and Chandramoni Narayanaswamy continue to fight for identities. Mallikarjuna and Reddy obviously love traditions and values and so create women characters that fight out for liberty but ultimately surrender. Women characters of Prem are valiant fighters who fight and die but rarely succumb to pressures. Narayanaswamy's women are decent, graceful and love traditions and so in a subtle way try to adhere to the value system. Within these parameters of relations, married life is lived. There is a subtle attempt on the part of authors to establish a sort of harmony in married life in spite of irritations while a quest for independence and a separate identity continues to haunt women most of the time.

Carving out a separate individual identity is not new among the women but it has gained new dimension and meaning for obvious reasons, for; now relations are being determined at the physical and material level and naturally, in years to come, this thought will define relationship in fresh contexts. In Hindi literature, while Ageya, Bharati, Vishnu Prabhakar and Mohan Rakesh hold strong down-to-earth views on men-women relationship in trouble and opine that all are entitled to respective independence and individuality, they at times challenge a traditional analysis. Lakshmi Kant Verma, Sarveshvar Dyal

Sexana, Shrikant Verma and Rajendra Yadav talk of ordeals of relations at the physical and psychological level between men and women empathetically. Here, one is inclined to observe that Desai speaks of Indian heritage, sensibility and culture while focusing on the life and feelings of women harmonizing and integrating jarring notes in relations, and this is Anita Desai's inimitable quality of creative writing.

Works Cited

Auster & Davis, Paul Auster and Lydia Davis. *Jean-Paul Sartre- Sartre in the Seventies, Interviews and Essay.* London: Andre Deutsch Limited, Great Russell Street, 1978. Print.

Desai, Anita. *Voices in the City.* New Delhi: Orient Paperbacks (A Division of Vision Books) 1990. Print.

_______ *Where Shall We Go This Summer*? New Delhi: Orient Paperbacks (A Division of Vision Books), 1988. Print.

Ram, Atma. *Morality in Tess and Other Essays.* Delhi: Mittal Publications. 1996. Print.

Singh, R. A. *Anita Desai's Bye-Bye Blackbird (A Critical Evaluation).* Bareilly: Prakash Book Depot, Bara Bazar, 1999. Print.

2

Unmasking Women in Kavita Daswani's *A Girl Named Indie*

G. Dominic Savio & S.J. Kala

In the beginning, Indian novels in English were novels of social realism because they catered to the social need. It is also to be highlighted that the rise of the Indian novel has its association with not just the literary sphere but also with the political and economic spheres. It is to be underscored that the first novel in India, *Alaler Gharer Dulal* (1854) published in Bengali was written by Pyari Chand Mitra. Thereafter many novels were published in other Indian languages and also in English.

Rajmohan's Wife was the first novel in English by Bankim Chandra Chatterjee. Both *Rajmohan's Wife* and Lal Behari Day's *Govind Samanta* discuss the women of their age and their sufferings. Bankim's novel deals with the condition of a middle-class Hindu wife who suffers in the hands of a hardened husband. Following the publication of *Govind Samanta*, that is in the later years of the nineteenth century, women writers who were influenced by the social reforms of William Bentick and Raja Rammohan Roy emerged announcing the emancipation of Indian women. Educated women like Toru Dutt, Krupabai, Sathianathan, Shevantibai M. Nikambe, Raj Lakshmi Debi, Swarnakumari Ghosal and Cornelia Sorabji took up efforts "to communicate to the world their own bitter experiences as women as well as their ideas of social reform, turned writers" (Ramamurti 67).

If these women writers focused on emancipated women, the novelists both male and female who followed them portrayed women from a different perspective. In the pre-independent era, novelists like Tagore and Romesh Chunder Dutt in the north depicted women who played the roles of wife, daughter-in-law, sister-in-law, sister and daughter in the Indian society and of women who loved to be subservient to men. However, the novelists of the pre-independent period mirrored the tragic life of the women of their times.

Even the Big Three (as addressed by William Walsh)—Mulk Raj Anand, R.K. Narayan and Raja Rao; the women novelists—Kamala Markandaya, Ruth Prawer Jhabvala and Nayantara Sahgal; the novelists of the sixties—Manohar Malgonkar and Attia Hosain; and the novelists of the mid-sixties—Chaman Nahal and others, documented women and their outer conflicts in the social, political, cultural, economic and educational arena. But it was only in the mid-sixties that Anita Desai probed into the inner self of her characters and projected their inner conflicts in her works.

Anita Desai's characters are more feministic. Her women continuously revolt against the patriarchal society. Maya in *Cry the Peacock*, Monisha in *Voices in the City*, Nanda in *Fire on the Mountain* and Sita in *Where Shall We Go This Summer?* break away from all binding shackles and in the process do not hesitate to even destroy themselves. Anita Desai's women are not those who are labelled "outsiders." Other novelists who project feministic perspectives in their novels are Ismat Chughtai and Shashi Deshpande.

In the novel, *The Heart Breaks Free*, Ismat Chughtai makes her characters Qudsia and Shabir rebel against tradition and offers them a new life creating a feminist Utopia. Shashi Deshpande's characters are also rebellious. Saru in *The Dark Holds No Terror* quite differently protests against matriarchy. Deshpande's Indu in *Roots and Shadows* undertakes an inward journey and defies the role of a wife. Shoba De also delineates defiant women. If in *Starry Nights* Shobha De picturises a woman who shuns patriarchy, then in *Socialite Evenings*, she sketches Karuna as a new woman who outdares all traditions.

Coming on to yet another group of novelists, it is to be noted that their focus is changed. With the whole world transformed into a global village and with more and more people moving from one part of the globe to the other, in search of a better job, writers get to write on new subject matter. In the process of settling down in the land of their choice they faced insurmountable odds that are adeptly dealt with by immigrant writers.

Novelists like Bharati Mukherjee, Amitav Ghosh, Rohinton Mistry, Salman Rushdie, V.S. Naipaul, Vikram Seth, and Kavita Daswani highlight the longings and yearnings of the immigrants. Their novels "represent the diasporic condition, the agonies of the diasporic people, being stranded in an alien land, who had to adopt the alien culture either willingly or unwillingly. . ." (Nara and Ghanshyam 112). Thus the women presented by these writers and the issues pertaining to them also differ from the women depicted so far in the Indian fiction. Readers get to see the changed face of women in the alien land that is captured in their works. One such writer who presents different Indian women in her novels is Kavita Daswani.

Kavita Daswani was born in Hong Kong to Bombay-based parents in the year 1968. After her marriage she moved to Los Angeles and is now settled there with her husband and her two sons. Her passion for fashion fetched her a job even at the age of seventeen as a fashion editor for *South China Morning Post* in Hong Kong. Subsequently, she became a freelance journalist. She has also served as a fashion correspondent for CNN and CNBC and has contributed fashion related articles to *Los Angeles Times* and *The International Herald Tribune*. Besides her contribution to the field of journalism, she has also to her credit three novels

– *For Matrimonial Purposes, The Village Bride of Beverley Hills* and *Salaam Paris* and a teen fiction, *A Girl Named Indie.* All of these works are devoted to women, their quest for identity and their experiences of being culturally torn apart.

This paper aims at recognizing the changed face of the female writer, Kavita Daswani who tries her hand as a woman at a different genre, teen fiction. On the other hand, it also unmasks her female characters—Indie, a teenager and second generation immigrant; her mother, a first generation immigrant and Aaralyn Taylor, a renowned fashion editor in the land of the immigrant's choice and the growing complexities that rise among the trio. The paper specially throws light on the relationship between Indie and her parents because of her undying attempts to chase her dreams in the land of their adoption.

A brief look into the first three novels of Kavita Daswani will facilitate a better understanding of the change in her as a writer of teen fiction. In *For Matrimonial Purposes,* she deals with Indian women and provides the age-old dilemma of arranged marriages a modern perspective. Anju, the protagonist of the novel, lives a Janus-faced life in New York shuttling between the roles of the sophisticated American girl in New York and the role of the traditional daughter when she returns to her parents in Bombay. During her visits on five-day family weddings, she is forced to accost a prospective suitor whom the ultra modern Anju cannot withstand. Eventually, it turns out to be a long journey of self discovery that is well punctuated with hilarious moments.

Her next novel *The Village Bride of Beverley Hills,* a rollicking romantic comedy, also discusses the theme of arranged marriage highlighting Indian women. Priya, the village bride from India, is taken to California after her arranged marriage where she lives with her husband and in-laws. Despite being in California she is expected to play all the roles of a typical Indian woman and in addition is insisted on to take up a job as long as she is free from pregnancy. But her attempts to fetch a job at a glossy Hollywood magazine that reflects the predilection of Kavita Daswani does not please her in-laws. Hence she is impelled to lead a life in the glitzy world without the knowledge of her new family. Simultaneously she also has to continue living with a husband whose affections are shared between his parents and his new wife. Throughout the novel one comes across the complications of the arranged marriage and an Indian woman who daringly combats them.

Quite different from her first two novels that discuss the issues of arranged marriages in India and its aftermath on Indian women is her third novel *Salaam Paris*. In *Salaam Paris*, the protagonist Tanaya Shah wriggles out of the clutches of arranged marriages. Following suit of Audrey Hepburn in *Sabrina*, she is lured by the awesome world of Paris. Very soon she seizes an opportunity to fly to Paris when there is a proposal for an arranged marriage with a man living in Paris. But, on her arrival there she severs all ties with the man and enters the glamorous world of modeling. Accolades, recognition and fame come on the way of this traditional Muslim girl who soon realizes her folly of disowning her family and the man chosen by them. She is wary of the engulfing evil in Paris. The novel ends with how she steps into the comfort zone one she gets back to her roots.

If the first three novels of Kavita Daswani revolve around the concept of arranged marriages and their repercussions, her next publication *A Girl Named Indie* focuses on an altogether different issue, the parent-teen relationship of the immigrants. Indira Gandhi, a second-generation immigrant is the protagonist of the novel. The fifteen-year old who is happy only when she is addressed Indie dreams of becoming a fashion reporter. On the road untrodden by Indians, especially Indian women, Indie dauntingly trods to pursue her dreams and experiences bumps of great and small. Initially her parents find it hard to come out of the tremors that quake them when she announces her decision to babysit Kyle, the two-year old toddler of Aarlalyn Taylor, a much acclaimed fashion designer and editor of a fashion magazine, *Celebrity Style*.

Gradually Indie learns the art of babysitting that she struggles with at the outset. With the course of time she also understands that Aaralyn's magazine is inclining towards its demise because of its loss of juicy news to a rival website, gossipaddict.com. Precisely at that moment when she wonders how she could save Aaralyn from the snare laid for her, she gets the opportunity to accompany Aaralyn to Milan as Kyle's babysitter. Fortune knocks at her door when she grabs a scoop that comes her way and redeems *Celebrity Style* from being doomed. *A Girl Named Indie* is different from Kavita Daswani's other fiction not only thematically but also generically. It is her first teen fiction, a genre not tried by many women novelists.

Teen fiction is otherwise called Young Adult Fiction. These novels are also referred to as problem novels or coming of age novels as they highlight the challenges of youth. In 1802, it was Sarah Trimmer who first described the group of youth between 14 and 21 as experiencing "young adulthood". The terms "Books for Children" (for those below fourteen) and "Books for Young Persons" (for those between 14 and 21) were introduced by Trimmer in her own Children's Literature periodical, *The Guardian of Education.* In spite of the lack of books being marketed specifically for young readers, there were many books published in the early nineteenth century like *The Swiss Family Robinson*, *Oliver Twist*, *The Count of Monte Cristo*, *Great Expectations*, *Alice in Wonderland*, *Little Women*, *The Adventures of Tom Sawyer*, *Heidi*, *Treasure Island*, *Adventures of Huckleberry Finn* and the others that appealed to young readers. Only in the 1950s, the two novels, *The Catcher in the Rye* and *Lord of the Flies* were successful in exclusively attracting adolescent readers. Later, between the 1950s and 1960s with the publication of S. F. Hinton's *The Outsiders*, the modern classification of young adult fiction came into existence.

But, presently, according to the young Adult Service Division of the American Library Association, a young adult is considered to be a person between the age of 12 and 18 years and so young adult fiction is written for and marketed for youth pertaining to that age group. The term 'young adult fiction' encompasses the literary form of novels or short stories. The significant attributes of young adult fiction distinguishes it from adult fiction, middle grade fiction and children's fiction. Irrespective of the basic elements of fiction such as characters, plot, setting, theme and style the following are certain features that are unique to a young adult fiction. A young adult fiction:

(a) Is always written in first person.

(b) Has an adolescent as a protagonist.

(c) Deals with the experiences of the adolescent.

(d) Sidelines adult characters.

(e) Covers a short timespan.

(f) Makes use of adolescent language, expressions and slangs.

(g) Hardly has any sub-plot.

All these mentioned characteristics find place in Kavita Daswani's teen fiction, *A Girl Named Indie.*

Unlike Kavita Daswani's earlier fictions, the narrator of *A Girl Named Indie* is a 15 year-old Indian girl, Indie and the plot of the novel revolves around her and her experiences. Indie's parents and Aaralyn, the fashion designer and the editor of the fashion magazine *Celebrity Style* are the main adult characters who feature in the work. Compared to Aaralyn the other adults are never in the limelight. Next to Indie it is Aaralyn who is given importance in the young Adult fiction because the teenager craves to be in her vicinity most of the time. The story begins with Indie eagerly awaiting the arrival of Aaralyn Taylor at the Meadow Lake High School on ". . . a beautiful March day when the chill of winter had passed . . . into the full bloom of spring. . . ." (2).

Indie avidly waits for her just to grab the summer job that she had applied for then. After three months on 30 June of the same year, the story comes to a close. Towards the end of the novel she announces it to the readers through the lines, "The 'inkys' and I were flying to Kolkata on the afternoon of 30 June, tomorrow, the day before the internship job would actually start" (180).

Within this short timespan Indie, a young Indian girl sketched by Kavita Daswani, follows her oscillating fortunes to hit at her target. It is Kavita Daswani's linguistic style that facilitate in the creation of the teenager's world. The writer is adept in using the typical expressions and slangs used by the teenagers in the United States to create a verbal picture of the teenager and the people around her. It is astounding to note how an Indian girl is proficient in using them. In an attempt to pay whole-hearted attention in delineating Indie, she has not introduced any sub-plot in the fiction. Above all, *A Girl Named Indie* focuses on the challenges courted by Indie a diasporic youth in her relationship with her parents while opting for a career of her choice. Indie is not depicted as a stereotyped Indian woman who usually appears in the Indian fiction.

This diasporic teenager with dreams of interning with *Celebrity Style* for the teen fashion department has to eyeball innumerable challenges as a second generation immigrant at home and outside. For Indie, the picture of India and the Indian culture and heritage that she has are mostly restored from the cherished memories of her parents. But her parents are equipped with first-hand experiences of their fond memories by upholding their indigenous culture in the land of adoption. Before taking a peek into the diasporic parent-teen relationship it is imperative to study the basic difference between the first and second generation migrants.

First-generation migrants do not integrate. They settle and preserve as much of the 'home country' as possible, regulating daily family life to ensure the continuity of culture and tradition, language, custom, etc. It is a form of exile of question of identity for the next generation broadens, in the sense that the individual has to adjust both to change within this own community as well as in the larger context that is nation (Thumboo 448).

With such a widened gap between Indie, the teenager and her parents she is wrenched to encounter countless hurdles and overcome them.

The physical transition from a child to an adult and the uncertainties of the forthcoming adulthood that threaten any teenager in reality make the relationship with his / her parents strained. In the novel, Kavita Daswani does not get into the details of bodily changes in Indie nor does she project Indie as a teenager who is quite apprehensive about her future. Instead, Indie is projected as a girl full of dreams. Accomplishment of her goal is the only propellant in Indie throughout the novel. She finds it too hard to convince her traditional Indian parents at each and every stage of her journey towards the purpose. With too many "first times" in the lives of teenagers, the parent-teen relationship in general is challenging. It demands hoards of understanding, patience and perseverance on the part of the parents.

Indie's father Rajkamal, a neurosurgeon, and her mother Nanda, a home maker, sustain their originality and retain as much of Indianness as they can. Twenty years ago when they came from India they had tugged with them Indian culture, practise and religion and had set themselves a standard of living. To them eating out was luxurious, a practice and attitude Indie says they have towed from India. Delving into their religious practices one discovers them as fervent followers of Hinduism that they try to pass on to their children. But the children hardly practise it. In Indie's house there is a sanctified place for praying where she rarely goes. Only before leaving for India on her mother's insistence when she enters the prayer room she keenly gazes at everything there. She states, "I looked around at all the photographs on the wall and lined up on tiny shelves, Durga and Krishna, Ganesha and Lakshmi, their beatific faces and brightly coloured clothes. . . . My parents came in here every morning after they had bathed and last thing at night before going to bed" (152-53).

Her first-generation immigrant parents love to relive the lives of their past / roots. They also see to it that in the United States they rear their children as true Indians. This vision of their parents is intermittently defied by Indie. Still, Indie's parents eternally express their admiration for their friend's daughters, Rinky, Pinky and Tinky who are fondly referred to as "inkys" in the novel and hearts of hearts want their daughter to be like them who are more Indian. Their comparison of Indie with the "inkys" throws light on their yearnings and longings for the past. Indie declares, "My parents, for all their mostly modern outlook on life, thought that I should be more like the 'inkys,' closer to 'the community' and less involved in what they often described as 'American nonsense.' The 'inkys' they would often remind me, could read, write and speak fluent Hindi, had learned all the lyrics to the Om Jai Jagdish Hare Aarti, and knew how to work a pressure cooker perfectly" (52). These lines justify her awareness of the conflict at home. But she likes to be more like an American but still remembers all what her parents have instilled about India by frequently taking them to community get-togethers that they never miss nor do they encourage their children missing them. Apart from this her inquisitiveness in knowing why her dad's friends even when they are not blood relations are called uncle nags her. She innocently inquires of her father:

> Dad, uncle Mohit isn't even my real uncle. My father couldn't argue that point, but it didn't make a difference. I knew that my brother and I had to call all my dad's random friends 'uncle', whether they were related to us by blood or not. And I knew just what kind of a party it would be; all the men clustered around the bar, talking about how interest rates and high property prices and all the women in the living room, discussing Saif Ali Khan's latest film, and whether frozen parathas could even be as good as the freshly made ones. (48)

These community gatherings are places for the diasporans to air out their longings for the past and to create a group identity.

The tug of war between the first generation and the second generation immigrant is a prolonged and a universal process. Anything that is acceptable to the second-generation immigrant is unacceptable to the first generation immigrant. For instance, Indie loves an old aerosmith T. Smith that she got from a garage sale but her parents can never commiserate how she could spend eight dollars on that particular piece of cloth that is someone else's junk. Apart from imparting all these values, Indie's parents want her to recognize the worth of money and so they are very strict with her pocket money or gifts. Her father perpetually reminds her of the simple life that he led in the past. Undeterred by all these agonies, Indie discloses her admiration for her parents when she compares them with Aaralyn Taylor. She is so bewildered to learn that Kyle, the toddler is not permitted by his parents to enter into the immaculate living room and attached dining area in his house. She instantaneously recollects how her parents never had "baby-free zones" while rearing them:

> It was probably normal in these circles to have 'baby-free' zones. I thought back to my own upbringing, where the entire house was one big playpen for Dinesh and me. To this day, my father would remind me of how many times he had stepped on tiny Matchbox cars and heads of dolls that I'd pulled off. My mother would cover the couch with an old bed sheet, and the carpets with tarp, and we would be allowed to paint and sketch and roll and giggle wherever we wanted. My father had a small office at home, converted from a bed-room off the den, and even when he was in there, going over reports or researching some obscure medical condition, his door was always open to us. As a consequence, we learned to respect where we were and knew instinctively what we could touch. Our home was never zoned for attention and love. (39)

Through this significant contrast, Kavitha Daswani, while glorifying India and Indian values also, underscores on how Indie, a second-generation immigrant grows, mature enough to appreciate the Indian standards of parenting.

For Indie's diasporic parents tackling their teen daughter with the aspirations of becoming a fashion reporter in America was a new experience. The father-daughter relationship in general is one that is warmer than the mother-daughter relationship. But, in the novel one notices that Indie is comfortable with both her father and mother. Typical of any Indian father Rajkamal also feels he has lost the "right authority and obligation to inform her when she is making a mistake" (86). In addition he also has dreams of his own for his daughter which is evident in the following extract:

> When I had started complaining about how old-fashioned my first name was, my father had told me that in deciding what to call his firstborn child, it had been his hope that I would embody all that he admired about his native land and the other Indira—Indira Gandhi—who once led it. He wanted me to be strong, virtuous, compassionate, intellectual. And while he had originally wanted me to choose what he would constantly refer to as a 'noble profession'—something in medicine or engineering or government—his views had started to change recently when his nephew Naresh had landed a six-figure job in New York in the digital media arena . . . (3)

Being the first child Indie's parents pin all their hopes on her. Her father's ceaseless reference to the 'noble profession' is his subtle way of telling his teen daughter what he wants her to be. Contrarily, Indie is shown as a girl who breaks the established norms followed by Indian girls of her age. She chooses to babysit Aaralyn's toddler just to intern with *Celebrity Style*. Indie's father exclaims, "Babysitting? . . . 'You're getting the best education, you excel at your studies and now you're going to do babysitting? Indira, what has come over you?" (31)

To a first generation immigrant it is quite disagreeable. To begin with Indie's father logically reasons it out. He asks her how she would be able to babysit when she has never evinced interest in helping her younger brother in any way. But observing Indie's determination and her confidence he concedes to her request of babysitting and drops her at Aaralyn's house. He does not grumble or shout at her resolution. Instead, on their drive to Aaralyn's house, he lectures on her "poorly considered decision." It is undoubtedly evident how the Indian father has mulled over it sufficiently and tries to convince Indie to opt out of babysitting. However, Indie sticks to her decision and babysits Kyle. But, when her father boozes in a party at uncle Mohit's house, he musters courage. Probably he feels secured only in the company of the members of his community. Giving vent to his feelings he brings to fore his hurt at Indie's decision and her will power to attain her goal even at the expense of breaking away from tradition.

> 'I'm just *ravenous!*' he said. 'This daughter of mine kept me out of the house for hours today driving her back and forth to her new job.' I prayed that my father would stop right there. He had said just enough to give me a little respect in the eyes of the 'inkys'. But Johnie Walker obviously had a mind of his own. 'Yes, babysitting,' he said, using a large wooden fork to pull out vegetables from a salad bowl. 'In our day, no girl would ever consider babysitting as a job. But our Indie here, that seems to be how she wants to spend her time. She came home today with dried paint and pee-pee stains all over her clothes!' And with that, my father let out a big, inebriated guffaw and moved on. (55)

Above all, Indie's father loves her so much that he does not want to intervene with her whims and fancies except when circumstances demand. He rarely intimidates her with his own views. Even when he wants his daughter to know how he detests dating, he does not warn Indie directly of it. Rather, as is his usual style he meanders aimlessly through illustrations to reach his point. After one of her babysitting rituals when Indie owing to weariness offers excuses for not attending the community party, he becomes annoyed and makes it conspicuous to her. He clarifies:

> 'It is your uncle's birthday and we are all going!' my father had said sternly, even though I started to protest and told him I was tired. 'And yes, my dear child, may I enquire what it is you have done today that has caused such fatigue to come over you?' Whenever my father felt the need to be sarcastic, he would often lapse into the very formal English he learned at boarding school in Kolkata. After twenty years in America, he still wasn't able to shake that off. (48)

Indie's remarks about her father being unable to "shake off" the boarding school English reveals the concealed desire of Indie's father to go back to his origin and his perpetual passion for his roots. But to the second generation immigrant, Indie, it appears to be ludicrous that even 20 years of her father's living in America has not made him an American. His connections with his birth place are so strong that he adores anything that is Indian. The first generation immigrants incessantly dangle between the land of origin and the land of adoption in all aspects because of their continual struggle to adapt themselves in the new land and their frequent search for their identity. On the contrary, Indie notes, "My birthday was on 12 April, a date that I was thrilled to share with the ever-stylish Claire Danes, although my father was far always more excited that some ancient Bollywood lyricist called Gulshan Bawra was born on the same day as me, albeit like, three hundred years earlier. It was a blessing Dad hadn't named after him!" (96). Like her counterparts in India who struggle to get into the mainstream, Indie, the second-generation immigrant too tries her best to be part of the primary group in the land of their adoption. She is quite comfortable in associating herself with them even if she is not integrated into the group.

Rajkamal, Indie's father is depicted as an Indian father who cares and dreams for his daughter. He is so protective about his daughter that he cannot visualise letting a sixteen-year old on her own like other American girls.. He is just staggered when Indie proposes to go to Milan all by herself but Indie defends her cause. This drives him so crazy that he openly admits that he is an Indian father. He tells her:

> Indie, I don't see another way. I have been very accepting of your choices up until now, but I don't know these people. And from what I have seen so far, I am not very impressed with them. You know, most Indian parents would never allow such a thing. I am trying to be open-minded, but I am still an Indian father after all. In Kolkata, a girl of your age wouldn't be able to go to the next town by herself, much less another continent. (145)

Time and an alien milieu has not brought in any change in this Indian, Rajkamal.

Even Indie's mother Nanda plays an important role in shaping her daughter. It is generally believed that the mother-daughter relationship is a soared one but, in the novel Indie's mother is her best confidante. Indie with all admiration for her mother proudly describes her and the marked changes even in her attire as:

> My mother was not one of those mothers. She had arrived in America from India as a shy bride and had worn simple cotton saris until I was three years old, when her *pallav* had gotten caught between the base of a merry-go-round at a local street and she had then decided that she couldn't possibly be an effective mother if she had to be constantly worrying about six yards of fabric on her body. So she had packed up all the saris gifted to her by her parents as part of her trousseau, stashed them in the attic, and had gone to K. Mart to stock up on classic cut jeans and T. shirts . . . (56)

For Indie her mother is a perennial source of inspiration and from this spring of stimulation she draws simplicity, humility, good manners, courtesy and all that she epitomises. It is she who understands her daughter's ardour for fashion and guides her at all instances. One day when Aaralyn makes a raving phone call to Indie and pleads her to babysit Kyle, it is Indie's mother who convinces her husband to send Indie. She also goes to the extent of empathising with her. Like other Indian mothers, Nanda is not even protective about her daughter. She gives her daughter the due liberty and also understands her ardent desire for fashion.

There are moments when she chastises Indie especially when she tries to be more like an American. She turns crazy even when she hears Indie answering the phone with a 'Hey' instead of 'Hello'. She being a distinctive Indian feels that saying 'Hey' immediately after picking up the phone is an abnormal activity. Probably that is her way of repelling from Americanism.

At the end of the novel, the Indian woman, Nanda is typified as an Indian mother who can tackle anyone for the sake of her daughter even in a different land. Profuse motherly love and the anguish caused due to the mistreatment of her daughter by Aaralyn is thrown light at the end of the novel. Throughout the novel Nanda is seen as a docile woman who hardly raises her tone even on her children. Whereas, at the end, she startles everyone when she challenges a renowned and distinguished American journalist that too politely and courteously all for her daughter. She boldly expresses her heart and thus establishes her daughter's identity:

> 'Ms. Taylor, may I say something?' she asked instead, coming, to my side and putting her arm across my shoulders. 'Our Indie, she has done so much for you', my mother said quietly. 'And she has asked for nothing in return. We have never quite understood her fascination with this fashion thing, but we have always respected her choice and chosen to support her. But I must say, Ms. Taylor, your mistreatment of our daughter has saddened me deeply. You have never given Indie her due. We are both mothers, after all. Our children are everything. We would die to protect them from being hurt. Surely you agree?' (187)

Kavita Daswani is successful in painting an Indian woman who unlike her predecessors does not remain a silent sufferer. Instead, Nanda is bold enough to confront an American in a land that is not her own.

A study of the writer Kavita Daswani as a young adult fiction writer or as a teen fiction writer has facilitated in the recognition of the transformed face of the writer. When most of the writers try to mirror Indian women as typical upshots of the Indian society—quite docile and resilient, Kavita Daswani tries to portray them differently in a varied setting and through a less adopted literary genre, teen fiction.

In the discussed teen fiction, both Indie and her mother Nanda skilfully aclimatise themselves in America. The success of their delineation lies in the way Kavita Daswani juxtaposes distinctly the outer and inner conflicts of the first and second generation immigrants in her literary work. Nanda at the surface level might seem to be a replica of other diasporic Indian women but it is her zeal for homemaking particularly her intermittent struggle to upkeep the culture and tradition of her roots, her care and concern exhibited in upbringing her children and above all her inner strength with which she champions the cause of her child in an alien land make her different. On the other hand, Indie with her dreams of becoming a fashion reporter appears different from her counterparts in India who either want to become an engineer, a doctor or the safest of all a teacher. Her perseverance to pursue a goal unheard of in India by Indian girls makes her unique. In fact, Nanda and Indie are illustrations of changed faces of Indian women. Aren't they?

Works Cited

Daswani, Kavita. *A Girl Named Indie.* New Delhi: Puffin Books, 2007. Print.

"*A Girl Named Indie*: Book Description." 18 Aug 2010. <www.infibeam.com/.../A-Girl-Named-Indie/9780143330530.html>.

"Indian Writers in English – Kavita Daswani." 18 Aug 2010. <www.paritoshuttam.com/indian-writers/kavita-daswani.html>.

"Indie Girl." 18 Aug 2010. <www.fantasticfiction.co.uk>.

"Kavita Daswani." 18 Aug 2010. <www.kavitadaswani.com>.

Nara, Rakhi and G.A. Ghanshyam. "Narrating the Diaspora: Amitav Ghosh's *The Glass Palace.*" *The Quest* 24.1 (2010): 112-17. Print.

Ramamurti, K.S. "The Women Novelists." *Rise of the Indian Novel in English.* New Delhi: Sterling Publishers Private Limited, 1987. 66 -111. Print.

Thumboo, Edwin. "Diaspora and Creativity: Notes on Variations." *Diaspora: The Australasian Experience.* Ed. Dreiser, Cynthia Vanden and Ralph Crane. New Delhi: Prestige Books, 2005. 439- 55. Print.

"What is Young Adult Fiction?" 21 Sep 2010.
<www.suite101.com/content/what-is-*young-adult-fiction*-a135786>
"Young Adult Fiction." 21 Sep 2010. <en.wikipedia.org/wiki/*Young-adultfiction*>

3

The Flaming Spirit of a Woman in Jhumpa Lahiri's *The Namesake*

Aju Mukhopadhyay

Introducing the Flaming Woman

Among the four characters in Jhumpa Lahiri's debut novel *The Namesake*, Ashoke Ganguli, his wife Ashima Ganguli and their children, elder Gogol and his sister Sonia, the greatest change with the passage of time comes in Ashima, the housewife. The husband is already in America as a PhD student and his wife reaches there after their marriage in India. While Ashoke Ganguli becomes a professor, Ashima goes as a housewife. Their children are born there. Both the children become American citizens by birth. While the husband and the wife manage their lives in Indian style, their children are mostly American in their habits.

The subject of the novel is the cultural mix among the Indian and American people. Ashima, a simple girl married while she is on the way to graduation, does not know the ways of life as an adult woman, even in her own country, what in America. She makes immense strides in her life, educating herself to become a librarian, learning to drive and run her household to the satisfaction of all friends and relatives. Silently the woman has undergone a change appropriate to her position to claim herself a representative of educated Indian woman of international standard. When she finally decides to come back to India after the death of her husband, she is a different woman; courageous and straightforward, friends to all, guiding others.

The Story of the Novel

The story is quite interesting, popular as cinematized. The first part of the story runs through the thread of birth of a child and naming him. While in India there are two or more names given leisurely to a child, at least one pet name and another official one, in America the name has to be finalized at birth. The honour for naming the child in this story rests with the grandmother of the child's mother. But her naming part never materializes. The real naming remaining pending, his father names him at birth after his very favourite Russian author, Nikolai Gogol. He becomes Gogol Ganguli. Being teased by schoolmates for his name, Gogol begine to hate his name. After reaching the appropriate age he changes his name legally to become Nikhil Ganguli. But for all practical purposes he remains Gogol to all old acquaintances, family circle and friends.

But the antecedent of Gogol's birth is the marriage between his parents. Ashima Bhaduri is married to Ashoke Ganguli, both from Calcutta, through negotiation and arrangements made by their parents and guardians. They have a long joyous conjugal life in America. After the death of her husband the wife cries alone, feeling lonely at the severance of the permanent bond of life. Their daughter and son both have a short but troubled married life resulting in divorce; such marriages are the results of free mixing, dating and then selection as per American custom. While her daughter Sonia has another contact, a new boyfriend with whom she is going to be married, her son Gogol at the age of 32 is quite uncertain about the marital status of his remaining life. Apparently, he has suffered frustration in life. Their mother, a changed woman after undergoing all cultural transformation due to assimilation of foreign tongue, manners and customs, while maintaining her own tradition and culture, is an independent, loving woman standing on her own legs unlike before her marriage, returns home alone after throwing her last party to entertain her children and friends and well wishers.

The Subject Matter of the Novel

Besides the story, the novel has a message to give; it is the subject matter of the work. *The Namesake* is a tale of cultural mix and its result; sometimes happy due to new adventure, sometimes unhappy as full of conflict and disaster, sometimes contradictory between the American and Bengali-Indian tradition clashing at different stages of life, enacted mostly in America. It is a story of cultural mix and clash. At the same time it is a story of changing time for none can stick to olden time and practice in a moving world. The characters of the novel, specially those reaching America after growing up in India up to their youth, certainly learn new things, undergo transformations while remaining in their original station of life. It is a novel to test how far they change, the old as well as the new ones born there; how they feel their lives, where they stand, how Indian life is in contrast with American life. Even for the second generation immigrants the life is not smooth, perhaps as they are born with strife. They do not live exactly as the Americans. It is a story to taste how they interact with each other. In life nothing is static, more so due to globalization. With the individuals the society too changes.

Cultural Mix and Contrast

Through her works Jhumpa Lahiri has shown the result of mixed culture upon the first and second generation Bengali Indians, not only in this novel but elsewhere, in almost all her short stories. Most of them could not assimilate the whole of the foreign culture, had some inherent dilemma in them. Some of them suffered for causes which may be applicable anywhere; exposure to an exotic culture without anyone to guard against or without caring for anyone's advise in the background of immense freedom enjoyed. Usually the first generation Bengalis maintained their identity. And this identity, the cultural practices, the writer has shown vis-à-vis other cultural habits as contrast which happened in the unrolling of the stories. Some dazzling contrasts may be cited from *The Namesake*:

> Seeing the two of them curled up on the sofa in the evenings, Gerald's head resting on Lydia's shoulder, Gogol is reminded that in all his life he has never witnessed a single moment of physical affection between his parents. Whatever love exists between them is an utterly private uncelebrated thing. 'That's so depressing,' Maxine says when he confesses this fact to her (138).

Maxine is one of Gogol's girl friends. Gogol and Maxine, on their way to vacation for two weeks, come to visit Gogol's parents on special request, before the departure of his father to Ohio on grant for research.

> 'Hi, Ma', he says, leaning over, giving his mother a quick kiss. 'This is Maxine. Max, this is my mother. Ashima.'
>
> 'It's so nice to finally meet you, Ashima,' Maxine says, leaning over and giving his mother a kiss as well (146).

Let us now see a meeting among Bengali friends:

> The families drop by one another's homes unexpected on Sunday afternoons. They drink tea with sugar and evaporated milk . . . . They sit in circles on the floor, singing songs by Nazrul and Tagore, passing a thick yellow clothbound book of lyrics among them as Dilip Nandi plays the harmonium. They argue riotously over the films of Ritwik Ghatak versus those of Satyajit Ray (38).

Now a contrast between the gatherings at two different parties, seen through Goglo's eyes:

> They are an intelligent, attractive, well-dressed crowd. Also a bit incestuous. The vast majority of them know each other from Brown, and Gogol can't ever shake the feeling that half the people in the room have slept with one another. There is the usual academic talk around the table, versions of the same conversation he can't participate in, concerning conferences, job listings, ungrateful undergraduates, proposal deadlines (236).
>
> How different they are from his own parents' parties, cheerfully unruly evenings to which there were never fewer than thirty people invited, small children in tow. Fish and meet served side by side, so many courses that people had to eat in shifts . . . .They sat where

> they could, in the different rooms of the house, half the people having finished before the other half began (140).

Teenager and young Gogol is against his parents but as he grows older and gets experiences he concludes that there is nothing absolutely good in any side. His mother, Ashima, who is a housewife only, learns too through time, by experiences. She fears not to go back to Calcutta alone.

We may say that this has been the experience of Gogol of the novel though his sister Sonia is going to have fresh life again with another marriage and her mother expects that relationship to last long.

There are many types of experiences the emigrants and their children have there as she has shown in her different works. These experiences together are the subject matter of Jhumpa Lahiri's fictional works, the subject still vibrant at different levels and stages of life.

The Growth of Ashima into an Inspiring Lady

As we come to the end of the novel we find Ashima is ready to quit the field she has occupied for 33 long years, growing from a neophyte young Indian wife to a matured host of large number of guests, often visiting her. She is on the verge of quitting her favourite job of a librarian, even ready to give up her post of a mother to her children and their friends.

> This will be the last party Ashima will host at Pemberton Road. The first since her husband's funeral. The house in which she has lived for the past twenty-seven years, which she has occupied longer than any other in her life, has been recently sold, a Realtor's sign stuck into the lawn (275).
>
> Ashima has decided to spend six months of her life in India, six months in the States . . . .True to the meaning of her name, she will be without borders, without a home of her own, a resident everywhere and nowhere (275-276).

Now it occurs to her that the next time she will be travelling alone for the first time since her flight to meet her husband in Cambridge, in the winter of 1967. The prospect no longer frightens her. She has learned to do things on her own, and though she still wears saris, puts her long hair in a bun, she is a different woman now. And this time she will return to India with an American Passport. In her wallet will remain Massachusetts driver's license and her social security card.

She is arranging to give away all her treasures accumulated so long to friends and relatives, not eventually to embrace the life of a sanyasini or female ascetic but to lead a simpler life without much responsibility, in coherence with the situation of her life.

> For the past month, she has been dismantling her household piece by piece. Each evening she has tackled a drawer, a closet, a set of shelves. Though Sonia offers to help, Ashima prefers to do this alone. . . . There is a thrill in whittling down her possession to little more than what she'd come with, to those two rooms in Cambridge in the middle of a winter's night. Tonight she will invite friends to take whatever might be useful, lamps, plants, platters, pots and pans. Sonia and Ben will rent a truck and take whatever furniture they have room for (277-278).

No, she is not frustrated to dedicate herself to the other world. Even after crying for the loss of her life-companion she laughs in entertaining guests, in talking to them and in feeding them to her heart's content. It is expected that she will take her position up to her capacity in society, even remaining humble.

At the end of the novel we are told that the guests have come. Gogol realizes that his mother would come any moment to his room to call him. After the divorce he has become disinterested about many things of the past, maybe temporarily. He is entirely undecided as to his marital life even at thirty two. Here a great thing happens to make a full circle of his father's love for Nikolai Gogol's short story, 'The Overcoat' and his coming back to it. Gogol even disliked the author like his own name, though without trying him. His father presented the book, a collection of short stories by Nikolai Gogol, during one of his birthdays which he shunted in a corner. With a disinterested mood he thinks that he would, soon after the guests go back, come to his room to read the book he had once forsaken.

> Until moments ago it was destined to disappear from his life altogether, but he has salvaged it by chance, as his father was pulled from a crushed train forty years ago. He leans back against the headboard, adjusting, a pillow behind his back. In a few minutes he will go downstairs, join the party, his family. But for now his mother is distracted, laughing at a story a friend is telling her, unaware of her son's absence. For now, he starts to read (290-291).

Biographical in Essence

Jhumpa Lahiri herself speaks of the novel thus: "*The Namesake* is, essentially, a story about life in the United States, so the American setting was always a given. The terrain is very much the terrain of my own life—New England and New York, with Calcutta always hovering in the background. Now that the writing is done I've realized that America is a real presence in the book; the characters must struggle and come to terms with what it means to live here, to be brought up here, to belong and not belong here." The naming part of Jhumpa Lahiri's only novel, *The Namesake*, also has some autobiographical essence about it. It is a force in her novel. She may now be working on another novel but that is talking in the future. Of all her works so far *The Namesake* seems to be the most autobiographical in nature. "'The Overcoat' is such a superb story. It really does haunt me the way it haunts the character of Ashoke in the novel . . . . Of course, without the inspiration of Nikolai Gogol, without his name and without his writing, my novel would never have been conceived. In that respect, this book came out of Gogol's overcoat, quite literally," she said during an interview.

But there was a spark perhaps before her embarking on the name of Gogol. And here it is: "The original spark of the book was the fact that a friend of my cousin's in India had the pet name Gogol. I wanted to write about the pet name / good name distinction for a long time, and I knew I needed the space of a novel to explore the idea," she said during the same interview.

She wanted to write about the pet name/ good name distinction perhaps because she suffered an indentity crisis during her early years in school. Jhumpa, like Gogol, is her pet name which her school authorities recorded as the official name as the easier one than her other names like Nilanjana or Sudeshna. It cast a shadow in her mind to deal in it in future. For this and for some other reasons she felt neglected. As a young child, she felt her Indian part remained hence she made a vow to herself to clarify the position through a novel in time. Thus Gogol carries a special significance in the story as in the life of the writer. Ashoke, Gogol's father, while reading Gogol meets with a serious accident during a train journey. He is saved by chance when someone of the search team finds him among the wreckage, slightly moving involuntarily with pages from the book in hand. He is inspired to read Russian writers by his grandfather. Gogol of the novel who immensely dislikes the book, "The Short Stories of Nikolai Gogol", presented to him by his father once on his birthday, opens it to read with interest long after the death of his father, just before his mother's parting for Calcutta while she is busy hosting her last party from their Pembarton Road house which was sold by then. This is also the first party thrown after the death of her husband.

The Place of *The Namesake* in Jhumpa Lahiri's Works

Jhumpa, it seems, is an admirer of Russian literature. Some critics have compared some traits of her writing with Tolstoy, Chekhov and Hemingway. So Gogol fitted in her scheme perfectly.

She has worked with characters she knows, knows the areas she has traversed. She is a true realist, writing without resorting to secondary ways of myth or symbol in fiction, ways of one who usually does not know the details of the path he or she tries to cover. Her broad areas of writing—cultural mix and clash among ethnic Bengalis and Americans—is a very interesting area of learning and study of people, race and culture, without any bias. It leads to further understanding among the people which leads towards the establishment of peace.

Many of the characters in her stories and novel wish to mix up or marry within their community. They come back to that even after some misadventure somewhere else as do Gogol and Moushumi in here, though that does not last. Lahiri is nostalgic about the past and it seems that she strongly wishes to go back to that origin, in this life or later; a love unshakeable.

In her works the tendency to preserve one's heritage and ethnic identity is strongly felt which is very natural for the human existence. The life is savoured best in varieties, not in uniformity. There should be efforts to maintain ethnic identity in all its colours rather than losing them through generations which will be an irreparable loss to humanity. On one hand *The Namesake* is like any of her short stories in extended canvas as on the other hand the three short stories, 'Once in a Lifetime,' 'Year's End' and 'Going Ashore,' comprising the second part of her second book of short stories, *Unaccustomed Earth*, together make complete whole of a novel which perhaps is more interesting than *The Namesake*. All are stories, after all. But *The Namesake* has some core value, specially as her debut novel. Even when she writes more novels the value of this novel as a record of cross culture will not be diminished.

Work Cited

Lahiri, Jhumpa. *The Namesake*. London: Flamingo, 2003. Print.

4

Lear's Daughters by the Women's Theatre Group and Elaine Feinstein: A Subversive and Feminine Re-visioning of *King Lear*

Aleyamma John

Literature, especially women's writing, is a cultural construct which provides valuable insights into the development of societies and which brings psychological understanding. Our civilization has been described as male centred and in all its cultural domains, women have been put into subordinate and secondary positions. Simone de Beauvoir in *The Second Sex* has argued that "the concept of 'woman' was culturally produced rather than biological" (qtd. in Baker & Wolfreys).

In the twenteeth century there was an unprecedented upsurge of women's resistance to collective male authority in theory as well as in practice. In the initial stage of the women's movement, the focus was on social and political changes and only very little attention was paid to literature and literary criticism. But soon enough, they widened their political action to the cultural field as it is here that gender differences are created and naturalized. Women's subversive appropriation of the male voice has been viewed differently in relation to different literary forms especially in drama.

This article proposes to discuss how Shakespeare's dominant patriarchal culture in *King Lear* is re-visioned and re-structured from women's perspective by the Women's Theatre Group and

Elaine Feinstein. Of the many retellings of *King Lear*, *Lear's Daughters* stand out as an independent story. It delivers an interesting contemporary story and makes the reader feel the shift in emphasis on different aspects of the earlier ones. It creates a feminist version of *King Lear* giving a voice to those otherwise unheard and maligned princesses.

"Re-vision—the act of looking back, of seeing with fresh eyes, of entering an old text from a new critical direction—is for us (women) more than a chapter in cultural history . . .," says Adrienne Rich (qtd. in Gelpi and Charlesworth 18). It is the theory and practice of pulling a text out of a previous text and fighting for a location on the ground already occupied by other varieties of language. Reading becomes something which exists between a text and all other texts to which it refers and relates. Intertextuality, however, is not an "intended reference by an author to another text, intertextuality is the very condition of signification, of meaning, in literary and indeed all languages" (Graham 82). Feminist criticism discovered many ways of discussing Shakespeare. It has proved not only to re-read the text themselves but to scrutinize the way in which the meaning of those texts has been determined by later generations. "Any feminist reading of Shakespeare positive or negative repeatedly moves back and forth between text and society, our society, or Shakespeare's or both" (Taylor 343). In so far as new approaches are concerned, they conclude that Shakespeare's works have no fixed inherent meanings but rather an open "play" of signification from which different versions of the story can be reconstructed. Today women's work in the theatre includes revision of the classics and re- working of Shakespeare to offer the same stories from a female perspective.

Lear's Daughters (1987) is one among such plays written by the Women's Theatre Group in London, based on an idea by poet and writer Elaine Feinstein. The Women's Theatre Group is one of the largest standing contemporary women's theatre companies in Great Britain. It differed significantly from other women's groups and concentrated on the promotion of new women playwright's work. Their works exist on the margins of mainstream culture and mainly operates as an oppositional force in relation to a dominant male ideology. It is against this backdrop that the *Herstory* Volumes seek to work. During the 1980's they have decided to recover women's herstories and the six plays published in the two *Herstory* Volumes originate from this period.

Lear's Daughter's appears in Volume I of *Herstory* along with two other plays—*Witchcraze* by Bryony Lavery and *Pinchdice and Co* by Julie Wilkinson. The two *Herstory* volumes "seek to place centre stage women who, until the act of 're-visioning' became a demand of the Women's Liberation Movement, were 'hidden from view,' whose work was lost and whose lives went unrecorded" (Aston and Griffin 8). The play was first performed by The Women's Theatre Group on 12 September 1987. It is divided into 14 scenes with subtitles, takes its form from the mysteries, gaps, and points of ambiguity that stir a need for a timely elaboration and explanation. The play focuses on women, power and criminality, Shakespeare's play *King Lear* focuses on the patriarch and is sympathetic to the king and his youngest daughter Cordelia. Jonathan Dollimore points out "*King Lear* is above all a play about power, property and inheritance" (197).

The play *Lear's Daughters* centres on the three daughters from whose perspective we discover the hidden truths about the royal family. The play is deconstructed in a way to show how King Lear treated his daughters as mere objects and possessions and imprisoned them in the role of daughters. Shakespeare polarizes the daughters into representatives of good and evil. King Lear wants to make a tripartite division of his kingdom among his daughters. Goneril and Regan perform precisely according to the desires of the king but Cordelia whom Lear expects to outshine in the game is passive. In the conflict between the father and the daughters we may wonder where the mother Queen has disappeared. The calamity of wrong decisions falls on the entire royal family and is extended to the kingdom as is often seen in history.

The central objective in re-writing *King Lear* is to provide an understanding of the two older daughters and in doing so The Women's Theatre Group has created a feminist version. The play *King Lear* is revised and refocused to the princess and is re-told by a hermaphroditic Fool who moves in and out of the tower refusing to be defined. He proceeds to define in child like simplicity the happenings of the play. He first holds up three fingers, indicative of the three princesses, then two to designate the servants; a further one, an offstage king and another finger, "One Queen dead" (WTG and Feinstein 21). The fool then stops the action and begins to think and again repeats the finger business to identify the characters. Hence from the very opening scene of the play, it is clear that *Lear's Daughters* stresses on analysis and re-structuring.

The Fool again begins a game of blind-man's buff catching in turn each daughter, who then addresses the audience one by one. They introduce themselves in monologues about their passion for art. Cordelia begins her speech expressing her delight in the shape and solidity of words, every one of them distinct and different. She conveys the articulation of her desire as logos rather than as shapes, colours or textures. It is noteworthy in terms of the plays representation of the youngest daughter archetype.

> Cordelia: I like words. Words are like stones, heavy and solid and every one different, you can feel their shape and their weight on your tongue. (22).

Her desire for logos can be identified with the male or father figure. When she is made a silent captive, she turns over words to find another voice, her own voice. Father daughter relations are central both to *King Lear* and to *Lear's Daughters*. This special relationship between the father and the youngest daughter forms a de-constructive discourse re-inforced by the shift in focus to the elder daughters Goneril and Regan. Their alliance0 with each other and with the nurse keeps Cordelia as an outsider. Regan, the middle and the marginalized one, lacks identity and desires to carve a shape for herself in wood. Throughout the play she looks into a mirror, searching for an image of herself.

> Regan: I love the feel of wood, of bark cracked and mutilated by lightning or curve smooth and worn by wind and rain. (23)
>
> Goneril, the oldest one speaks last and she expresses her desire for a world which breaks into colours "When I look the world breaks into colours" (23).

Nanny, a surrogate mother figure who loves to tell stories, makes a retelling of the childhood incidents related to the princesses. It points to the possibility of the different ways of perceiving the past and present. The first story that Nanny tells is of the daughters' births, which offers idyllic readings of family life. In the course of the narrative, they are elaborated and shifted to such an extent that any sense of reality is undermined. Goneril, she tells, shot out form her mother "like a dart" (24), all scarlet with blood. It was midnight when Regan was born. The Queen was sitting on her velvet throne and Regan dropped out like a ruby. When Cordelia was born, the Queen was outdoors and she grew like a red rose out of her legs. A portent indicated each birth, a comet with a red trail rushed through the sky for Goneril, a volcano erupted for Regan and a hurricane for Cordelia. Significantly for Cordelia's birth Lear was present in contrast to the birth of her elder sisters.

The princesses spend their days up in a tower attended by the nurse and the androgynous court jester. The parents rarely interact with the daughters. The fool acts the part of Lear who therefore never appears as a distinct and separate figure and also of the Queen who looks faded and ghostlike even before she dies in child birth. Both Lear and the Queen are pervasive and distanced figures. Lear's concern to each of his daughters has determined the course of her personality and her relationship with her sisters. Initially Lear focused his interest on Goneril, his first child but later rejected her in favour of Cordelia. The case with Regan is also the same and they jointly form an alliance. Behind the ill treatment and the rejection of Goneril and Regan, The Women's Group locates a fundamental problem of how patriarchal society traditionally has viewed father-daughter relations. The social structure works to maintain and preserve patriarchy at the expense of slighting the daughters. Goneril finds the tower and the cellars that underlie the down stair rooms as an extension of Lear. When one day she has visited these cellars in Lear's company, he pushed her into the room which was filled with gold and closed it. He promised that one day everything would be hers, but wanted to keep it as a secret and put his hand on her shoulder. When Goneril returned to the room later, instead of gold there were bars through which hands came clawing and scratching. Her telling silence before the words 'on my shoulder' (57) reveals a form of sexual abuse by the king and she is incapable of making a connection between Lear's abuse of herself and his wider abuse of power. Her experiences in keeping accounts taught her to make a shrewd assessment of her own and Regan's worth to Lear. He will get them married to the Duke of Cornwall and to the Duke of Albany respectively and thereby gain powerful allies.

Regan also had unpleasant experiences form her father. Her first memory of downstairs was that she had a glimpse of her father while he gropes a castle woman on the very day of her mother's funeral. Regan rebelled against Lear by turning to sensual and sexual experiences. She reacts to the attitude of the never favoured daughter by grasping every available opportunity and eventually becomes pregnant. Goneril insists that she should get rid of the baby since Regan with a bastard child is valueless. Marriage for Goneril and Regan is a way out of the father tower but still it represents another form of patriarchal imprisonment. Neither Albany nor Cornwall is represented on stage and it is the Fool who speaks the lines of the officiating clergyman and Lear.

The marriage service is disturbed by the frequent speech of Nanny and the sisters. The dialogue is intercept from the preceding lines of the play. Nanny announces the words 'Cordelia the favourite' (63) which remind us of Lear's betrayal of the other two daughters. Goneril and Regan take the opportunity to hit out at Lear. Both Goneril's and Regan's actions fall short of patricide, though they reaches the boundary, are unable to cross it. Until Cordeila became the favorite of Lear she had a voice of her own. But Lear has fashioned her voice and language to his liking. Still, hidden in the recesses of her memory there is another voice and words which she has never spoken to anyone. The concept of motherhood is another concept that *Lear's Daughters* deals with. It can be observed that the absence of a so-called nurturing figure is the reason for the decline of the family of King Lear. A significant concern with both the plays is the inability of women to bear sons. In *Lear's Daughters* the Queen fails to bear sons and miscarries several times in the attempt to give birth to a male child. This leads to her death. She goes through the kingdom's account books and waits around in case Lear returns for his "wouldn't give up on her having a son" (55). The mother usually gains power in a family by giving birth to a male child, but the child must be legitimate to inherit the power and wealth of the male line. While the indeterminate period of time spanned in the play moves on, the parental neglect and isolation on the tower takes its toil. In Shakespeare's play *King Lear*, Lear asks, "Is there any cause in nature that makes these hard hearts?" (3.6. 76-7) In *Lear's Daughter* we get the answer to his question. The motivating force is Lear himself. The daughters can act only in the way they were taught by their father. Alterative structures will not be effective to free them from the experience of oppression. Goneril is what Lear has made her and Regan is the very stuff whom Shakespeare wants to anatomize " in order to see what breeds about her heart" (3.6.75-6). " The two monster sisters will however remain bound together by their herstories until their deaths" (Cousin 112).

It is from the figure of the Fool who functions both as master and mistress of ceremonies that most of the plays style emanates. In between the fun ad the frolic, the Fool takes control of the play's action. Since the Fool and the Nurse are both paid for their respective jobs, they offer a materialistic discourse which serves as a critique of capitalism. They are employees in the household of a dictator who is responsible for the poverty in the land and for establishing a regime of the haves and have-nots. When the Nurse is dismissed, she throws away the money at the Fool who desperately gathers it.

The re-visionary paradigm which The Women's Theatre Group makes use of in *Lear's Daughters* underlies an experience within a global hybrid culture. The play is an analysis of the manner in which the cruel daughters in *King Lear* have come to behave like that. The play also presents self-estrangement, a crisis of self-hood that is expressed in social and cultural division. *Lear's Daughters* portrays different roles of women with opportunities to play at different ages and explores the deeper emotions and physicality of women. This fairy- tale sort of play makes a stylistic way of presentation which seeks to make some valid points regarding the changing role of women in contemporary society. Even though located in times past, the play converses with the present in incidents like the Fool's obsession with money, father's oppressing daughters and the like. The dialogue is often poetic and catches our attention. The play initiates an encouraging note in terms of an all female presence. The men's world is reported and established as an offstage space. Their unseen presence constitutes the defining factor that leads to the existence of the female characters. The play focuses on women and otherness, which depends on perspectives. It foregrounds a space that a patriarchal culture has defined as peripheral. "As herstory unfolds against a backdrop of male power—the shadow of Lear . . . offers an alternative and celebrating image" (Aston and Griffin 18).

Works Cited

Aston, Elaine, Griffin Gabriele. *ed. Herstory Volume I.* Great Britain: Sheffield Academic Press, 1991. Print.

Baker, William, Wolfreys Julian, eds. *Literary Theories: A Case Study in Critical Performance.* London: Macmillan, 1996. Print.

Cousin, Geraldine. *Women in Dramatic Place and Time.* London: Routledge, 1996. Print.

Dollimore, Jonathan. *Radical Tragedy: Religion, Ideology and Power in the Drama of Shakespeare and his Contemporaries.* Brighton: Harvester P, 1983. Print.

Graham, Allen. *Inertextuality: The New Critical Idiom.* London: Routledge, 2000. Print.

Rich, Adrienne. "When We Dead Awaken: Writing as Revision" Adrienne *Rich's Poetry and Prose.* Eds. Barbara Charlesworth Gelpi and Albert Gelpi. New York: Norton, 1993. Print.

Shakespeare, William. *King Lear.* Ed. Kenneth Muir. London: Methuen, 1972. Print.

Taylor, Gray. *Reinventing Shakespeare: A Cultural History from the Restoration to the Present.* London: Hogarth, 1990. Print.

5

Voice of the Silenced: A Reading of Shashi Deshpande's Novels

Asha Susan Jacob

The novels of Deshpande are focussed on the issue of silence, chosen and thrusted in marital, filial and social relations. Yet silence does not mean feelings cease to exist. Though education, feminism and Westernization have effected in breaking the silence of Indian women we find them sheltering under silence as a secure haven to safeguard the delicately balanced man-woman relationship in the society. While some of the characters ascribe to the patriarchal pattern, the self-conscious woman tries to break silence and starts to speak, marking a definite change. The eternal silence of the infinite crowd can be categorised as the silence of ignorance, despair, surrender, anger, protest, pain or combinations of any of them.

Each of the marriages is marked by silence. "Silence is a symbol of oppression, while liberation is speaking out, making contact. Contact is what matters. A woman who lies or who is silent may not lack a language, but she does not communicate" (Cameron 7).

Through Saru, the doctor protagonist of *The Dark Holds No Terrors,* Deshpande highlights how emancipation and success for woman in the patriarchal Indian society can cause subversion of roles in the family and destroy happiness. The social status and recognition Saru gleans as a doctor and the demands on her time cleave a wedge in her marital life. Though education elevates her status in the community, it does not alter her status in the family. The decaying silence makes its first entry into the newly formed Saru-Manohar life when her achieved position conflicts with the ascribed position of the husband. The narrative itself vocalizes the silent physical and emotional suffering of Saru only towards the end of the novel. Analyzing her 20-year-old married life she realizes the purity of her self–assessment: "I had learnt it too, to create an image of myself for the world, to live within it hiding my real self so resolutely that at times I forget myself it was just a facade" (88). This split personality springs from the sourness and silence that pervade her marital life.

Back in her ancestral home, which she left on her rebellious love-marriage to the low-caste Manu, Saru reflects on three specific incidents instrumental in transferring her marital bliss to a monstrous invasion of her body in the silent night. The explosion of the factory near their first residence elevated Saru from the young bride to the doctor while Manu was reduced to the status of the 'doctor's husband.' The self-esteem which made her inches taller, made him much shorter. The ego clash accelerates once she proves to be something more than a tagged wife.

Manu's "marginalisation from the centre to the periphery" (Ghan 250) is augmented by the tart remark of a friend's wife. The envious remark on Saru's career not only destroys the charm of their first holiday after the initial economic difficulty and dearth of time, but also unleashes his hurt ego that exerts its animal power over her body. But the dichotomy between the solicitous daylight husband and her own bruised body keeps her silent. Her inability to discuss the matters of sex and her yearnings and frustrations creates a wall of silence between them. With each nightly assault a fresh brick is added until, as she fears, one day she "will be walled alive within it and die a slow, painful death" (96). With all her unrevealed expectations, betrayals and bruises she feels like an uncleaned and unopened house.

The estrangement between them is accelerated by her doubtful relationship with her mentor Boozie. Though Manu does not question or protest in any way, the very complacency of Manu against the provocative behaviour angers her. The extrinsic tranquillity proves to be the harbinger of a gathering storm. Saru recalls "And they began then . . . the silences that grew between us. Just great grew and grew like Jack's beanstalk" (94). The estrangement reaches its climax with an interviewer's casual query, "how does it feel when your wife earns not only the butter, but most of the bread as well?" (182). The comment undermines his confidence and status completely that the wounded pride surfaces only through his bestiality on her. Yet Saru shelters under her silence for an articulation of her nightly terror would certify her mother's prophecy against love marriages. Children and mother force her to close the cupboard with the skeleton inside.

Indu of *Roots and Shadows* too feel suffocated and disintegrated in a marriage that fails to render her physical or emotional gratification. Marriage denies her fullness of experience when she is compelled to conceal her "responses and emotions as if they were bits of garbage" (38). Sandwiched between tradition and modernity, illusion and reality, Saru finds her rebellious love-marriage deteriorating to a mere mechanical affair when she is forced to curb herself as if there is something shameful in total commitment. Despite being the land of the *Kamasutra* woman is never expected to initiate sexual intimacy in the conservative Indian society. Indu is forced to conceal her real feelings behind the mask of passivity for the male ego in her husband refuses to accept passion in a woman. The pain, anger, frustration and disappointment over the absurdity of her life develop an emotional polarity with her husband. When a woman is expected to negate herself and to behave in accordance with the male construct of woman, she finally fails to recognize herself.

Marriage transfers Indu from the sharp tongued to the toned, from an independent woman to a dependent one. It has bestowed on her an immense capacity for deception for the sake of survival. The persistent denial of the right to express herself "compels a duality of life" (Hiremath 18). Her genuine responses and sensations remain suppressed as if an expression of them would profane their relationship. Emotional restriction reduces her to an automaton responding in the way it is conditioned to do. There is no effective communication between them. His knowledge of her is limited only to those areas that are open to him. Fear of rejection prevents her to reveal her troubled inner world to him. Silence becomes an integral part of their life. Indu ruefully remarks: "That was one thing I had learnt now. One thing my marriage had taught me. The gift of silence" (30). Even the thoughts that destroy her sanity and certainty remain unconfided, grating her insides. Instead of providing harmony and happiness marriage has disintegrated her for she is forced to relinquish her identity before his masculinity.

The desire to have a child, though goes uncommented, becomes explicit when she talks about Jayant's attitude to it. The realisation of the need to conform and the awareness that conformity is the great destroyer of selfhood make her cry out, "I can never become myself" (34). The determination to remain silent to avoid conflicts issues from the earnestness to keep the façade of a successful marriage before the indomitable Akka who prophesied catastrophe for an inter-caste marriage.

Child wives are forced to succumb to the will of the husband in silence despite the tenderness of her mind and body. Indu's Akka endured and submitted to insults and humiliation with a deadly, stoic silence. Her inability to bear a child belittled her status and was forced to witness has liaisons for "man considers it as normal behaviour to satisfy his desire at both the emotional and physical levels outside marriage" (Arora 61). Child marriage stifled her childhood. The tender soul withered under the sexual advances of her husband.

In *That Long Silence* the narrator-writer-protagonist recalls her transformation from a carefree girl to an ideal wife who hides her true self. She too joins the Deshpande club of split personalities vacillating between the two selves, 'Suhasini' steeped in tradition and 'Jaya' trying to break the shackles of tradition. Sex once again becomes an instrument of power or an alienating element. Marriage and sex are two sides of the same coin, but men and women see it differently. While men consider marriage as a licence to physical intimacy, women demand to be guided to sex through emotional intimacy. The difference in their attitude to sex pervades throughout their married life though it remains an undiscussed area. Sex becomes a mechanical action which forces the woman to hide her feelings leaving her both ashamed and terrified of frenetic emotions.

The differing cultural background too contributes to the silence between them. However educated the men in Deshpande are, they still hold on to traditional notions of wifehood where woman remains in her constricted space catering to the needs of the male. Any attempt to cross the chalked out lines would disturb the man-woman relationship. In the Indian cultural concept there are clearly segregated areas for men and women including areas of work. The first quarrel between Jaya and Mohan, she recalls, resulted from her suggestion to cross his gender ascribed role by asking him to cook during the first months of her pregnancy. By reciprocating to his anger with the same degree of wrath she once again transgressed her role. Mohan's accusation "my mother never raised her voice against my father, however babbly her behaved to her" (83) becomes a patriarchal discourse on the need of female silence. Thus the vocabulary of love and that of anger pass them by. After the first disastrous foray into verbalizing emotions that almost ripped her marriage apart, Jaya becomes tuned never to go" beyond that first basic mudras" (116). Basically a modern woman rooted in tradition, Jaya finds herself succumbing silently to the male ego for she has been groomed of the importance and necessity of the 'sheltering tree' of a husband. Even a perusal of her diaries provide only skeletal outline of that like leaving behind the essential core, the agonised cries of "I can't cope, I can't manage, I can't go on" (70).

The enormity of Mohan's crime and the retreat in shame to her flat erects a barrier between them. Communication becomes limited to the essential level. Jaya admits: "The fact of what he had done, of what lay before us came between us, an awkward, silent third, making conversation impossible" (55). In fact the whole novel is built around silence. Herself tossed up in an emotional turbulence, she fails to function as Sonia of *Crime and Punishment.* Confronting her own ghosts, she can only listen to his attempt at exorcising his ghosts. But her long silence is seen as an act of defiance which provokes him to leave the flat throwing a league of accusations.

That Long Silence is not only about Jaya's efforts to obliterate the silence that is suffocating her, but also about the despair and resignation of other "victims of patriarchy and also their silence" (Palkar 168). Behind the facade of toughness, nonchalance and surrender of her mother–in-law, Jaya perceives a despair too rooted to be articulated. The invariably pregnant mother symbolizes the powerlessness of the woman who has no say over her body. The desperate attempt to abort the foetus leads to her death in shame. The silence in which Mohan's sister bleeds to death with an ovarian tumour links her to her mother for she too is aware of the conditioned response of a patriarchal system to a barren woman.

Thematically as well as ideologically Deshpande novels exhibit a continuity. Once again the novelist concentrates on the meaninglessness and sexual confusion confronted by women in tradition bound institutions in *The Binding Vine.* Urmi finds it difficult to cope with her marriage to one who fits into her life a few months a year, and goes out again leaving nothing for herself. The very first might instilled in her a sense of the distance between them. His parodying of marriage as a trap supported the trapped look on his face. It was her strong determination to prove him wrong that made her walk out of her nuptial bed the very first night. Despite their years of familiarity the first walkout remains undiscussed. The permanent detached look on his face stifles her emotions. Lack of communication crumbles their relationship. Her attempts to articulate her emotional insecurity during his absence are answered by an assertion of his sexuality. But it remains only a temporary answer. Experience forces her to realize her inability to remove Kishore's mask: "Kishore will never remove his armour, there is something in him I will never reach" (14). Silence stretches between them. Marriage suppresses her human demands. Like any other normal human being Urmi too is haunted by erotic feelings during the long absence of her husband. The intensity of her bodily hunger during his absence is not communicated. When love degenerates to a mere physical affair, woman withdraws silently to her cocoon never revealing her needs to him.

Deshpande argues how the invasion of female body "even though sanctified by marriage, can be as traumatic as rape" (Reddy 97). Forced sex in marriage is not wrong to the traditional male psyche governed by the dictates of Manu. The poems and diaries of Mira, Urmi's mother-in-law, echo the age old cry of women silenced and suppressed under the veneer of marriage. The voluminous pile of writing left by Mira enables Urmi to reconstruct the tragic tale of a bud withered before blooming in an incompatible marriage. Urmi finds in Mira a predecessor to herself who tries to hide her true self. The diary reads: "I give him the facts, nothing more, never my feelings" (67). The ill-matched marriage sows in her only distaste for love, when it is misunderstood by her husband as mere lust or physical passion. He never realises the need to develop an emotional bond with the sensitive girl before expressing his passion for her body. The objectification of her body instils in her only fear about the dark, clouded, engulfing night. While Saru and Mira silently suffer rape in marriage Shakutai, a woman belonging to the lower strata of society, is forced to remain silent about the rape on her daughter for fear of social stigma.

A Matter of Time also projects the silence hovering over three generations of women in the Big House. Varying degrees of silence are felt through different, yet connected experiences. It is the unexpected desertion of the husband that forces Sumi to retreat into a shocked silence. Her refusal to crumble to pieces and her unperturbed composure indicate a kind of blankness that has come over her. In the absence of Gopal, her husband, the swift flowing stream of her life begins to slow down. Though her ancestral home gives her physical security, she experiences "an air of being lost, of having no place in her childhood home" (33). Desertion of the husband engenders not only pain but a sense of humiliation as well. Ironically the disgrace falls not on the man who abandoned his wife, but on the wife who is left behind to moor the despair–filled hearts. Sumi copes admirably with her status as a deserted wife and her role as a single parent sheltering inside her silence. The very silence, however, speaks eloquently of her pain than words ever can.

The fate of Kalyani's marriage is more poignant than that of her daughter. The cultural devaluation of girls in the Indian society is reflected in the marriage of Kalyani to her uncle Shripati to safeguard her mother's marital status (she does not have a son) and to retain the property within the family. Marriage degenerates into a pawn, without taking into consideration the girl-child as a being with her own individuality and desires. The silence in their marriage has emanated from the loss of the ten year old, abnormal child in the medley at a railway station. Refusing to forgive her negligence, Shripati left her on the pattern forcing her to return to her parents with her daughters. That act of public desertion is "a memory so painfully blotted out that to bring it back to life would be as painful as the process of childbirth" (144). Shripati's return has only extended the public desertion to the privacy of the home with the husband and wife living in the same house on two different floors with stony silence between them. Life in the tomb-like house is worse than widowhood for Kalyani. She is punished to live with the psychic wound of guilt and forced 'widowhood.' For 35 years she has remained a silent sufferer. Her mysterious silence regarding the incident denies her a chance to exonerate her of the accusation. The great wall of silence erected between them remains intact till his death.

Silence becomes an insistent metaphor in Deshpande. To her protagonists it becomes a part of their lives, a distinguishing mark. Most women in India leave behind them only silence. Deshpande does not extol this Indian habit of silence on the part of woman, but shows how it can become a weapon in the hands of man, a punishment inflicted upon women. While it is used as a protest against the threat to their individuality or as a strategy to maintain their troubled marital life by the other protagonists, the silence that is imposed on Kalyani is not companionable.

The same destructive silence permeates into the life of Madhu and Som in *Small Remedies*. The parting scene at the railway station, as Madhu departs to Bhavanipur on an assignment, reinforces the nature of their relationship: "There's no pretence of conversation between us, he stands outside silent and motionless" (20). In her attempt to reconstruct the life of Savitribai Indorekar, Madhu unfolds her own story; a life transformed in one traumatic moment which took away her son and her marriage. The almost perfect married life of Madhu crumbled down with a "nightmare that is the beginning of the nightmare" of their lives (259). The past which her present complacent life had overtaken returns with the nightmare of a man who slept with her at the age of 16. Articulation of the terror of that gruesome nightmare shoves her from the pedestal of the chaste and untouched girl he had married. Suddenly the familiar becomes the stranger.

Our society is conditioned to accept male immorality while the slightest deviation or rape by the same male categorises the female as immoral. As in the other novels sex is used as an instrument of vengeance. If the brutal sex of the post nightmare period has been an expression of his anger at the destruction of his belief in her chastity, refusal of physical contact which immediately follows symbolizes his total estrangement. When he starts suspecting her of post marital infidelity dragging even her cousin Tony into suspicion, the wall of silence rises between them. Sumi recalls: "It's when he adds in desperation, I now think, Tony's name to the list that I retreat into silence. I will no longer answer him, I will say nothing, I will deny nothing" (256).

Women sometimes retreat into silence for reasons other than martial disharmony and threat on individuality. The ennui experienced by bereaved mothers forms a recurring motif in Deshpande. Madhu's nightmare not only annihilates her marriage but causes the loss of her only son, Adit. The emptiness that fills her with his death remains unexpressed for his death has been a consequence of their matrimonial friction. Death of her son is "like a nuclear devastation, there's nothing left (211) except silence. Even the silence and darkness around her speak eloquently of her loss.

Grappling with the death or the loss of a child is a theme that connects *Small Remedies* to *The Binding Vine* and to *A Matter of Time*. Agony caused by the death of her little daughter dominates the consciousness of Urmi, distancing her from others. A sense of hopelessness haunts her with the realization that nothing on earth can replace a lost child. Both Urmila and Madhu want to deal with their grief single-handedly. Madhu fiercely guards her agony from any one as there are no words to express the void and the emptiness. The single moment of death has transformed the world of the living. The sense of silence that pervades *A Matter of Time* also emanates from the loss of a child. Though the pain over the loss remains unexpressed, the mother had to pay a heavy price. Saru's mother in *The Dark Holds No Terrors* also retreats into silence in the A.D. (After Dhruva), after the death of her son Dhruva.

Right from childhood a female child is indoctrinated to be passive, submissive and silent. Gender discrimination at childhood affects the entire attitude of women, conditioning them to mask their feelings. It is the same parental partiality that, in a way, leads to the guilty conscience in Saru regarding the death of her brother in *The Dark Holds No Terrors* which permanently darken her adult life as well. The negation of the living daughter for the dead son causes indelible scars in Saru's mind which remain unarticulated. It is in fact the protest against the forced silence that takes her to her marriage to Manu which too ends in a deeper silence. It is the rejection as a daughter that instills in her a fear of rejection as a wife which in turn forces her to remain in silence to be labelled as a successful wife.

Indu of *Roots and Shadows* too continues in her unhappy marriage to disprove the prophecy of the matriarchal tyrant shedding bits of her self each day. Kalyani of *A Matter of Time* became a victim of her mother's failure to produce a son. The numbness out of terror sealed her future twice: first when her education was abruptly stopped for her marriage to Shripati and the second when Shripati deserted her. Her children Premi and Sumi are also victims of childhood scars. Watching her children's unconscious attempt to lower their voice to the exact decibel required to keep them away from their 'upstair' grandfather, Sumi ruefully remarks: "I don't want my daughters live with a hand clasped over their mouths, like Premi and I had to" (59).

Lack of freedom as a creative artist can make a person silent. As writers both Indu of *Roots and Shadows* and Jaya of *That Long Silence* feel marginalised. Without the freedom of expression they are succumbed to dance to the tune of others, either the husband or the editor. On the threshold of establishing herself as a successful writer Jaya is forced to masquerade behind a safe 'Seeta column' because her husband fears a close resemblance between her stories and their life. Hesitation to jeopardize her marriage compels her to be silent though the skimming over life like sketches provides only an escape hole. If societal expectations of woman as a writer alienate Jaya from her job, for Indu too her journalistic profession ceases to be a vocation when she is forced to cater to the demands of the editor.

Remaining forever in silence is like sitting on a heap of hot charcoal. The articulation of their problems releases the developing pressure inside. The journey to Bhavanipur equips Madhu to confront her own chaos, "to make sense of it, to speak of it, to convert the fractured images, the vague shapes and sounds into a coherent word pattern" *(Small Remedies* 29). Though the cause of his death remains uncommunicated the very sharing of the agony of waiting for Adit enables her to confront her future. She learns from other bereaved mothers that many are forced to conceal their suffering. The letters from Som calling her back acknowledges their need for a renewal of their relationship. Once they speak they will be able to recreate Adit through their recollections. Intense self–examination enables Urmi also to alleviate her pain and to break her silence in *The Binding Vine*. Both Kalyani and Sumi learn to cushion themselves against the cruelty of patriarchy through their involvement with other things. Nostos helps Saru of *The Dark Holds No Terrors* to review her past which equips herself to confront her ghosts. With the confession about her guilty conscience about the death of her brother and the disclosure about her marriage Saru gathers enough strength to squarely face the reality. Her last decision to boldly face her husband itself marks her shift from the periphery to the centre. Homecoming helps Indu to realize that under the guise of independence the rebel in her had been conditioned to be as submissive as any other Indian woman. The realization that there is nothing to be ashamed of her sexual needs liberates her from a sense of guilt.

Withdrawal from quotidian life enables Jaya of *That Long Silence* to review her life with Mohan and to examine her inner self. Together with the system she too has participated in victimising her and in making her silent. Writhing out of the emotional upheaval Jaya comes to terms with herself and breaks her silence through writing. The very act of writing bestows a sense of liberation. Her decision to listen and to speak definitely envisages a change in her lifestyle. The decision to give up her 'Seeta column' heralds the quitting of Seeta role also. The decision to discard prakrit (the language of the minor characters in a play) suggests the march towards the centre.

The fictional world of Deshpande embodies the essence of the cultural milieu of India with all its complexities. Caught in a world of transition, the women folk of different classes and age groups are in a process of redefining and rediscovering themselves. From the traditional gender based roles the Deshpande protagonists struggle to emerge as individuals. Deserting the oppressive environment of their families where gender discrimination conditions a girl to silence, they tread into another realm of silence by the willing acceptance of the mantle of an ideal wife. But an intense self-review, occasioned by some incident in their lives, help them to cast off their restricting role models. Reconciliation with their own selves enables them to discard their silence too which is a strong symbol used by Deshpande for submission, anger, pain and frustration issuing out of helplessness. The decision to break the silence is the first sign of liberation.

The novels are not mere documentations of female resistance to patriarchal ideologies but are the attempts made by women to forge an identity of their own, to voice themselves. From a state of passive acceptance they move to active assertion. By refusing to succumb to societal pressures and by creating space within the matrix Deshpande women succeed in establishing their identity by expressing themselves.

Works Cited

Cameron, Deborah. *Feminism and Linguistic Theory.* London: Macmillan, 1985. Print.

Deshpande, Shashi. *The Binding Vine.* London: Virago, 1993. Print.

______. *The Dark Holds No Terrors.* 1980. New Delhi: Penguin, 1990. Print.

______. *A Matter of Time.* New Delhi: Penguin, 1996. Print.

______. *Roots and Shadows.* 1983. New Delhi: Disha, 1992. Print.

______. *Small Remedies.* New Delhi: Viking, 2000. Print.

______. *That Long Silence.* New Delhi: Penguin, 1988. Print.

Ghan, A. G. "Shashi Deshpande's Heroines: Prisoners by Choice." *The Fiction of Shashi Deshpande.* Ed. R. S. Pathak. New Delhi: Creative, 1998. Print.

Hiremath, Ujwala. "Victim Consciousness in Shashi Deshpande's Novels." *Victim Consciousness in Indian English Novel.* Ed. Usha Bande. Jalandhar: ABS, 1997. Print.

Palkar, Srala. "Breaking the Silence: *That Long Silence.*" *Indian Women Novelists.* Ed. R. K. Dhawan. Set I. Vol. 5. New Delhi: Prestige, 1995. Print.

Reddy, Y. S. Sunita. *A Feminist Perspective on the Novels of Shashi Deshpande.* New Delhi: Prestige, 2001. Print.

6

The Intricate Web of Human Relationships in Githa Hariharan's Novel *The Thousand Faces of Night*

Avis Joseph

The intricate web of human relationships, as it was instrumental in the development of the self, was a dominant concern in Githa Hariharan's novels. Each of her novels is focused on different issues—loneliness, clash with male ego, the degree of freedom within marriage and the extent to which one could approximate independence. My primary aim in this article is to excavate the labyrinthine relationships that existed among the characters of the novel, *The Thousand Faces of Night.*

Of all the human relationships the most significant is man-woman relationship. Of the various relationships existing between man and woman husband-wife relation comes first. The husband-wife relationship begins with marriage. According to the Indian concept, marriage is a lifelong companionship based on mutual love, sharing of each other's happiness and sorrow, working together to build a kind of life one considers desirable for oneself. Matrimonial happiness requires time and happiness coupled with a sense of forbearance. The sense of forbearance and adaptability in a character and the approach of both the husband and wife, save marriage from being wrecked.

In India, marriage is not an independent affair of a young man and a woman but an affair of the relatives of both the spouses. They have been seeking to strengthen their relations that already exist or create new relations through matrimonial alliances. This leads to an elaborate restrictive control on the sexual and marital norms. One of the defects of this type of arranged marriages is that the parents give importance only to the social and economic status of the partners. The intellectual personalities of the bride and bridegroom play hardly any role.

Despite the spread of education, the Hindu family structure still continues to be traditional, especially with regard to marriage. Even the educated people in India prefer arranged marriages. The traditional system of arranged marriages with the consent of and in consultation with the young partners seems to be an ideal type of marriage for the Indian society. Marriage arranged to please everybody except the principal partners in the union doesn't mean companionship. It excludes human warmth, caring and understanding.

Man and woman need each other's love for maintaining a harmony in their physical and mental health. The maladjustment between the husband and wife leads to various problems. The dissimilar tastes and interests of the couple if not spanned in time may lead to unhappy situations. No couple can remain united, unless there was a spiritual rapport between them.

Similar was the case of Devi, the central figure in Githa Hariharan's novel *The Thousand Faces of Night.* Devi, the daughter of a traditional South Indian brahmin family, returned to Madras from America, to live with her mother, Sita. Sita arranged Devi's marriage with Mahesh. The dream like life came to an end when Devi was married to Mahesh after her return from America. Devi was impressed by Mahesh's frankness when he talked about his expectation of marriage. But very soon she realized that there were no heroines in his life, only wives and mothers. Her life was ripe for disillusionment when she walked into an arranged marriage. It hit her that if Dan was too un-Indian, Mahesh was too Indian. Through the life of Devi and Mahesh, Hariharan threw light on the shortcomings of arranged marriages.

Mahesh had everything a young lady could wish for: an executive job, a mansion in Bangalore and enormous riches. But the cold and indifferent attitude of the husband was more than she could bear. She heard many stories of harassment at the hands of husbands, but she was not prepared for such a kind of treatment from her husband. Mahesh was brought up in a family atmosphere that considered the role of a wife as being confined to the house with non-interference even in the activities and business of the males. Devi considered the total neglect and indifference on Mahesh's part as an ultimate insult to her. He went on long tours for weeks together on business. Devi confessed herself that her education had left her "unprepared for the vast yawning middle chapters" of her life. Mahesh could not understand her feelings and thought that she was leading a contented life with comforts at her disposal. He teased her once thus: "why don't I pray to be born a woman in my next birth. . . . Then I won't have to make a living at all" (Hariharan 54). More than his long absences, it was his coldness that left Devi utterly dejected. Devi's urge for a strong sense of revenge is manifested in different forms. She grew wild in her fantasies and sought an escape in her weird imaginings: "I will grow a garden of weeds, those single-minded, wild, common-blooded weeds that plunge their tenacious roots deep, deep into the helpless soil" (Hariharan 58).

Devi had an extramarital relationship with Gopal, a musician. Condemning Mahesh to a lonely life without wife or child for trampling on the marital vows, Devi went away with Gopal hoping to find her own emotional voice through music, which in itself was 'a non-conformist mode of spiritual expression'. The fascination of the new relationship lasts until Devi understands her place in his life. She realizes that the time has come to leave Gopal otherwise she would be drifting between worlds. She throws the peacock coloured sari that she tied over the mirror to cover the images that reflected the surroundings to which she no longer wishes to belong. Her leaving the sari behind shows that she no longer wants the memories of the past to be carried in to the future as she wants to start life in a new way. She is no more a reflection, no longer on the run. She is a survivor now, bent on to become a conqueror (Nityanandam 181).

While leaving Mahesh she felt bold as a heroine. Now she is not on the run, but she feels like a fugitive escaping from captivity to a stage of self recognition. Indira Nityanandam describes the changes in the life of Devi in these lines:

> . . . however, it is Devi who is the modern feminist. Though she lacks the will to choose and her early decisions are faltering, we note a development in her character. Initially she is easily influenced by societal role expectations. She quits the U.S and leaves behind Dan because of a sense of filial piety, marries Mahesh as a good daughter should, attempts to be a full time wife and house maker as an Indian *pativrata* should. Gradually she shows her resolve in walking out with Mahesh and even greater determination in walking out on Gopal. (191)

In the novel *The Thousand Faces of Night*, Githa Hariharan displayed her mastery in presenting an inextricable link between a mother and a daughter through the characters of Sita and Devi. This novel looked at a renewed conceptualization of the mother-daughter bond from a different perspective. It celebrated the female bond and attempted to create a new paradigm for the recreation of woman's identity. The mother-daughter relationship was redefined in this novel. In a patriarchal set up, mother-daughter relationship was 'deformed' and motherhood had a limited meaning. It possessed neither economic nor social status and at the same time, it was away from the notion of sexuality. The restoration of a mother-daughter bond even after the facts of gestation, birth and suckling was important, because this displayed persistent effort against sexism.

The Thousand Faces of Night challenged, generalizing definitions of motherhood by re-conceptualizing the definition of the mother-daughter bond. In contrast to isolation and loneliness as the only response to the woman's condition in a patriarchal set up, Githa Hariharan sought other solutions that proposed rejuvenation and joy in a set of different circumstances that subvert existing social patterns and values. She realized that womanhood was different from motherhood. In *The Thousand Faces of Night*, it was the stifling presence of the mother as a social figure in a patriarchal setup that made the protagonist, Devi, questioned herself. In the end she subverted the dictates of patriarchal system and sought to empower herself by giving a new meaning to the mother-daughter relationship. In the Indian cultural context, reviewing this relationship was particularly symbolic when it concerned about the relationship between a mother and a married daughter. Daughters were conventionally brought up to believe that their parents' home was a temporary abode and it was the husband's house that needs to be eventually considered as home. Once married, they were treated as 'visitors' when they 'visit' their parents. But 'returning' married daughters caused shame to the family's reputation and was a source of despair for their mothers.

Devi propitiated to the conservative widowed mother and was soon sucked back into the maternal love. Sita was always Devi's anchor rock, never wrong, never to be questioned, a self-evident fact of her existence. She "believed most in the power of her own magic". Sita made discreet inquiries and thorough investigations of all candidates before Devi's marriage. Leaving behind the freedom that the U. S offered her, Devi returned to India because "Amma's letters brought with them an unspoken message of loneliness, poignant in its quiet dignity . . . . That she might need me, my hesitant, self-doubting presence was intoxicating" (Hariharan 16). A bagful of certificates and a scholarship to study abroad were also deft strokes of her mother who planned and executed everything to perfection. Devi would grow and prosper in "the wholesome rays of a scientific antiseptic sun" (Hariharan 106). It was for the mother's fond hope that the daughter was sent abroad for higher education.

Unable to bear the chauvinistic behavior of Mahesh Devi eloped with Gopal, a singer of classical music. There too she failed and she realized that she had done wrong. A passing relationship with Gopal gave her the superficial feeling of freedom. In Dan or Gopal she merely looked for instant adventure and gratification. She had a mundane attitude towards her lovers or husband and failed to connect with them mentally or emotionally. The lack of commitment that characterized Devi's intimate relationships with men were probably because of her reaction to her mother's smothering control of every relationship in the family.

As Devi entered her mother's house in Madras, she heard the faint sounds of a veena, "hesitant and childlike, inviting her into the house" (Hariharan 139). Her mother knew that Devi would ultimately come to her and was prepared to receive her as she came out with her real self by retrieving the long forsaken veena and by identifying with her daughter. She thus realizes that woman is not primarily a wife or a mother but an individual with her own world cut out for her (Viyayasree 190).

Commenting on the psychological implications of mother-daughter identification, Sudhir Kakar observed:

> The special maternal affection reserved for daughters contrary to expectations derived from social and cultural prescriptions, is partly to be explained by the fact that a mother's unconscious identification with her daughter is normally stronger than with her so in her daughter the mother can re-experience herself as a cared–for girl. And, in Indian society a daughter is considered a guest in her natal family, treated with the solicitous concern often accorded to welcome outsider, who, all too soon will marry and leave her mother for good. Mindful of her daughter's developmental fate the mother re-experiences the emotional conflicts her own separation once aroused, and this in turn tends to increase her indulgence and solicitude towards her daughter. (61)

It was the constant indulgence that Devi sorely missed in her married life and the subconscious feeling to turn back to her mother for emotional sustenance prominently guided her future actions.

Luce Irigaray suggested that "a mother must give a daughter more than food. She could give her the gift of a language in place of suffocation and silence" (24). In *The Thousand Faces of Night* it was the gift of music that the mother eventually learnt to give her daughter that symbolized this new language. In this way, both mother and daughter could be represented as self-referential subjects and not as exchangeable objects for men. Luce Irigaray claimed that another language was required outside the symbolic order. It constructed a maternal identity but that would also include sexuality. It was only such a mode of expression that could permit the forging of a bond between mother and daughter and at the same time assured each a separate identity. In *The Thousand Faces of Night*, music symbolically provided a solution of an alternative language associated itself both with the feminine and the maternal. Devi came back to her mother to the inviting notes of the veena. The language that Sita renounced as a symbolic gesture of her self-denial was what she eventually adopted as she waited for her daughter to return to her. The novel made a full round to culminate in the picture of the awaiting mother and the homecoming daughter.

Hariharan had succeeded in tracing the battles of woman in her relationship with man and society, not to urban existential angst but to times immemorial. The primacy given to motherhood in contemporary fiction in terms of power or vulnerability was a major theme in Hariharan's novels. Thus Paulina Palmer's opinion, "the identification of femininity with an experimentally fluid form of writing which subverts the reader's expectations of linear, rational discourse, merging identities and ego-boundaries in a manner similar to that which occurred in the pre-oedipal, mother-infant bond," (97) is coherent with Hariharan's novel *The Thousand Faces of Night*. The study analyzed how Hariharan traced the battles of women in their relationship with men and society. Hariharan's mastery in presenting the relationship among the individuals and problems and inner tensions that a woman had to face in her life was taken into account.

Works Cited

Hariharan, Githa. *The Thousand Faces of Night.* New Delhi: Penguin Books, 1992. Print.

Indira, S. "Walking the Tight Rope: A Reading of Githa Hariharan's *The Thousand Faces of Night.*" *Indian Women Novelists,* Ed. R. K. Dhawan. New Delhi: Prestige Books, 1995. Print.

Irigaray, Luce. *Speculum of the Other Woma.* Ithaca: Cornell UP, 1985. Print.

Kakar, Sudhir. *The Inner World.* Oxford: Oxford University Press, 1981. Print.

Nityanandam, Indira. "A Search for Identity: Githa Hariharan's *The Thousand Faces of Night."* *Indian Women Novelists,* Ed. R. K. Dhawan. New Delhi: Prestige Books, 1995. Print.

Palmer, Paulina. *Contemporary Women's Fiction: Narrative Practice and Feminist Theory.* London: Harvester Wheatsheaf, 1989. Print.

Vijayasree, C ."Revisionist myth making: A Reading of Githa Hariharan's *The Thousand Faces of Night." The Post modern Indian English Novel: Interrogating the 1980s and 1990s.* Ed. Viney Kirpal. Bombay: Allied Publishers Limited, 1996. Print.

7

Women Characters in the Works of Sarat Chandra

Bhaskar Roy Barman

In order to discuss how the women characters in the works of Sarat Chandra Chattopadhyay, one of the major Bengali novelists who pioneered the Bengali novel, let us peep deep into his literary domain.

No mean number of books have been written and published since his death to deal from literary and historical perspectives with his life, literature and art, but no book, so to say, has not touched the core of his literature and art. The standards that we have adopted or adhered to stand in the way of delving deep into his work. The writers, more or less conversant with Western literature, have attempted to discern the influence of western literature and philosophy in the works of Sarat Chandra Chaattopadhyay, and quoted Dickens, Herbert, Galsworthy, Spencer and other Western writers to show that Sarat literature is as realistic as theirs. Sarat literature is certainly realistic, there is no denying this fact. But the realism in it greatly differs from the realism in western literature. Perhaps the realism characteristic of Sarat literature may have eluded the grasp of majority of the writers having written treatises on different aspects of Sarat literature.

But the question is: what kind of realism is revealed in the work of Sarat Chandra? If we cannot grasp that kind of realism, it is not possible to get through to the heart of his work, let alone interpret it in its proper perspective.

Realism is possessed of different meanings and they are apt to overlap with one another. The first meaning of realism consists in creating in the reader's mind perception of characters and situations and in this sense folktales are, too, realistic. The second meaning is enlivening of characters and incidents through meticulous description. The third meaning is vivid portrayal of contemporary life and society. The fourth meaning consists in making action and reaction of characters consistent with psychology. There are many other meanings of realism that could be mentioned here, but the four meanings of realism will do at this moment to interpret the kind of realism Sara Chandra took into consideration in delineating his characters, particularly female characters. Many critics are of the opinion that all realistic works hinges on the flow of consciousness.. Sarat literature mirrors life, as it is lived and, thus, is realistic is his portrayal of characters and his works abounds in contemporary problems, social, economical and political.

In dealing with the work of Sarat Chandra we find ourselves confronted with two pertinent questions, one posed by Rabindranath himself and the other by a young novelist belonging to the 'Kollol' group.

In a letter addressed to Sarat Chandra, Rabindranath Tagore said, "You may rest content with exacting prices out of the present time; what will you leave behind for other times that follow?' Still today unparalleled is the popularity of Sarat literature, but popularity can never vouchsafe literary worth. The problems and the questions that deeply stirred the consciousness of Sarat Chandra and impregnated his work with richness—racial antagonism, casteism, cruel social canon, social humiliation of widows and fallen women, the hauteur of the British rules and the pangs of dependence—are losing their intensity to cope with the changing of time and are being replaced by other problems and questions cope with the changing of social and political and social milieux. The rural life portrayed so dexterously in his work has considerably changed and the concept of joint family which is the mainspring of his work is rapidly dwindling away. Now economic problems monopolize man's attention and thought and overshadow social problems. Human values are being drowned in the whirlpool of poverty, ignominy, misrule, class struggles and other social evils. Though his work hints at this social decadence, the problems are now threatened with a possibility of receding into history.

The second question was thrown into the gauntlet, as I have said a bit earlier, by a young novelist belonging to the 'Kollol' group. He said, "If any mess in Kolkata had had a maid servant like Savitri we would have stayed on in that mess for ever, forgetting our families." We cannot put this comment down to the young novelist's intrepidity, for in this comment there is a suspicion of truth. This comment stands on the question: Are all the characters Sarat Chandra has portrayed in his novels and short stories real or true to life? Is undaunted love of a step-step mother for her step-son, of a sister-in-law for her husband's brother real or psychologically proven?

Jadav Mukerjee of the short story 'Bindur Chhele (Son of Bindu), is the record-keeper of the zemindar and has doubled the ten thousand rupees of Bindu by laying it out on interest, but he is indifferent to worldly affairs. Girish Chatujje of the short story Nishkriti (Deliverance) is a just-established legal practitioner. But he cannot distinguish between the broking in straw and the broking in jute and is indifferent to property and money, to boot. Human mind and body are controlled by biological needs. But a majority of Sarat Chandra's main characters, both male and female, have transcended the biological barrier.

Though the side characters and social backgrounds are starkly true, it is well-night difficult to analyse his major characters on the same scale. The truth to tell, we should not analyse the works of Sarat Chandra on the same scale as we analyse other works. We should not search for the likes of the characters in our real life and in the society we are living in. On his mind's background there remained painted the primeval images of ethereal love and affection and the idols that symbolize unworldly indifference such as Maheshwari, Uma, Jhasoda Gopal, Radhika. These idols culled from the epics, *Puranas*, Sakta literature, Vaishnav literature and Indian philosophy got entangled with his mental set-up. Different philosophical thoughts and their contradictions did not cast shadows over his imagination. He has embodied these images in his characters by synchronizing natural and supernatural entities and placed them in contemporary social milieu. His characterization aims to bridge the gap between heaven and earth.

Sarat Chandra was interested in social sciences and well-conversant with western literature and philosophy. But the roots of his literature are struck deep into the soil of his country As I have said earlier, he owed the primeval images of his characters to Indian literature. Philosophy and Puranas. To bring home this point, I shall mention two characters here; they are Savitri of 'Charitrahin" (Characterless) and Saraju of 'Chandranath'. The character of Savitri gave rise to a controversy much before the novel was published. Even the editors of 'Bharatbarsha' did not dare publish the story around Savitri, the maid-servant of the mess. In reaction to this controversy, Sarat Chandra wrote from Rengun to his friend Pramathnath Bhattacharya: "You have seen Savitri as the maid servant of the mess, Pramath, but you have mistaken the diamond for a glass-piece." In his letter dated 13 May 1913 to Upendranath Gangopadhyay he compares the character of Savitri to diamond, as in: "You have seen Savitri as the maid servant of the mess. If you had had that eye...if they had understood which priceless diamond comes up from which coal mine, they would not let slip that diamond."

Many years later in a letter written from Samataber to Radharani Devi, Sarat Chandra compares true love to diamond:

> True love does not come in the life of all men. If this rare thing comes in one life and if one can recognize it, then his life achieves success. You know many ignorant people throw a rare diamond, mistaking it for a glass piece. True love is tasted in sacrifice.

In our eyes Savitri is a maidservant of a mess and a fallen woman. But is the eyes of Sarat Chandra she is an embodiment of ethereal love and affection, never profaned and polluted by human craving. He had recourse to a folktale in delineating the character of Savitri.

> Behari was devoted to Savitri and addressed her as Maa. He regarded her as a cursed goddess.
>
> (*Charitrahin*, Chapter 28)
>
> Behari was saying, 'It is written in the scripture that Mother Laxmi (Goddess of Fortune) once worked as a maid-servant, cursed by Narayana for a certain fault My mother (Savitri) too, for a certain fault, had come over here to work as a maid-servant and went away, subjected to much suffering'.
>
> (Charitrahin, Chapter 38)

Sarat Chandra mentioned this legend in a letter to Dilip Kumar Ray:

> Buddhadev Basu wrote if we had had a maid-servant like Savitri in our mess we would stay on in the mess....The boy...doesn't understand that Savitri doesn't belong to the maid-servant class. The legend has it that even Laxmi had but to work at the house of a Brahmin.

The primeval images of the goddesses Laxmi and Annapurna and the unchaste Radhika have got juxtaposed in the character of Savitri. Wrote Radharani Devi in her 'Sarat Chandra: Manush o Shilpi', 'The character of Savitri resembles that of a girl of Bankura. Her brother-in-law brought her over to Calcutta on the pleas of marrying her. She was a very spirited girl and a girl of a rural well-to-do -family.' Sarat Chandra mixed freely with prostitutes. He might have seen in a prostitute an inkling of the character of Savitri. He has synchronized his real experience and the primeval images in creating his women characters and they remain ever-fresh. This synchronization is vividly exemplified in the story of Chandranath. Chandranath abandoned Saraju for fear of public scandal; Ramchandra, too, sent Sita into exile for fear of public scandal.

> They must go down to the station before dusk, to catch the train. The old sarkar (accountant) wrapped a few cloths in a napkin and sat beside the coachman. He found himself thinking of the plight of Sita and his eyes were sopping wet with tears.
>
> (*Chandranath*, Chapter Ten)

The primeval images are clearly and vividly perceptible on the background of the characters of Savitri and Saraju, but they did not dominate the portrayal of the characters in other novels and short stories, though we can discern a suspicion of their presence in them.

> You are talking about my scandal. No. I have no scandal. If people calumniate me for my meeting you clandestinely, this calumny won't touch me.
>
> (*Devdas,* Chapter VI)
>
> Then I could not understand the plights of Sita and Dayamanti, nor did I believe in Jagai-Madhai.
>
> (*Devdas*, Chapter 13)
>
> We did never see the wish-yielding tree of Heaven. The people in Brjababu's family have got a wish-yielding tree. They stretched their hands out beneath it and returned, smiling.
>
> (*Baradidi—Eldest Sister*, Chapter 3)

I could give so many examples to show how unworldliness and worldliness mingled in the characters, particularly women characters, but I did not, because they would not add much and would burden this article.

It is much easier to draw pictures of sin, ugliness and poverty, in as much as we are gaining first-hand experience of these things day by day in our society. The unworldly Sarat Chandra painted in his characters are not reduced to mere puppetry; they are rather imbued with the vibrating rhythm of life. In the words of Rabindranath, body and mind is full of rapturous joy. Human life strives after spiritual consciousness. Humân beings have enslaved themselves to passions and incarcerated themselves in the prison of selfishness, self-centredness and narrowness. Other contemporary novelists drew upon these wonted pictures in writing their novels and short stories. In the midst of these wonted pictures Sarat Chandra embodied his idols

Annapurna, the bestower of all happiness and bliss, is a well known divine image manifested in women characters. Unworldly is Annapurna's love and it cannot be daunted and profaned by selfishness. Sarat Chandra presented us, readers of his novels and short stories with a good number of mother-images, such as: Shubhada (Baradidi), Abhaghi (Abhagir Swarga – Abhagi's Heaven), Haima (Dena-Paona – Assets and Liabilities), Bhubaneshwari (Parinita) and so on. But his portrayal of these characters was not tainted by unbridled imagination, suffice it to say. In our country motherly love is given a unique place. Sarat Chandra knew from his intimate knowledge of social sciences that love and affection are vulnerable to physical attachment and dominated by narrowness and selfishness. Sarat Chandra gave expression to this physical attachment in a few stories. To bring home this physical expression he had recourse to jest and cruel ignorance displayed by his woman characters.

> Elokeshi said, There would have been no delay, Chhotobou (Youngest daughter-in-law, there would have been no delay. By this time he could have passed four examinations.
>
> He could not pass them because of that wicked master....Out of jealousy he kept him in the same class.
>
> (*Bindur Chhele*, Chapter 4)

> Kadambini was saying in anger, 'Khuri (aunty) is our own woman. Panchugopal is very Fond of the head of a rui fish, didn't she know it. Not giving it to him she cast the pearl into wilderness.
>
> (*Mejdidi,* Chapter 3)

I think these two examples will suffice to drive home how Sarat Chandra revealed the narrowness and ignorance spearheaded by physical attachment.

But Annapurna stands at the opposite pole. Her unparalleled nature is not confined within biological bounds. Sarat Chandra searched for her place in those relationships which transcended the narrowness and selfishness .She is presented in women characters as an image of love and affection. The love of step-mothers for her step-sons is vividly revealed as in Devdas, Baikunther Will, Panditmashai, Shrikanta. The earthliness of Annapurna is manifested in the undaunted love for brother-in-laws and bother-in-laws' sons, as in Ramer Sumati, Mamlar Phal, Nishkriti, Shrikanta (Third Volume). They appear unnatural and unbelievable to us. The following instances serve to beguile the readers into thinking of the characters portrayed as unnatural and unbelievable.

> You're fondling your brother-in-law, but your own son is loitering hither and thither.
>
> (*Ramer Sumati*, Chapter 2)
>
> As mother is, so is her son. I have seen so many boys, but have never seen such an ungrateful boy as he is
>
> (*Bindur Chhele*, Chapter 7)
>
> Hearing the description his smiling pace paled. Have you got mad, Barothakurum?
>
> I thought you would say something else. They have taken their son, what will you do?
>
> (*Nishkriti,* Chapter 8)

There is some similarity between 'Ramer Sumati and 'Mamlar Phal' in the treatment of theme. Against the background of these two stories is the manifestation of Govinda-Jasoda eternal love. But in the character of Narayani in Ramer Sumati the jasoda-image of Annapurna vividly reveals itself. In Mamlar Phal, Shibu and Shambu are own brothers; but in Ramer Sumati Shyamlala and Ramlala are step-brothers.

Devotion to one's husband harmonizes with the unworldly love of Annapurna. The pictures of all-renouncing Shiv and Annapurna proud of her husband scattered over Sarat Chandra's novels and short stories. But Sarat Chandra thought that love and chastity are not the same thing; full-fledged humanness is by far greater than chastity. Devotion to one's husband is glorified in many short stories and novels of his. Annapurna in Bindur Chhele said, bubbling over with anger, "Sati committed suicide. I swear I would rather eke out my own living by cooking in other house than eat your rice. What did you do? You humiliated him!" Deserving of mention here are Annadadi (Shrikanta), Shubhada (Baradidid), Kangali's Mother (Abhagir Swarga), Bimala (Darpa Churna), Sati (Bipradas), Surabala (Charitrahin), Siddheshwari (Nishkriti) and so on. Women like Siddheswari and Annapurna are blessed with the presence and love of their husbands who endear themselves to their wives. Annadadi, Mohini (Birajbau) and their likes are deprived of this blessedness, but they do not deviate an inch from their devotion to their husbands and their devotion touches deeply the heart of the readers. The woman who glorifies and idealize the chastity amidst trials and tribulations in Annadadi in Shrikanta.

> I turned round and saw Indra's elder sister (Annadadi). She appeared to me as if she were an ash-covered fire, as if she had spent many years in meditation and had just risen up from the meditation.
>
> (*Srikanta, First Part*, Chapter four)

In the eyes of the society, Annadadii forsook her family with a man. But she eloped with her own husband. This is an example of undeviating love, reminiscent of the love of the unchaste

Radhika for Krishna. According to the Vaishnav religion Krishna is the real husband of Radha. Rup Goswami has shown Srikrishan in one of his plays as having been married to Radha. But on the earth and in the eyes of the society she is the forsaker of the family. Rup Goswami and Jib Goswami have not supported the extramarital love between Sriikrishna and Radha; they have referred to it as marital love. But the Vaishnav religion and literature has given prominent importance to extra-marital love. Sarat Chandra had a deep attachment to the Vaishnav religion and literature

The aim of the Vaishnav-Sahajiya sect is to delve deep into the nature of the love between Radha and Krishna. Sarat Chandra did not enter into this complex theory, but was mesmerized by natural and preternatural love and romance and this love and romance reverberates in his novels and short stories.

Sarat Chandra collected histories of many forsakers of families and behind his search for the histories ware the inquisitiveness of social sciences and his compassion for the fallen women. He saw the extreme ugliness of the prostitutes, but their greatness and steadfastness in love did not evade his notice. In delineating the characters of Tagar Bostabi (Shrikanta, Part 2), Kamini Bariuli (Charitrahin), Mokshoda((Charitrahin) and so on, he pinpointed the ugliness and dirtiness of the society. Still today the influence of Sarat literature has not diminished with general readers, as is evident in selling like a hot cake of his novels and short stories. The influence is greater, so to say, with women readers, inasmuch as, they love to consider themselves like the women characters aggrandized by the image of Annapurna.

Sarat Chandra is a magician in delineating of characters. But he is not immune from adverse criticism levelled against his works by the critics who interpret the characters portrayed in his wok from the viewpoints of their own experience; their criticism is more or less moulded by Western literary criticism. But they could not deny the popularity of works of Sarat Chandra with the reading public. Here I reproduce a comment (in English) by Buddhadev Basu, quoted by Himabanta Bandyopadhyay in his book, Galpa Niye Upanyas Niye published in 2005 by Bangiya Sahitya Samsad, Kolkata on page 39, which testifies to the popularity of the novels and short stories of Sarat Chandra: "No other authors, not Rabindranath himself had Saratchandra's measure of immediate success. Like Dickens he was the idol of the public."

Side by side with the never-diminishing popularity of his works, there have erupted some adverse questions centring on the delineating of characters divorced from the reality we often find ourselves confronted with. Readers and critics are divided into two groups. One group lavishes unreserved praise on Sarat Chandra's novels and short stories and the other group subjects them to their knife-sharp criticism. They opine that Sarat Chandra wrote novels and short stories just to cater to the transient needs of ordinary people who love spending their time in poring over them. Some of them have gone to the extent of calling Sarat Chandra a script writer. But they seem to be not literarily or rather, critically tutored enough to be able to judge Sarat Chandra's works. Even Buddhadev Basy did not do proper justice to his work by merely saying 'immediate success.' Again he sort of beiittled Sarat Chandra as in the following passage quoted by Himabanta Bandyopadhyay on page 40 and I reproduce it:

> This, however, is worth mentioning that the early Rabindranath and Sharatchandra do not represent two different schools of fiction… . Sharatchandra defiantly lacks the predecessor's poetry. He has been lucky in so lacking, for it had made him a Rabindranath Made Easy, and won him a spectacular success through those heart-Wringing and tear-bringing qualities in which he has had many imitators, but not a competitor.

It is certainly wrong in calling Sarat Chandra 'a Rabindranath Made Easy.' By any stretch of imagination we cannot call him 'a

Rabindranath Made Easy', for Sarat Chandra never suffered himself to be influenced by Rabindranath's short stories and novels. As we have seen he drew upon the epics, the *Puranas,* in delineating his characters. The critics have been so mesmerized by uniqueness of Rabindranath's creativity, they seem to be seeing the ghost of Rabindranath in the works of Sarat Chandra Chattopadhyay.

Rabindranath and Sarat Chandra ascended two different flights and, thus, different are the modes of their expression and their uses of language. There is no denying the fact that Rabindranath's subtle philosophical thought is completely absent from Sarat Chandra, but Sarat Chandra had the power giving vivid expression to human appeals which made his works so popular with the readers and their popularity stubbornly persists. His novels and short stories were translated into many Indian languages. He is perhaps only Bengali novelist to have almost all his works translated into major Indian language, which proves the undiminishing popularity of his works.

Though I have set out at the initial stage to write on his women characters and how they influence his readers, particularly, women readers, I could not resist the temptation of dealing with the nature of his novels and short stories.

It should be noted in this connexion that the genius of Sarat Chandra manifests itself in his novels. Though he has written no mean number of short stories, they are more or less imbued with the characteristics of novel. Though 'Parinita', 'Arakshaniya' 'Baikunther Will' were written in the form of a short story, many critics object against considering them short stories. The editors of the centenary edition of Sarat Works placed them in the short story section, but did not place 'Birajbau' in the short story section, even though Shrikumar Bandyopadhyay considered it one of the best short stories. Srikumar Bandyopadhyay, on the other hand, regarded 'Darpachurna' and 'Kashinath' as novelettes, but many won't agree with him in regarding them as novelettes. It is really well-nigh difficult to distinguish in case of Sarat Chandra's works between short stories, long stories and novelettes. There is no denying the fact that no writers contemporary with Rabindranath could succeed in writing short stories, conforming to the characteristics of short story. Perhaps no writer can create anything worthwhile by doggedly adhering to the standards foisted on them. We should not bother about which are short stories, which are long stories, or which are novelettes We should leave this distinction up to the critics who bother about it and write treatises, classifying them.

Nowadays computer and TV adorn every house and dominate social and literary spheres. The romantic films of the sixties and seventies telecast over TV still appeal to middle-aged middle-class Bengali people. Sarat Chandra's love stories likewise attract them; no theory can explain this attraction

What had made his short stories and novels attract readers is his compassion and respect for woman. Sarat Chandra developed a compassionate mind for woman and this compassionate mind appears sort of backdated. In his novels the questioning and protesting women characters could not stick to the zeal and sort of pale into insignificance towards the end. Achala of 'Grihadaha' or Rama of 'Pallisamaj' is not different from the intellectual Kamal of 'Shesh Prashna'; they speechified on the value of woman, but could not become free women. Perhaps it was not historically possible for them to turn into free women. In a feudatory state governed by foreigners it was not possible for any woman to achieve rights. In the male-dominated society female rights were suppressed and the socio-economic aspects of the society chained them to male and familial needs. Sarat Chandra could not completely go beyond the social strictures on women, yet, through delineation of women characters, he fuelled their inherent desire to slide out or the Slough of Despond. Standing on the ground reality they could find in him a saviour of their downtrodden self. Intellectuals tend to brand his love for women fake, but they can't bring themselves to deny the fact that he brought into the lime light those women who were socially and economically oppressed by society and he very subtly paved the way for women liberation movement.

Sarat Chandra tried to vivify the plights of young widows and prostitutes who forsook their families. The plights were not of their own willing, but foisted off on them by the male-dominated societies. Though Vidyasagar had had a law enacted in favour of widow marriage, the law has not still been executed. The traditional customs and the greed of male people scattered thorns along the path for women to tread on. Rama of 'Pallisamaj' and Aparna of 'Mandir' were torn to pieces by the sword of the conservative society. More wretched was the fate of Savitri of 'Charitrahin' and that of the family forsaking Gauri of 'Ekadashi Bairagi'. Their premature widowhood drove them into taking to a wrong path. In fact the short stories and novels of Sarat Chandra abounds in the characters of prostitutes like Chandramukhi of 'Devdas'. Though they did not claim respect in the society, Sarat Chandra gave them the respect that they deserve in his short stories and novels. We cannot put it down to a 'heart-bringing, tear-bringing' quality.

It is not possible to deal with all the short stories and novels of Sarat Chandra, we would rather touch upon a short story entitled 'Sato' Sarat Chandra wrote towards the end of his life. In our culture and tradition there is no male equivalent for the term 'Sato'. The word 'sati' cannot be taken to connote 'chaste' or 'virgin'; it is unique in itself. Sarat Chandra himself pondered over the tem 'Sato' , while writing on 'Narir Mulya', that is, value of woman. He thought that there is some hidden aspect associated with the term 'Sati'. 'Sato' does not merely imply chastity, something else, as well. To stress that 'something else' he wrote 'Sati'.

'To remain sexually chaste' is regarded here as a criterion for judging human character. But every one knows it is next to impossible to adhere to chastity throughout one's life. This concept passed down through generation after generation has bound men and women to the cruel social strictures and tugs at them. Before the desire to remain chaste pale into insignificance other aspects of life. Harish in the story 'Sati' is a flourishing pleader and belonged to a well-to-do family. He was now close on forty. When he was young he had fallen in love with a girl of the name Labanyaprabha. Their love did not culminate in marriage.. Though Labanyaprabha was equal in respect of education to him, his guardians married him to a certain girl, Nirmala. But their marriage did not turn out to be happy. Nirmala suspected her husband and this suspicion made his life hellish

One day Harish was afflicted with smallpox. When every one was busy nursing him, Nirmala came out of the room and announced to the world, "If I am sati (chaste), my mother's chaste daughter, no one can wipe the vermilion mark off my forehead." Saying this she lay down before the image of the Goddess Sitala at Her temple. No one blamed her for her irresponsible and blind behaviour, but rather congratulated her, because coincidentally Harish completely recovered from the small pox. Then her chastity stood asserted to the village people.

Nirmala increased her mental torture of Harish and on every opportunity used harsh and ugly words on him. He gradually grew fed up of the humiliation and harsh and cruel words. He started seeking an outlet from this torture and humiliation.

He did not wait long for the outlet. The outlet appeared before him of its own accord. Labanya came back as an iinspectress of the girls school. She was a widow. He refreshed his love for her in order to get relieved from his humdrum and humiliating married life. His visits to her got spread through the village. When this news reached to the ears of Nirmala, she stood as if transfixed and her pride of chastity left her.

Here in this story Sarat Chandra mocked at the concept of chastity that the society imposed upon women and how it shattered their conjugal life.

Works Cited

Bandyopadhyay, Asit Kumar. *Sarat Prasanga o Anyanya Prabandha. Kolkata:* Sahityashree, 1976. Print.

Bandyopadhyay, Bhabatosh. *Sarat Sahityer Swore.* Kolkata: Rupa & Co, 1980. Print.

Bandyopadhyay, Himabanta. *Galpa Niye Upanyas Niye.* Kolkata: Sahitya Samsad, 2005. Print.

8

Perspectives on the "Mestiza" Consciousness: Bharati Mukherjee's *Desirable Daughters*

Eliza Joseph

Of late, the literary world of English is flooded with diasporic writing from South Asia. In their works, writers of Indian origin have narrated their experiences of what it means to live in a "borderland" (Anzaldua *Borderlands/ La Frontera: The New Mestiza*) where they have to straddle two cultures, each diverse in starkly significant ways. Though they struggle to re-root themselves in the alien land, for expatriates and immigrants home is an uncertain territory which they must discover for themselves somewhere between two cultural locales, failing which they will find themselves alienated in their adopted country.

A person who has crossed boundaries eventually learns that unless he is flexible he cannot survive. A migrant continually walks out of one culture into another. Such an individual, according to Anzaldua is marked indelibly with the "mestiza consciousness" or in other words, a consciousness of the "borderland". The "new mestiza" shifts "out of habitual formations from convergent thinking . . . to divergent thinking . . . from set patterns and goals. . . towards a whole perspective . . ." ("La Conciencia" 766).

While the immigrant struggles to celebrate his present in the adopted country, an expatriate drowns himself in the memories of his native past. Expatriation is actually a complex state of mind which includes a wistful longing for the past, often manifesting itself in a struggle to maintain the difference between oneself and the new unfamiliar surroundings, refusing to accept in totality the identity forced on one by the new environment. He builds a cocoon around himself, to keep himself protected against the cultural dilemmas to which he is exposed. He clings to his ethnic identity as a strategy for survival in the adopted land.

Unlike the expatriate with nostalgia for the past, the immigrant plunges into the present and gets involved in the environment around him. Immigrants are alive in the new world and they are energetic and have a resilient spirit, a readiness to accept and adapt to the changed environment. Yet assimilation of the new culture by an immigrant does not mean a complete denial of the past. So, despite their decision to become Americanized, writers like Bharati Mukherjee who has integrated into American culture struggle continually to reaffirm their Indian roots. The shift in the geographical space brings about a change in the individual's sensibility. For the South-Asian immigrant, life is "all about straddling one's sense and sensibility in a way that connotes a peripheral distancing from one's own cultural moorings and a superficial accommodation to the adopted culture" (Celly153). Yet, as Salman Rushdie notes, "Exiles or emigrants or expatriates are haunted by some sense of loss, some urge to reclaim, to look back… [to] create fictions… not actual cities or villages but invisible ones, imaginary homelands —Indias of the mind" (10).

Carol Davies Boyce believes that migration creates desire for home "which in turn produces the rewriting of home" (113). Longing for home, therefore has become the motivating factor in diasporic writing. She also adds "the figure of the displaced, homeless person is the most poignant, tragic representation of the transnational capitalist post-modern condition" (113). Gloria Anzaldua endorses the view and explains the dilemma of the displaced as follows, "Cradled in one culture, sandwiched between two cultures, straddling all three cultures and the value systems *la mestiza* undergoes a struggle of flesh, a struggle of borders, an inner war . . . . Like others having or living in more than one culture, we get multiple, often opposing messages" ("La Conciencia" 766). W.E.B. Du Bois, the African American thinker and sociologist of the 19thC expresses a similar view with his concept of the "double consciousness" in his book *The Souls of Black Folk* and it echoes in clear tones the concept of the "mestiza consciousness' theorized by the twenteeth century Chicana feminist thinker Gloria Anzaldua. Caught on the border between two cultural areas, between exile and home, these writers evoke the dress, the food, the rituals, the cultural forms and the stories of their native land. The description of such mundane activities that include food preferences and social etiquette are infact attempts to recreate the "self" in the new environment.

Although exile is the creative source that has generated novels like *Mimic Men*, it is for Naipaul an experience of loss and isolation. Gloria Anzaldua has remarked, "living in a state of psychic unrest in a 'borderland' is what makes poets, writers and artists create" (*Borderland* 73). However, writers like Salman Rushdie and many expatriate women novelists like Bharati Mukherjee and Chitra Banerjee Divakaruni from the Indian sub-continent transform the trauma and agony of dislocation into a celebration where exile, despite its attendant pain, help them to discover new territories of experience. Gloria Anzaldua in *Borderlands/La Frontera: The New Mestiza* has admirably summed up the dilemma of women living in an increasingly multicultural world in the present milieu of globalization. She writes:

> I am a border woman. I grew up between two cultures, the Mexican (with a heavy Indian influence) and the Anglo (as a member of a colonized people in our own country . . . . It's not a comfortable territory to live in, this place of contradictions . . . . However, there have been compensations and certain joys. Living on the borders and in the margins, keeping intact one's shifting and multiple identity and integrity, is like trying to swim in a new element . . . . I have a sense that certain "faculties". . . dominant areas of consciousness are being activated and awakened.
>
> (Unpaginated Preface)

So the protagonists in a number of novels written by expatriate women writers from India are not represented as being overcome by despair and disillusionment. On the other hand, they are imaged as being ushered into an arena of great freedom, independence and self-assurance. Though most of the protagonists in Bharati Mukherjee revel in the unlimited opportunities open for them in their adopted land, Jhumpa Lahiri's women are plagued with nostalgic longing for their motherland. Seeking a home in a new land, some of these women therefore find themselves without moorings.

It is interesting to note that most of the protagonists in the novels written by contemporary Indian immigrant women, struggle to discard their old selves and forge new ones. It is a change that is painful, yet inevitable. Gloria Anzaldua has rightly remarked that an expatriate woman should be flexible. She should be able "to stretch the psyche horizontally and vertically" ("La Conciencia" 766). The new "mestiza" copes by developing "a tolerance for contradictions . . . she learns to juggle cultures" (766) and she constantly attempts to work out a synthesis. Poised on the borders, all expatriate women writers know that they can never melt away into the increasingly diverse melting pot of the West because of the fragment of their Asian homes that they carry into their new homelands. Anzaldua remarks that they have a plural personality and they operate in a pluralistic mode. They sustain contradictions and turn "ambivalence into something else" (767). In the process, they have broken boundaries and refused to limit themselves to any specific categories. Instead they emerge as pioneers of newer territories, experiences and literature.

My attempt in this paper is to use Bharati Mukherjee's *Desirable Daughters* to highlight how Indian women in America whether they are expatriates or immigrants cannot sever their links entirely with their mother culture. They have to reconnect and reclaim their cultural roots and their links with their past to experience true fulfilment in life. So, however Americanized one may proclaim oneself to be, his/ her sense of home will be an inextricable part of his/her being.

Even though it is more than three decades since Bharati Mukherjee left India for the American continent, familial ties continue to bind her to the country of her birth. She is greatly attached to Calcutta, since she was born and brought up there.

Mukherjee's writing career began in 1971 with *The Tiger's Daughter* which was followed up by *Jasmine, Wife, Days and Nights in Calcutta, Leave It to Me* and *Holder of the World.* However, she came into literary limelight with *The Middleman and Other Stories,* which bagged the National Book Critics Award of America in 1988. The book is remarkable in that it attempts to dramatize the "immigrant experience" in America. In an interview, Mukherjee stated that:

> We immigrants have fascinating tales to relate. Many of us have lived in newly independent or emerging countries . . . . When we uproot ourselves from those countries and come here, either by choice or out of necessity, we suddenly must absorb two hundred years of American history and learn to adapt to American society. I attempt to illustrate this in my novels and short stories. My aim is to expose America to the energetic voices of new settlers in this country.
>
> (*The Times of India* 1 Oct. 1989)

Bharati Mukherjee has created "new immigrant literature" that embodies her sense of what it means to be a woman writer of Bengali origin who has been exposed to life in Canada and the United States from a very early phase of her life. In fact, Bharati Mukherjee had to struggle to come to terms with her own identity in an alien land, caught as she was between two conflicting cultures. Like Gloria Anzaldua, she situates herself in a metaphorical borderland where the migrant who has shifted from one cultural place to another lives in a state of discomfort as they try to negotiate between the conflicting forces on the margins where they are located.

Desirable Daughters is set both in America and India. As a book-jacket review notes, "It is both the portrait of a traditional Brahmin Indian family and the contemporary story of an American woman who has in many ways broken with the tradition but still remains tied to her native country" (Rupa Books 2003). The book delineates the dilemma of three sisters caught between cultures. Parvati, the second of the Bhattacharjee daughters shocked the family by choosing her own husband, and strangulated the father's efforts to find her a suitable bridegroom. Tara on the other hand divorced her father-chosen husband in America. As for Padma, the most beautiful daughter now relocated with her husband in America is supposed to have given birth to an illegitimate son in her teens, whom she had left behind in an orphanage. His unexpected arrival at Tara's house in search of his mother, many years later sets her upon a quest for her family's past and her cultural roots.

Though the story revolves round the three 'desirable daughters', the focus is on Tara, the youngest of the three. Of the sisters, Tara is the most removed from her family's traditions and its legacy until events cause her to examine her tenuous relationships with her homeland, her two sisters and her divorced husband.

Tara had a proper 'English' education in a private, elite Catholic School in Calcutta and was married at the age of nineteen to Bishwapriya Chatterjee. After their marriage, they immigrated to the US for Bish's graduation. In America, she emerged as the most 'un-Indian' of the three. After her divorce from Bish, the Silicon Valley millionaire, an ideal to all Indian immigrants, and a sort of 'ethnic' Bill Gates engaged in trying to create a network of communication via the internet, she stayed in San Francisco with their son Rabi, and Andy, her live-in lover—a Hungarian Buddhist.

Before their marriage Bish was acknowledged by her father to be "the best husband on the market" (26). Though Bish was protective and generous towards Tara, somehow they couldn't match with each other. For him love was secondary. Tara says, "Love to Bish is the residue of providing for parents and family, contributing to good causes and community charities, earning professional respect, and being recognized for hard work and honesty. Love is indistinguishable from status and honours" (27). Bish was very rarely supportive of Tara's wishes. For Tara living in America was like living in chains. He was a thoroughly conservative Indian at home and when she expressed her desire to go out for work Bish could not approve of it. He probably didn't want people to think that he couldn't support his wife. Tara felt lonely and neglected. When she had arrived at Stanford with Bish, as a young bride, she was thrilled that she was becoming part of "the life [she had] been waiting for . . . the liberating promise of marriage and travel and the wider world" (81). Eventually, after a decade of marriage, when she realized that the promise of life as an American wife was not being fulfilled, she divorced him (82). She had by then turned her back on all those stereotypical images of how married women of India ought to be – obedient, submissive, self-sacrificing, chaste and so on.

As a single parent, Tara faced problems in bringing up her son. Rabi was not happy with the school in San Francisco. He was terrified with the freedom in the school. Tara said, ". . . he was going to school with the children of San Francisco's bohemian elite kids who had never harbored an illiberal thought, nor suspected the existence of repressive social codes and norms of behavior" (153). In fact, such schools are not easy for Bengali mothers who are over-protective and over- possessive. Though Tara in her quest for freedom had distanced herself from Bish, she was not ready to jeopardize her son's well-being by giving him access to unlimited freedom.

Tara led a rather mundane life trying to balance herself in the borderland between her American and Indian identity until one day a sinister boy appeared in her home as guest of her son. He said he was Christopher Dey, and was looking for Tara's eldest sister, Padma whom he claimed to be his mother. Rabi and Tara got confused and doubted the genuineness of his claim. Chris gave proofs as evidence of being the son of Ronald Dey, who was Padma's lover during her teens. But Tara was shocked and outraged as it was certainly unimaginable that her sister could become pregnant out of wedlock especially because they were groomed in an orthodox Bengali brahmin family that taught girls to be docile and virtuous. She feared that the stranger was trying to blackmail her.

Hoping to uncover the truth about the "new" relative, Tara travelled to East Coast to visit her eldest sister. Less assimilated than Tara, Padma was a member of the New Jersey Indian cultural elite. During the visit, she reminisced that her eldest sister, in her youth, was far more adventurous than she had ever imagined. Tara sometimes felt that her Didi could possibly be the mother of the stranger. The search for clues about the young man's parentage led Tara back to the Calcutta of the late 1950s and early 1960s period when with their parents, they had attended the fabulous parties during the winter "social season" (33). And she remembered her Didi being very close to one Ronald Dey, her friend's brother.

Tara was confused about her strange new 'nephew' and when she cross-questioned him, he always came out with unsuspecting, apparently reliable answers. Chris Dey carried a letter from Ronald Dey, which contained clues about his mother. He had got Tara's address from Parvati in Bombay, her second sister. But when contacted, over the phone Parvati remarked that no such man had ever approached her. And it confirmed Tara's suspicion that he could be an impostor. Even Andy endorsed the view. Whoever the stranger was, he had brought the distanced Banerjee sisters together and Tara felt the urge to consult Bish even, because as a mother with strong Indian roots she worried that the friendship between Chris and her son Rabi would jeopardize his future. When Padma was contacted, she admitted casually that Ronald Dey and she had some nice time together and she even wanted him to be her lover. But it was just that and nothing more. She also added that just a few days before she had received a letter from Ronald revealing that he had an illegitimate son, but had not divulged who the mother was.

To tide over the present tension in her life, Tara who had strayed away from her husband met him once again in their house. Both were apologetic for having ruined each other's lives. Both blamed themselves for the mess they had created. Tara consoled Bish, "Bish please, it was my fault, my head was turned. I was so naive I had too much time and not enough to do—" (265). But all the time she knew that Bish also accused himself for his failure—"He had failed in his dharma, the basic duty in the householder phase of his life, to support and sustain his marriage" (265). In their joint effort to solve the mystery of stranger "nephew", both Tara and Bish realized the value of relationships. However, a terrible explosion in the house rocked the moment of their reconciliation. At first, Bish thought it was an accident caused by the cooking-gas that was left open carelessly by Tara.But it was not that.The next day's newspaper reports confirmed it was maliciously planned by Andy, her jealous lover who felt alarmed to find him being slowly replaced by Bish (274). Sexual jealously and frustration probably drove him to the desperate action. As Mukherjee writes: "What set him could well have been the attempted reconciliation of the Chatterjees" (275). The unidentified body that was later discovered on the beach was that of Christopher Dey. Whether he was the real one or just an impostor would always be a mystery. However, rumours were rampant that Abbas Sathar Hai, member of a terrorist gang operating from South Asia, had murdered him.

Tara realized her mistake and nursed her husband, who was injured in the blast when he attempted to rescue both Rabi and

Tara. Her experiences in America had taught her to rethink the need for sustaining familial bonds. Eventually, they returned to Calcutta for a change, to forget all the misfortunes that overtook them in America. There, Tara's mother advised her about the values of marriage and its duties. Her parents explained why she felt alienated. It was because she had moved away from them in her heart. On the other hand, Bish never fooled himself into thinking he was totally independent (304). However, they got the desired happiness in life when they reconnected to their cultural roots. The alien country had changed them into perplexed and emotionless beings. But the power of their cultural roots restored them to a state of calm and silent bliss. The violent incident forced Tara to look back at her family's past and she comes to terms with her history and legacy from which she was almost separated by her passionate drive towards Western acculturation.

Desirable Daughters is at best an exploration of Tara's quest for identity as her traditional brahmin roots and the American interlude coincide. When she lives in San Francisco, she intermittently reminisces spells of her Bengali brahmin childhood, thereby portraying the contrasting cultures and the emergent migrant dilemmas. Tara's dilemma of straddling the two divergent cultures is symbolically represented by her links with Bish, her ex-husband and her live-in lover, Andy. The novel sends out the message that in the adopted land, one must not entirely reject the traditional well-springs of ones family and one's ethnic origins, that very often help in transcending the traumas and the sense of rejection experienced while navigating the alien world. Tara's uneasy idyll of assimilation and its supposed glories come to an end with her lover's alleged bombarding of her house. The crisis in her life propels her back towards her family and her cultural origins, which eventually reconciles her with her estranged husband.

Though Mukherjee was criticized for not representing in her early works, the problems of assimilation faced by South Asians in America, *Desirable Daughters* is apparently an answer to such negative perspectives. Her strength as a writer cannot be overlooked as she has written extensively and imaginatively about their successes and failures and have offered fascinating glimpses into the lives of immigrants. Her protagonists are depicted as negotiating not only the possibilities of fresh starts and new beginnings but also of the hazards of dislocation and loss. *Desirable Daughters* proclaims that both expatriates and immigrants cannot sever themselves entirely from their cultural roots and their ethnic past. To wind up with a cliché, I would readily endorse Gloria Anzaldua's statement that immigrants carry home on their back as a turtle does, wherever it goes. And with that vibrant note on the indestructibility of man's links with his cultural roots despite his moorings in an alien geographical / cultural space, I seek to conclude this study.

Works Cited

Anzaldua, Gloria. *Borderlands/La Frontera: The New Mestiza.* San Francisco: Spinsters/Aunt Lute, 1987. Print.

_______. "La Conciencia de la Mestiza: towards a new consciousness" *Feminisms.* Eds. Warhol Robyn R. and Diane Prince Herndl. Hampshire: MacMillan, 1997. 765-775. Print.

Celly, Anu. "'Struck in Dead Space':The Sense and Sensibility of the Indian American in Bharati Mukherjee's Short Stories." *Indo-American Review* No.12 (2006). 153-167. Print.

Davies, Carole Boyce. *Black Women's Writing and Identity: Migrations of the Subject.* London: Routledge, 1994. Print.

Mukherjee, Bharati. *Desirable Daughters.* New Delhi: Rupa, 2003. Print.

Rushdie, Salman. *Imaginary Homelands: Essays and Criticism (1981-1991).* London: Granta, 1991. Print.

Times of India. Interview with Bharati Mukherjee. Oct. 1, 1989. Print.

9

Disintegration of Female Psyche: A Study of Co-existence of Multiple Identities in Indian Women of Postmodern Era with Respect to the Plays of Girish Karnad

Kavitha Gopalakrishnan

> One is not born, but rather becomes, a women . . . it is civilization as a whole that produces this creature . . . which is described as feminine.
>
> (Beauvoir 249)

Postmodern era provides a fertile ground for "writing back to the centre," as it ushers in a centreless space. The demarcations like the "centre" and the "margins" do not hold now. As a result women who were the "other" have become active and have begun to make their existence felt. Postmodernism thus gives ample space to present, express and develop their repressed identity.

Karnad through his plays like *Nagamandala, Hayavadana, Fire and the Rain* and *A Heap of Broken Images* tries to place woman's experience, her innermost feelings and unshared desires at the centre of attention. He questions the validity of traditions and customs that "circumscribe women in narrow slots," and "challenge the operating codes of morality which subordinate women in the social structure" (Rao 149). He is bold enough to expose the double standard of the patriarchal society in which men irrespective of his deficiencies get recognised, while the women regresses in the eyes of the beholder as an object, slave or even a goddess, but never wins her identity as a women. Superficially 'woman' is considered as 'mother,' respected in theory, while underneath they suffer as an 'object,' as the 'other'. Images of women tend to fall into two antithetic patterns. One, as an "idealised projection of man's desires" and the other, as "demonic projection of men's sexual resentments and terrors" (Abrams 90).

Karnad concerns himself with the state of Indian women, her problems of isolation and frustration and her search of identity. In *Hayavadana* and *Nagamandala*, he uses "traditional" performance conventions in the urban theatre, there by giving women characters a centrality that is absent in urban realist drama. His female portrayals fall mainly into two categories—one who finds solace in the patriarchal set-up and the other who questions the very same patriarchal norms. The former group slowly realizes and eventually reacts, while the latter reacts from the beginning. In both cases, his intention is to foreground how women manipulate the patriarchal setup to form an autonomous identity.

Indian society is not an individualistic society, and especially in case of a woman her claims to individuality is out of question. The emphasis is more on duty and this result in repression of individuality. Male patriarchal society considers women as 'the other.' She is always dominated suppressed and silenced. The norms, rules, conventions are all for women. Those who follow these norms are considered ideal women and those who flout these even if slightly are considered outcastes. Society upholds the methods of repression and oppression through institutionalised systems of marriage, family and heterosexuality. Society oppresses the women as inferior to man in all realms, at all times, and questions her words and deeds.

In *Nagamandala,* when Rani is impregnated by the cobra, Appana, her husband who has never touched her, drags her to the village panchayat to put her under trial. This patriarchal regulatory body asks her to prove her integrity by undergoing either the fire ordeal or the snake ordeal. Rani puts her hand into the cobra live and swears that she has never touched any other male in her life except her husband and the cobra. The cobra does not bite her as she speaks the truth. She thus comes out victorious by manipulating an instrument of oppression structured by the patriarchal society. Padmini also distorts the patriarchal value system. She poses a challenge to traditional notions regarding female decorum and male patriarchal control. In *The Fire and the Rain*, we see an outcast woman, Nittilai, is presented with beauty in figure, spirit and action. Thereby, Karnad brings to the centre the outcasts so far doubly marginalized, one by the patriarchal setup and the other by the cast system. He also shows how women may react violently if driven to the margins too far. Vishaka staying within her conventionalities avenges her anger upon Yavakri. When she realises that her lover, whom she believed to be sincere was betraying her, the repressed emotions within her burst out in the form of being the catalyst in his death. It is consciously unconscious attempt on the part of Vishaka to pour out the sanctified water.

In the plays discussed here, we find the disintegration of female psyche. It brings out the fact that repression of all sorts—physical, social or verbal—has had lasting impact on the psyche of women, whether it is Rani, Vishaka, Nittilai or Padmini. It also showcases the fact that women flout the patriarchal structures using the structure itself. For instance, Rani subverting the trial sequence. They also reinforce the fact that women are multifaceted. To describe them as just one or the other would not be justifiable. They can be docile, patient on one hand and at the same time may also be aggressive. Nittilai, Vishaka, Rani, Padmini all of them present multiple shades of their identity. Initially, being feminine, they imitate dominant structure of tradition. Being feminist they react against traditional standards, demand their rights. In the final stage of being a female, a self-discovery is made. In *Nagamandala*, we can see Rani transforming from an archetypal passive Indian woman to a bold woman. Rani says to Naga in the beginning of the play, "The pig, the whale, the eagle . . . none of them asks why. So I won't either" (*Nagamandala* 26). But gradually Rani transforms into a woman who speaks out boldly what she feels. She says to Naga, ". . . I was stupid, ignorant girl when you brought me here. But now I am a woman, a wife and I am going to be a mother. I am not a parrot. Not a cat or a sparrow. Why don't you take it on trust that I have a mind and . . ." (*Nagamandala* 32). From her early approach of being a passive one, she begins to attain activity. It is here that *Nagamandala* lends room for reading a feminist act of subversion.

In *Hayavadana*, Karnad has gone a step forward in disintegrating Padmini's psyche. The patriarchal society never addressed the physical needs of women. They ignored the fact that women had similar urges as that of men. Karnad in this play depicts women's urges and women's freedom. As tradition goes an Indian 'Pativrata' is expected to be 'pure' in thought and action. Though Padmini is a devoted wife, she is liberal in her thoughts. As she watches Kapila she states, ". . . and what an ethereal shape! Such a broad back—like an ocean with muscles rippling across it—and then that small, feminine waist which looks so helpless. . . . He is like a Celestial Being reborn as a hunter. . . . How his body sways, his limbs curve—it's a dance almost" (*Hayavadana* 25). Padmini thus is shown to trespass the boundaries of the value system that governs human society. She is not the traditional Indian woman who is shy and submissive, but one who is strong in mind and character. She thus breaks away from stereotypes.

Nitillai and Vishaka of *The Fire and the Rain* also do not fit into any stereotypes. Nittilai is presented as a tribal woman of a low caste, but with elevated thoughts. She is bold and breaks the rules imposed upon her by her community. Vishaka like Rani slowly evolves from passivism to activism in a subtle way.

Manjula of *Broken Images* is different from her earlier counterparts. *Broken Images* has an urban setting unlike rest of his plays. In *this play*, the psyche of Manjula, a modern professional young woman, is disintegrated and examined. This play effectively delineates the psyche of the protagonist Manjula Nayak, a Kannadiga-turned-English novelist. This play is noteworthy for the manner in which the protagonist's psyche is peeled layer after layer till the true self is revealed. The process may remind us of *Emperor Jones*, but the fact that this play delineates the intricacies and different shades of the psyche of a woman is what is worth mentioning.

The story line goes like this—Manjula has become an overnight celebrity by writing her debut English novel, *The River Has No Memories*. Her new commitments and busy schedule has made her leave her job of teaching English in a local college and also estranged her from her husband. Her novel has been filmed in Kannada and is to be telecasted. Before that, she is to deliver an introductory address. She takes of this as an opportunity to defend her stand, refute and replay to the allegation laid against her. She is accused of having betrayed Kannada for the sake of fame, fortune and a vastly expanded audience. Very cleverly she refutes all the charges levelled against her by posing counter questions to her critics.

After her address is over, her TV image refuses to disappear from the screen and holds she captive with probing questions. When after the interview she stands to leave, the image calls out, "Where are you going? You can't go yet." Manjula thinks it is a technical hitch and calls the assistants. But nobody responds. The truth is unravelled as she is entrapped in a whirlpool of questions from which she has no escape the only alternative left for her is to open up. When the image cross- examines her, fragmented and painful truths slowly emerge. In Karnad's own words "as layers of carefully cultivated pose peels off, the persona splinters" ("In His Own Voice" 53). The interrogation of the image brings out her repressed past, her repressed guilt and repressed fears buried in the unconscious to the fore. The image makes her admit that

Malini was more attractive, intelligent, vivacious, than her and that she was jealous of Malini because she was the favourite of her parents and she got the best of every thing. "She was always the focus" (*Collected Plays II* 269). The image also compels she to accept that she was an average in all maters compared to Malini. Malini's stay in her house for the last six years helped her to improve her English because Malini "breathed, laughed, dreamt in English" (*Collected Plays II* 271).

The TV image cleverly traps Manjula in the chronological account of Malini's death and publication of a novel. To the question of the image whether Malini new that Manjula was writing a novel on her life, Manjula replies that she hadn't even thought of it when she was alive. She further narrates that within a couple of weeks of her death; she mailed the typescript of the novel to the literary agent. The image wonders at Manjula's speed of writing—350 pages within two weeks—one hundred and fifty thousand words a day that was virtually impossible. Finally, Manjula loses her control and finding no way out, admits, "All right! I didn't write the novel. She did. She wrote it. Every word of it" (*Collected Plays II* 279). She further vomits out the truth that Malini had started writing the novel eighteen months before her death. He found the typescript in Malini's drawer, read it and sent it to the literary agents. Malini used to sign herself as M. Nayak. Manjula signs the manuscript as Manjula Nayak. The literary agent took her to be the author as they were unfamiliar with the Indian names. In this way, the TV image of Manjula makes her confess the fraud she has played upon her dead sister. She finds herself without any identity at all, almost dead. The image is Manjula's alter-ego, her hidden other self, her conscience, the reality. It sets her conscience working by asking questions or passing comments cynically and sarcastically which exposed the inner self of Manjula. Towards the end of the play, the virtual image grows more real and the 'seemingly' real image of Manjula seems virtual and fraudulent. In the climatic juncture, the screen breaks. Manjula looks into the broken mirror and it reveals bits and pieces of the personalities, some hers and some assumed from her sister. These are in contrast to real broken mirror parts that reflect the same image of the person in all the pieces.

The significance of the play lies in the manner of how the character of Manjula is conveyed through a gradual breaking down of her conscious ego and the revelation of her unconscious. In the beginning we see her ego—the conscious mind, dominating our personality, and she totally avoided the unconscious. When her image on TV questions her, her self created mask, the falls 'ego- image' shatters and her unconscious—the 'id' comprising memories come back to her. Thus, Karnad delves deep into the psyche of Manjula and bears open the workings her mind.

One cannot fully explain the essence of 'woman' as she is several things at the same time. Simone de Beauvoir in *The Second Sex* as speaking highly of the multifacetedness of women says:

> This unique woman at once carnal and artificial, natural and human, casts the same spell as the equivocal objects dear to the surrealists; she is like the spoon-shoe, table-wolf, the marble-sugar that the poet finds at the flea-market or invents in a dream; she shares in the secret of familiar objects suddenly revealed in their true nature and in the secret of plants and stones. She is all things. (264)

Rightly so Karnad in his plays present women attempting to affirm their multifaceted identity. The images of women in his plays are vivid. We find two different images: one, evolving gradually out of their cocoon to an awakening. Such characters flout the patriarchal system by remaining in it. The other comes across with a streak of boldness and violent reactions and then later succumbing to be a victim. The former category consists of Rani, Vishaka and the latter of Nittilai and Padmini. Both characters of women are needed as change can be steered only if there is a revolutionary streak in us, but treading more gently and diplomatically would be ideal as we belong to a developing world where systems and codes of conduct are different from the developed western world. Irrespective of the category, the women in Karnad's plays present streaks of boldness when the situation demands. Hence we see the co-existence of multiple identities in women of postmodern era, who are all set to "write back to the centre." One cannot pinpoint and say 'woman' is 'this' or 'that.' No longer can one define woman in a simple manner. Nor can, one generalise and state that Indian women are meek, submissive, pure, and simple. One is reminded of Toril Moi's statement: "What is a woman? Woman is not one" (114).

Works Cited

Abrams, M. H. *A Glossary of Literary Terms*. Singapore: Harcourt, 2000. Print.

Beauvoir, Simon de. *The Second Sex*. New York: Bentham, 1952. Print.

Chandra, Subash. "Theory, Movement, Context of women in Culture and Literature in India: An Introduction. *Intersections: Gender and Sexuality in Asia and the Pacific*. Issue 22, Oct. 2009. Web. 15 Jul. 2011.

<http://intersections.anu.edu.au/isssue22/chandra.intro.html>

Dharwadkar, Aparna. Introduction. *Collected Plays*. By Girish Karnad. Vol. 2. New Delhi: OUP, 2005. vii-xxxix. Print.

Karnad, Girish. *Collected Plays*. Vol. I. New Delhi: OUP, 2005. Print.

_______. *Collected Plays*. Vol. II. New Delhi: OUP, 2005. Print.

_______. *The Fire and the Rain*. New Delhi: OUP, 1999. Print.

_______. *Hayavadana*. Madras: OUP, 1991. Print.

_______. "In His Own Voice: A Conversation with Girish Karnad. Interview with Tutun Mukherjee." *Girish Karnad's Plays: Perfomance and Critical Perspectives*. Ed.Tutun Mukherjee. New Delhi: Pencraft International, 2006. 25-27. Print.

_______. *Nagamandala- Play with a Cobra*. New Delhi, OUP, 2002. Print

Moi, Toril. *What is a Woman*? Oxford: OUP, 1999. Print.

Rao, Vishveswara CR. *Indian Writing Today*. New Delhi: Indian Association for English Studies, 1996. Print.

10

Women's Empowerment and Personal Mobility in Shashi Deshpande's Novel *The Dark Holds No Terrors*

Khobragade Grishma Manikrao

Indian Independence produced radical and lasting changes in Indian social and cultural life. Besides new technology, knowledge, institution, beliefs and values also dominated the Indian social minds. Subsequently, many cultural practices changed slowly and they started acting as a barrier to successful social adjustment. Contemporary Indian English noveles portray images of protagonists confined to rigid tradition and orthodoxy. The novels produced after independence show that the Western culture has been partly assimilated by Indians. Post-Independence Indian society also witnessed a new social and economic empowerment of women coming into existence. It was also to see the emergence of new patterns of class structure and the formation of new communities, i.e., educated women community according to the changing patterns of life.

Up to the end of the eighteenth century, England was an agricultural country, subsequently on the way to industrialization, and there was a lot of improvement in the methods of production. The population of the towns increased with the migrants from villages thronging the towns in search of job opportunities. It resulted in the creation of a new social order—labour class and capitalist.

India too had a similar developmental phase. Although some of the class barriers have broken down in this country, it is a mistake to think that India is classless society. Social change takes many forms and each change in the structure and function of a society has effects on other aspects of the society. Thus urbanization and industrialization affected the patterns of social class as well as those of living and working condition. The increase in population in this period, the improvement in working conditions and the growth of trade unions has all changed pattern of social behavior.

The present study makes an attempt to read certain selected novels of Shashi Deshpande with an objective of locating the class and community structures embedded in them. It also tries to detect the class interest of the perspective that travels along her narratives as the point of view. The study is based on the hypothesis that her novels reveal her views and opinions on empowerment of women community and personal mobility. The basic methodology used in the study is those of analytical study wherein fiction is considered as valuable social document and by analyzing fiction, social structures too are analyzed. The scope of this study is the possibility of using the same parameters in analyzing the works of various other Indian English novelists and in making the study of literature an interdisciplinary exercise.

Shashi Deshpande's fiction focuses on a real-life situation of society. Her description of person of one class assimilating into another class is a realistic picture of modern urban society and cross-cultural social realities. She acknowledges that higher class and lower class or male or female gender can come together and they are closely interdependent. She has presented a variety of such images in *The Dark Holds No Terrors (*1980*)*.

This novel is about the homecoming of Saru, the protagonist. In this novel, Sarita, or Saru, a successful married doctor rejects her husband, Manohar. She returns to her father's home after fifteen years. By doing so, she tries the gap between herself and her father. This novel is also concerned with the suffering of the modern educated Indian woman who is in search of her individuality. Saru, who is such a woman, also tries to fight from the constraints of caste based traditional social system.

Sarita is a successful, well settled doctor. Her husband Manohar is an English teacher in college. she has two children. But she is not happy with her married life. She had left her parents in a fit of anger to get married to her lover. The novel opens with Saru returning after 15 years to her father's house. She had decided never to return but she has to change her mind with her mother's death. This homecoming gives her a chance to think about her past. The novel explores the various dimension of middle class family life and the liability which controls a woman's conduct and responsibility.

Saru is the narrator of the novel. She remembers her childhood experiences and her stay in her father's home gives Saru an opportunity to re-assess her relationship with her father, her dead mother, her dead brother, Dhruva and her children Renu and Abhi. She finds that Father lives along with Madhav. She tries to understand herself and others by redefining her relations. This makes her mentally strong to face realities. The darkness no longer holds any terror and Saru is highly self-determined and she discards traditional rules. She rejects her mother to become a doctor and she rejects caste to marry outside; and defies social limitation by using Boozie, her friend, to advance her career. These moves are possible for her because she is economically independent and it gives her courage to take an action against social system. Saru wants to become self-sufficient and her every effort in life is towards this goal. When she earns Manu's love, she feels that it is her great achievement. However, she is not a passive woman. However, she always tries to prove her individuality as a doctor. While Manu is anxious, she is aware of the facts of life. She observes: "And yet we stayed physically apart It's my painful middle-class inhibitions, I told myself, making marriage the open sesame of all enjoyment for me." (40)

Saru is interested in improving her financial and social status. She does not like to live a life of common person. When she realizes the inequality of success between herself and her husband is the cause of domestic squabbles. She marries him only when she thinks that he would consider her to be equal. She is also self-centered. She always tries to build up her self-image, so much so that she forces him to surrender his ego before her. She nullifies Manu's existence and makes him a cipher. She thinks that all the men are weak and inferior. Her profession makes her conscious of her self sufficient status and she learns to command the others.

Saru has a very gracious and receptive but very cautious personality. She lacks confidence as a middle class woman. She knows her limitations and abilities. She is ready to overcome strict traditional, social limitations and accept new modern vision wherein all are equal. She develops a sense of self image and cultivates self-confidence. She understands herself without exaggeration and without underestimation. The manner, in which she behaves, communicates and relates with others, reflects her personality and upbringing. Society, education, peer group interaction, mental and every physical characteristic add to her personality, sometimes positively, sometimes negatively. Her behaviour is not only governed by base instincts, but by higher motives or values. She rejects her father's home and her search leads her to realize the potential in human life. She wants to be free person and wants to prove her independent identity in society. She says:

> "My life is my own..." Somehow, she felt as if she had found it now, the connecting link. "It means you are not just a strutting, grimacing puppet, standing futilely on the stage for a brief while between areas of darkness. If I have been a puppet, it is because I made myself one. I have been clinging to tenuous shadow of a marriage whose substance has long since disintegrated because I have been afraid of proving my mother right." (220)

Saru's love for power can be acknowledged with her relationship with every character in the novel. She thinks that she may be responsible for all happenings. She says: "The helplessness of trying to go back into that time, that state of mind, trying to be definite about what I did and why" (184).

She celebrates her children's birthday party and games. When she goes away to her father's house, she remembers the need of her children. Yet, she is in favour of family planning. She says: "One boy and one girl. A family the right size. The right kind. Like the ads. A happy family. Healthy, happy, smiling and in colour" (20). She is also realistic. She believes that family planning is connected to liberation, empowerment of women, and with social and gender equality.

Saru makes efforts to raise her dignity and image in society. She realizes that her basic drive is the greed for money. Saru resorts to hard work and makes effective use of her skill to earn money. She recalls her frugal life: "It is a marvel how we managed to live. Manu's salary, never very much, barely covered our expenses. And for two years I was earning nothing. At first it didn't matter that I was out of all the things that were so much a part of student life—the parties, the eating out, the movies, casual trips" (92).

Saru who has a healthy personality approaches situations with a rational attitude, accepting them. She knows that success comes only with hard work and strives for long-term gains rather than immediate pleasure. She accepts her drawbacks and improves those in which she is strongest. She lives in the present, and does not turn back to the past. Saru is self-governed and is independent in her thoughts and action. She keeps her emotions under control and doses not harm her. She is able to meet frustrations without conflicts. She also develops tolerance towards stress, anxiety, depression, pain and emotional disturbance.

Saru also sets realistic goals. She acquires the knowledge, skill and qualification to reach her goals. She is well organized and consistent. She also makes the best use of their time and effort to achieve her dream. She remembers: "A year later I was his Registrar. In less than two year I passed my MD. Four years later

I was an Assistant Honorary at a suburban hospital" (92). At the end, she realizes that she has broken her past life and peaceful harmony. She is isolated in her own house. She always feels insecure, alone. She feels herself as homeless.

Saru plays different role at different times—one a successful doctor in a white coat by day and a trapped animal by night. She always depressed in her mind, even though she is a doctor, in the eyes of her husband, she is just slave. When she has been ill-treated and victimized by her husband, she wants to escape from her house. This is her difficult time when she has to face the inner crisis and conflict. She says:

> a+b they told us in mathematics is equal to b+a. But here a+b was not, definitely not equal to b+a. It became a monstrously unbalanced equation, lopsided, unequal, impossible. But is that the only reason, or would it have happened in any case, What happened to us later, he being what he is and I being what I am? I have a feeling I will never know the answer to that one. (42)

Saru represents a middle class girl in a modern Indian social structure. She has been trapped in a conflict between traditional idea and new. She is brought up in a traditional family. However, her education has changed her attitude towards life. She becomes rebellious towards mindless orthodoxy. However, she is a self-centred person. In her world, there are only her two children, her home, her practice, and her patients. Her circle of interest is very limited. Manu, her husband is out of her circle. She is responsible for her own critical situation. She is very professional. She tells Manu: "You want clothes, good food, lots of books and magazines, movie and plays, the best cigarettes. And do you get. All that without money?" (152). She gives preference to her job not for her family. She is first a doctor, then a wife or mother in her image. But because of her profession, she is motivated and that has courage to face her husband. Manu has to face the reality of his failure. Saru says: "I was too busy, I was too tired, I was too exhilarated with the dignity and importance that my status as a doctor seemed to have given me" (42).

People visit Saru's house for different purposes, which creates a gap between Saru and her husband Manu. She remembers a leisure time spent in the company of her friend. For her friend, "the only one she knew there, treacherously deserted her for others, cousins and closer friend" (47). She had attached herself to one group or another, hoping to be taken for one of them. Groups often develop because the individual members have one or more common characteristics. The members of the group interact and influence each other in collective pursuit of a common goal. The behaviour of each member of a group is influenced by the behaviour of others of the group. Social alliances extend outside the work situation: they can be based on similar age, gender, hobbies, religious or political affiliations. The only time she did belong to a group was when they all gathered together for a meal, a ritual. And then, when it was over, "the crowd dissolved into people who had nothing to do with her, shattering the semblance of belonging, of togetherness" (47).

Saru realizes that her superiority complex is the root cause of her predicament and suffering. At the end of the novel, she receives a letter from Manu. He decides to visit and to get her back home. He tries to compromise and she is ready even to go back. She asks her father, "Baba, if Manu comes tell him to wait. I'll be back as soon as I can" (221). This decision shows that she is psychologically prepared to admit the reality of her life. She emerges as a new different woman who can control herself and ready to surrender before her ego and her negative idea. Saru represents a middle class working person in post-Independence period. She revolts against customs and traditions. She is ready to understand a life outside the family and faces the critical life. She fights to make her free from social tradition and use her womanhood to show her identity and realize her self-image.

Saru is a career-oriented woman whose income and profession status is greater than her husband. Meenakshi Bharati observes:

> This is a gendered imbalance that sits in opposition to the socially prescribed ' right ' balance in which the scales of married life are, under ideal conditions, weighted equally by material provision at one end-the male end- emotional provision at the other end- the female end. If the roles are reversed, surely the scales remain balanced; but mathematical equations tend to operate in the field of the ideal, unaffected by the less than ideal conditions of social reality. (104)

Saru is presented an emerging female character. The novel starts with she visiting her father's home after a gap of 15 years. Now she is a well-known reputed established doctor and mother of two children. When she reaches father's house, she gets a cold reception. "She is confused, helpless and almost miserable." (15)

Shashi Deshpande believes that society will not change because men will never give anything to women. It is a desirable social duty of women that they should come forward and bring certain change in themselves to face the ground reality. It is observed that no one comes forward to make other free. Minakshi Bharati observes:

> I think consumerism is good in one way. You see a TV, you see all those things, and you say I want to have that. And how do you get that if you don't work and your husband alone is earning? You know, my servant who has been working with me for many years, whatever she wants she buys with her own money. She does not wait for her husband to buy it. Therefore, consumerism is going to be good in one way. Because if people want the goods, they'll need their own money. To earn the money they want to take up a job. Once you take up a job you become a independent person. (104)

After an intercaste marriage with Manu, they live in the room in the chawl and start their married life. But she is not satisfied in this environment and she tries to mobilize her life towards her destination to live in a flat.

In the novel, The *Dark Holds* No *Terrors,* the society presented is in transition. The women who are financially independent have always a choice to enjoy their life with pride.

Shashi Deshpande's Saru, the protagonist, finds her position as a married woman has certain limitations. But at the end of the story, the novelist has shown her character at two levels. Saru is sentimental and emotional: however, she is intellectual. She has to keep on struggling her own battle alone, redefine, and rediscover her life. Vijayalakshmi Sheshadri rightly states:

> This becomes crucial to the characterization of Sarita, who is presented as a woman with tremendous possibilities of movement, which match her desire for new places. In the terminology applied by black feminist critics, she could be described as an 'assimilated heroine' who has gained control over her life, a woman who apparently has combined career and marriage successfully. (61)

The novel could be considered as a social document as it adequately reflects the realities of life. It could also be considered as a cultural material which has in it the dynamics of social realities which are conditioned by factors like caste, class, gender and community. These statements are testified in the novels of Shashi Deshpande and reflect effectively the complex class system and the community patterns of India.

Shashi Deshpande's novel *The Dark Holds No Terrors* reveals a similar class system and communities. The protagonists in both the novels represent the middle class and they show urge for upward social mobility and interest in better education.

Saru, the protagonist in *The Dark Hold No Terrors,* represents this middle class. She also represents the community of educated, employed urban women who have their financial, independence and better freedom of choice. Shashi Deshpande makes such women the focal character of her narratives, and juxtaposes other characters with them to show how higher social class male gender and urban society afford certain privileges in Indian society.

Further, Deshpande also makes a micro segmentation of Indian society by bringing the variables such as caste, gender and geographical location which makes subtle differences with in a class. She also helps readers to look largely into the lives of Indian women, both employed and unemployed women. She also looks at various social institutions such marriage, education and religion and their influences on various class and communities. She implies that women of better education and financial freedom, though still victims of patriarchal bias, are less oppressed as compared to the less fortunate women. She indicates that women from lower cast and lower class are vulnerable as they are the victims of the domestic violence, rape and discrimination.

However, Shashi Deshpande focuses on the middle class women though she depicts men and women of lower economic strata; they merely provide a contrast to the main characters who are invariably picked from the middle class or upper middle class. Though Shashi Deshpande is not insensitive to the problems and the realities of women from the lower class, her focus seems to be on women as a community. In her novels, women of all class are marginalized though degree of marginalization differs from person to person.

Deshpande also indicates that the boundaries of class and community are not rigid. Character such as Urmu, Vanna and Saru frequently cross the boundaries of their respective classes to reach out and to understand the people other classes. Urmi in *The Binding Vine* takes a role of activist when she tries to help rape victim from a lower class. Saru in *The Dark Holds No Terrors* connects to Boozie who represent the business class. For a while she leaves with the dream of improving her social status. She also exercises mobility and freedom which are uncommon for the women of the class. She has extra marital affairs which are generally seen in the lowest and the highest class.

Deshpande also propels her characters across the divides of the communities. Most of her characters are at once the members of many communities. Saru, for instance, has a childhood spent in rural community and her later life spent in urban community.

Similarly, she changes her status from an unemployed girl to a professional woman with the help of education.

The novels of Shashi Deshpande also bring to light the specific behavioural pattern of people belonging to different class and community. The indifferent attitude of Shakutai towards the crime of rape is typical of her class. Similarly discriminatory attitude of Saru's mother towards her by privileging the male child is a typical behaviour of the rural community.

Shashi Deshpande also brings out the social sites where class and community intersect. She indicates in *The Dark Holds No Terrors* that certain social and individual behaviours are common to class and community. Marginalization of female, for instance, is seen in all classes and communities. Religious belief is another factor which cut across classes and communities. She depicts mostly Hindu family in her novels, the members of which are usually God-fearing and they follow most of the rituals.

Thus *The Dark Holds No Terrors* bring out the subtle implications of class and community in Indian society. This novel analyzes the basic fabric of Indian society and keeps away from the discussion of class and community of other countries. In this respect, Shashi Deshpande's novels have distinct Indianness. One can also say that She has used classes and communities of Indian society effectively in her novels. in the naturalistic tradition to locate her characters and to study the causes of their problems.

Works Cited

Bharati, Meenakshi, *Desert in Bloom:Contemporary Indian Women's Fiction in English*. Delhi: Pencraft International, 2004. Print.

Deshpande, Shashi, *The Dark Holds No Terrors*. New Delhi: Penguin Books, 1990. Print.

Sheshadri, Vijayalakshmi *The New Woman in Indian-English Women Writers Since the1970s*. Delhi: B.R. Publishing Corporation, 1995. Print.

11

Jagua Nana: An Archetypal Image of New African Woman

Kiran Thakur

Jagua Nana, Cyprian Ekwensi's iconic feminist text that tells the story of a socially ambitious prostitute Jagua, who is the central figure in the novel. She is the centre towards which everything points, and her fate is what supremely matters and structures the novel. Jagua is an aging high-lifer and a member of the seedy club Tropicana, and the novel is a brilliant trace of the confusion and intensity of modern life in Lagos.

Jagua is the daughter of a catechist and her father wanted her to marry a filling station assistant, who, by her father's standards is probably the best match for Jagua. The boy is also fascinated by her charms and ". . . wanted to take her back with him as wife" (Ekwensi, *Jagua Nana* 166). But Jagua "is a quest heroine" (Cox 229) who will not marry just any man and so is "her thrust into dangerous adventures by her search for the ideal hero" (Cox 229). She cannot be a perfect match for the poor man because, "Jagua was fond of changing her clothes often, and in those early days of make-up of painting her face . . . . All the girls in her age group had children but she resisted to the last, hoping ever, for some eminent man to come along to Ogabu to marry her" (166). The jeans-clad girl riding bicycles is representative of impact of the city lifestyle on the tribal villages of Africa.

Jagua's temperament and ambitions are unconditional. She can best be described as the child of modern Nigeria. Her fondness for stylish cloths and make-up has its origin in the rapid urbanization of Nigeria wherein the village life was fast giving way to an Anglicized way of living. Much against her wishes, Jagua was ultimately married to the man approved by her father, who had paid the bride price of one hundred and twenty pounds. But after marriage Jagua realizes that there is none to see her misery. What grieves her most was that unfortunately she failed in conceiving any child after her marriage. So living in a world around where " . . . children were the most important thing in the world . . . [and] that every man and woman must have as many as they could" (Akpam 6) Jagua turns out to be a failure. Though she knows that her husband takes periodical leaves and has relations with other girls as well, yet "she took the blame of sterility, and it was becoming a thing between them" (167). To the extreme of her frustration she becomes an exile in her own home when the husband takes a second wife. Once Jagua's husband marries for a second wife, it becomes next to impossible for her to bear the situation and she is left with no option but to leave him. However, in following a path of individual will she deviates from the traditional social norms.

Jagua is autonomous in nature and exercises her own free will in tailoring the track for her life ahead. Her infertility and her husband's second marriage mark the climax, which precipitate her into a world of free will. Marriage, children and family retreat into the backdrop with her and she steps up into a world of her own dreams. Allured by the charms of the city, she flees to city of Lagos and she has ". . . heard of Lagos where the girls were glossy, worked in offices like the men, danced, smoked, wore high-heeled shoes and narrow slacks, and were 'free' and 'fast' with their favors" (167). To many people including Jagua, 'Lagos' is related to many magic connotations that attract them to be therein. The novel therefore is an exquisite delineation of such a transitional phase in the life of an African woman.

Jagua suffers on account of the social set-up and mindset of the people. But with her migration to the city and search for her own identity she voices against the system. With her very act of deviating from the well defined confines of traditional role for 'a woman, she re-conceptualizes the very notion of womanhood.

Jagua makes the break from the tribal African woman who accept polygamy unconditionally by her rebellion. In fact polygamy was invaluable in the past. For instance, Okonkwo in *Things Fall Apart* (Achebe) had three wives and many children. In fact in the Ibo traditional society as depicted in Achebe's earlier novels *Things Fall Apart* and *Arrow of God*, (Achebe) a personal status was estimated in terms of the number of wives and children a person had. But such a practice is unsuited with the demands of modern life. So Jagua deserts her husband in search of better opportunities. Through her departure she makes it clear that women can function as individuals in today's society more easily in the town than in the rural and traditional areas. So she can be termed as "a magnificent woman full of the warmth and charm who also stands for the companionship in socio-political life" (Mutiso 72). Jagua can attain that 'magnificence' because of her spirits to think and go beyond the expected way of living and code of conduct.

Jagua Nana is bodily arresting and finds that village life is much too restraining to one of her talents and passions, and like many other similarly affected has come to Lagos to live there. The inherent "thirst for adventure in her blood" (167) deviates her from her traditional values, and she literally follows modern values, feels delighted in doing so and becomes addicted to Tropicana, the glaring nightclub in Lagos. This is the world of fast sports cars, the tired businessmen, the corrupt politicians and the hoodlums. The women who come here have their faces masked with powder, pencil and lipstick, their hair is combed straight and heavily oiled, and their feet are clad in high-heeled sandals through which can be seen the lacquered nails. And Jagua is always the best of the lot. It is a world that stands in total contrast to the world of the traditional way of life in the pre-colonial era, where Jagua plays the hectic game of survival.

It is in this Lagos that Jagua seeks a new life and is dazzled by the ways of urban living. She has her own norms of living and functionality and has come to the city from her village with a clear purpose, to carve for herself a place where doors of opportunities are open for her. In turn she also leaves no stone unturned in grabbing whatever opportunity comes her way, be that socially or morally acceptable or not, and seeks self-growth. She wants to live a full life and doesn't give up so very easily in spite of all odds coming her way. After the second marriage when she leaves her home, ironically she doesn't know that in the city she herself is going to be exploited by so many men analogous to her husband. But she accepts this situation open-heartedly and continues with her struggle for survival, asserting her individuality most daringly.

Through the character of Jagua, Ekwensi is able to flash out women's active participation in the socio-economic and political spheres. Throughout the novel Jagua's works are praiseworthy in social activities, especially during the election campaigns with Uncle Taiwo, and her act of bringing two warring villages to reconciliation. She remains successful in settling the battle between Chief Ofubara and his brother. Impressed by her, the Chief proposes Jagua for marriage, providing her yet another opportunity to becoms a respectable woman and to escape the sordid life that Lagos offers, but is rejected by her because she cannot compromise with whatever standards she has set for herself. Because somewhere she experiences an identity crisis and it is out of that urge to find her own individuality that she steps into Lagos and tries the make the best of every moment and opportunity that comes her way.

In the company of Uncle Taiwo, Jagua gets a chance to enter into the world of politics. Being aware of the existing squalor in politics, she warns Freddie when he announces his intention to compete with Uncle Taiwo in elections, tries her best to deviate Freddie from going ahead with her word of advice that "No Freddie, I no wan' you to win." . . . "Politics not for you, Freddie. You got education. You got culture. You're a gentleman an' proud. Politics be game for dog. And in dis Lagos, is a rough game. De roughest game in de whole world." "Is smelly and dirty and you too clean an' sweet. I speakin' frank to you Freddie" (103). And she goes on to explain, to Freddie, the tactics by which elections are won:

> Elections in Lagos were not won by wearing smart clothes and appearing distant from the people. You had to show them what you could do for them, before you won. You must associate with everyone, particularly the lowest ones, and regard them as your friends... give them the freedom of your time and thought, your car and your room .... Uncle Taiwo was working very hard indeed ... [he] was distributing many presents to the people .... The whole of Obanla was plastered with [his] pictures ... and all women had received match boxes and cooking stoves ... and the school children exercise books with his [Uncle Taiwo's] portrait. (102-3)

Jagua also assists Uncle Taiwo in this dirty game. A speech delivered by her to the Lagos market women during the election campaign sums up her awareness of the inequalities of modern Nigerian socio-political life. While addressing the crowd, she asserts:

> You see the sort of people you will be voting for, if you vote O.P.1 [Uncle Taiwo's opponent party] you will be voting for people who will build their private houses with your money. But if you vote for O.P.2, [Uncle Taiwo's party] the party that does the job ...will educate your children to Oxford and Cambridge, ... if O.P.1 ever comes into power ... your children will be sent to the slummy suburbs... you will continue to sleep on the grass mats ... will be bitten by mosquitoes .... And you will console yourself that you are struggling. (145-46)

The speech presented by Jagua shows her deep understanding about what politics actually is and what are the tactics implying which one could place oneself on the winning edge in the game of politics.

Though Jagua sells her body to earn money, yet she makes the best use of it for herself and others. She is economically independent and has bought a home of her own in Lagos. So she is able to give shelter to Rosa, who has come to Lagos for the first time and cannot afford to live without any support. Jagua does provide her this scope. Similarly, she is able to finance Freddie for his studies in abroad. Because she is good in public dealings, she takes active partnership with Uncle Taiwo during election campaigns and wins votes for him. Last but not least after her father's death she takes her household responsibilities on her shoulders, which her brother is supposed to shoulder. Back at the village home, "She had become housekeeper to the family, and more importantly still, custodian of her mother's will to go on living. Her duty was to look after the property, to avoid marriage, for that would take her away from home and mother" (180). Hence, all the struggle and the efforts she puts in during her stay at Lagos, enthuse new spirits in her and help in making her mentally and economically independent. Equipped with such vitality and strengths only she can afford to shoulder the complete responsibility of her mother and family after the death of her father.

Though Jagua is physically impure and always wants to 'bewitch' men and 'sap' them of their pennies and their virility, yet she is not completely devoid of feminine sensibility and emotions. The pain that she experiences for Freddie is not without human feelings. "She saw genuine tears in his eyes and she knew that when that happens to a man, the wound has gone deep. But she could not go near him. She had become unclean. For once she actually felt and he was to her a god with the power to pass judgment" (53). So Jagua, a name epitomizing the spirit of freedom and vivacity of personality with which she is born, and in the accomplishment of which she experiences sexual depravity, at last doesn't let moral depravity overpower her. In a moment of epiphany she grows much ripened. With her vision enlightened and perception enlarged she comes to envision something divine in Freddie. This helps her establish further parameters for her newly-found existence with the heritage of beliefs and attitudes of traditional ways of living with which she can operate in whatever social system she finds for herself.

In her struggle for independence and freedom she does experience the isolation and hollowness as rewards of the ways of urban living in which she and many other urbanites live. Even after leaving Lagos she feels its presence and feels isolated from her very roots.

> There was no choice for Jagua but to cast aside her city ways and settle down to living in Ogabu. For her it was no easy task. The people still looked on her as a kind of curiosity. The way she talked and dressed, her moods and manners of eating, they were out of keeping with Ogabu ideas . . . she remained isolated from the very surroundings (178).

Jagua is overpowered by a sense of guilt and sin when she finds herself in the circumstances after Uncle Taiwo is defeated in the elections following Freddie's death.

> How am I better? Jagua thought. She ought to have remained in Onitsha with brother Fonso and tried to become a Merchant Princess or better still, she ought to have married Chief Ofubara. Even before that, before she came to Lagos, she had a real husband. She thought of him now. She thought of her whole past life . . . (169)

Once the realization dawns upon her, she looks forward to sticking back to her roots in the village. What she could find in the traditional ways of living is absent in the modern living. Hence, finally she conforms to conventional morality in praising the purity of village life and condemning the decadence of the urban rat race. The novelist has tried to resolve the cultural calcification by identifying Jagua to traditional norms. This also completes her search for identity, though earlier she remains a rebellion against the system.

After retreating to her native village at Ogabu she acts like a responsible daughter and is all set to take care of her mother. Once she goes back to her home she "becomes housekeeper to the family, and more important still, custodian of her mother's will to go on living. Her duty was to look after the property [and her mother] . . ." (180). She shows courage and remains with her mother at the village and starts her own business for income. So in the search of an identity she keeps moving between city and village, between urban and rural life, and the real solace and tranquillity to her is, of course, provided by the blissful rural living only that makes her realize that "Ogabu was the home of her father and mother" (106). She rediscovers her roots and opts for a 'respectful' life. It is in the village that she experiences motherhood, although briefly, overcoming the stigma of sterility, and conforming to the conventional image of the African woman as mother. The birth of her child fulfils her craving for being a child bearer.

The novel thus focuses on the influence of the city culture on the aspiring natives like Jagua Nana. But what lies at heart towards the end is what Jagua herself experiences in her roots. Finally she conforms to conventional morality in praising the purity of village life and condemning the decadence of the urban rat race. The novelist has tried to resolve the cultural adulteration by identifying Jagua to traditional norms. This also completes her search for an identity, though earlier she remains a rebellion against the system. Jagua is no doubt orthodox, but the way she acclimatizes herself with all sorts of modes of living and cultural and socioeconomic classes, makes her an appealing figure. In a way, through her, the dominant social idea exemplified in the novel is the independence and freedom of women. Because of such women like Jagua other women can participate in politics, in fashions and even to some extent in the running of their families and the state. In short, such women make it possible for other women to become involved in public life.

In a nutshell, the novel is a radiant analysis of the social realities in post-Independent urban Nigeria and the ways in which traditional value system in getting restated as a result of the European infiltration in Nigeria experiencing the consequent socio-political and cultural changes. The character of Jagua has surely left Ekwensi sufficiently equipped with a ground where he can give way to all his ideas in black and white related to the true picture of Nigerian/African populace in an objective manner, thus making Jagua an ideal image of the new African woman.

Works Cited

Achebe, Chinua. *Arrow of God.* London: Heinemann, 1964. Print.

_______. *Things Fall Apart.* London: Heinemann, 1996. Print.

Cox, C. Brain. *African Writers.* Vol. I. New York: Charles Scribner's Sons, 1997. Print.

Ekwensi, Cyprian. *Jagua Nana.* London: Heinemann, 1975. Print.

Mutiso, G.C.M. *Socio-Political Thought in African Literature: Weusi?* London: Macmillan, 1974. Print.

12

Beatrice as the Image of a New African/ Nigerian Woman in Chinua Achebe's *Anthills of the Savannah*

Kiran Thakur

A good number of African novelists truthfully stand for their respective societies and social concerns expressed within them. Societal concerns form the core of the writings of many African/ Nigerian fiction writers. Chinua Achebe, a most commendable figure in Nigerian literature, is no exception to this trend. In his writings he has rendered considerable space to women characters but during his initial ventures, especially in his trilogy i.e. *Things Fall Apart*, *Arrow of God*, and *No Longer at Ease* women have been pictured in passive positions. In these novels he represents the practice of polygamy which by any means does not justify the existence of women and carries such ramifications that poses a challenge to women's equal share of participation in every sphere of their lives.

During pre independence period women were put in the periphery and have been portrayed as quiet beings because their autonomy was suppressed by the patriarchal and polygamous practices which indeed, played a negative role in allowing independent existence to women. As compared to pre independence era their participation is more explicit in the postcolonial era during which focus was centered on the woman's position in society and in projecting their self-reclamation. The depiction of women in Nigerian literature assumed a new dimension during the post-Independence period only and hereafter, women's roles could no longer remain unnoticed when the realization of their individuality and their contribution to the society dawned upon them.

The women were envisioned with a better perspective after independence which helped in imparting fresh dimensions to the post colonial Nigerian/African literature. The period around the late 1970s and so offers a more reasonable platform for the Nigerian literati to be liberal and modern in handling female personas in their writings. This paradigmatic shift could be seen mainly because of the fact that by now women themselves started off articulating the voices of their own with positive shades and anticipated the long cherished image of new woman that stood in absolute contrast with the image of a traditional woman. So the women partaking is more explicit in the postcolonial period.

One such representation of the image of new African woman is Beatrice in Chinua Achebe's *Anthills of the Savannah*. Through her character, Achebe conceptualizes a female image who is redeemed from all conventional restrictions. With an increased awareness about her spiritual, political, social or economic strengths Beatrice has exhibited a confidence in her own capacities and has come to secure a room for her where she could expect dignity and self respect.

Anthills of the Savannah is a manifestation of the ruling by military in Nigeria and the resultant consequence on the Nigerian populace in the last quarter of the twenteeth century. Even after independence, the socio-politic fabric of the society remained unchanged and the natives experienced the same kind of confusions and uncertainties about their existence because of the lack of proper and true governance. Nigerians were forced to adopt the ruling system that posed threats and challenges of varying degrees and kinds at every step. Achebe has brainstormed such challenging issues in the contemporary political life of

Nigeria and after a thorough critical analysis of the situation has arrived at the conclusion that any political set up which is led by self centered and hypocritical authorities is bound to fall as the ending of *Anthills* shows.

All this critical analysis is handled in the fictious place named Kangan, which actually comes to represent Nigeria itself. All this is represented through the life and experiences of four leading characters in the novel who are close friends among whom three are males and one female, named Beatrice Okoh. She is an official in the Ministry of Finance and the girlfriend of Ikem Osodi, a newspaper editor and one of the leading and revolutionary characters in the novel. The other two major characters are His Excellency, Sam, a military dictator and Chris Oriko, the commissioner for information.

The only female character in the novel in lead role is Beatrice who is quite a mature character and is pretty aware not only of her existential duties and responsibilities but is also well aware of her rights. It is because of her ripeness and awakened sense only she comes to signify her name which means "A Woman is also something" (*Anthills of the Savannah* 87). Beatrice is a character that imparts an opportunity to Achebe's long cherished desire of having such a feminine voice in his writings who could attach a meaning to womanhood. She does justice with her role and comes to beat the expectations of the readers because she feeds the reader's mind with uncommon and untraditional fruits. In handling the character of Beatrice, Achebe seems to be "responsive to the concerns of women" (Landry and MacLean 9-10). And Achebe's serious concern with this particular issue is discernible in the unconventional presentation of her persona in the novel.

Beatrice is a woman who wishes to exercise her free will in all spheres of her life so she cannot afford to be submissive to the convention. Because of her independent bent of mind she feels handicapped in accepting and subsequently performing the traditionally assigned roles for women. In all of Achebe's works before *Anthills of the Savannah*, women are not provided any important and dignified space and were given violent treatment as is evident in Okonkwo's beating of Ojiugo in *Things Fall Apart*. But there is an evident change in *Anthills of the Savannah*, where Achebe envisions an idea of women which ensures a respect and recognition to their identity. The women in Achebe's earlier works were sidelined but in *Anthills of the Savannah* Beatrice is put at the hub of affairs and she plays a lead role in the novel. Her presence is very central in reconciling the various threads of the plot of the novel. "The portrayal of Beatrice represents a woman shouldering the responsibility of changing the course of female emancipation" (Fonchingong 45). In a way through her character Achebe successfully projects the image of a modern woman who is liberated from all the shackles of patriarchal notions and norms of living.

In *Anthills of the Savannah*, Beatrice is the only character who can have the spirit of cross questioning His Excellency and reminding him of his duties and responsibilities, and who can dare to ask him to deliver his duties with utmost sincerity. Though it is difficult to state the reason that enthuses so much of strength in her that she can afford to talk such things to His Excellency yet it makes us admit her extraordinary daring spirit. She also tries her best to create such an environment in the society where women could look forward to equal opportunities as men do have.

All the four leading characters in the novel including are very close friends and hold very significant positions in the administrative set up. Their intimate friendship which began in England pushes them into positions of power in Kangan and that is what makes Beatrice comment upon the three male characters that "the story of the country, as far as you are concerned, is the story of three of you" (*Anthills* 22). She has earned an honours, bachelor's degree in English and she writes short stories that Ikem praises for their 'muscular' and 'masculine' style. She is also the central character in the novel who is closely linked to HE, Ikem and Chris, but a severe split comes up in their bond when Sam decides to announce himself President for life and comes to acquire supreme power since he "holds both the yam and the knife" (*Anthills* 127) as the white bearded Elder of Abazon puts it. She is the first to foresee the power of the political disaster building up in Kangan. She prophesies: "I see trouble building for us. It will get to Ikem first. No joking, Chris. He will be the precursor to make straight the way. But after him it will be you. We are in it. Ikem you, me and even him" (*Anthills* 114-5). This forecasting by Beatrice does have deeper ramifications and towards the end of the novel the storm sweeps off all other three in power and only Beatrice is left to direct the upcoming generation and relate them the stories of their sacrifice for the cause of the people. So she seems to have a better insight among them all. The portrayal of Beatrice as the leader of that group which comprised of three men and one woman is reflective of the much needed transition in the society which Achebe wanted to transform. Though all the major characters appear to be disillusioned with the contemporary socio-political situation in Kangan yet Beatrice's approach is grounded on sound reasoning and logic which enables her to withstand the problems more tactfully.

In the novel Beatrice also comes to represent the traditional faith because there is a reference to legendary character Idemili in the novel who is supposed to be the daughter of Almighty as the harbinger of redemption of mankind. And Idemili performs her role through Beatrice. Though Beatrice "did not know these legends and traditions of her people because they played but little part in her upbringing," (*Anthills* 105) however, she is chosen to perform such role because she is deemed worthy of it. When the goddess takes possession of her Beatrice undergoes great transformation and becomes instrumental in getting the divine purposes of Idemili complete. So it can be inferred that Beatrice has got such an aura that makes her special not only with her near ones but also with people like Idemili who have got something divine in them. Thus, Beatrice is a new woman who is not shaped in the "mould of an imported Western model of 'a feminist'" (Dhawan 66), but depicted as a reincarnation of "the village priestess who prophesies when her divinity rides her" (Dhawan 66). And through such incarnation the past traditional beliefs and practices and the present day reasoning and vision get together.

Achebe's evocation of the female sensibility through the disposition of Beatrice is his own affirmation that it was high time to render empowerment to women. Beatrice holds a significant position as secretary in the ministry of finance which provides her the ground to be an agent of social transformation and to check "man's unquenchable thirst to sit in authority" (*Anthills* 104). Very frequently she is seen discussing about the life of women and rights given to them with Ikem. In her reference to Sembene's film also she is seen to be critical of the secondary position given to women. It is due to this spirit in Beatrice to stand for the cause of women that she comes up with ideas and means to provide women with their due rights and consideration.

The problem of class difference and the exploitation of the lower class people have been depicted in the novel through various characters and incidents like in government's treatment of the delegation from Abazon, in the relationship between Beatrice and Elewa and in the interaction between Ikem and taxi drivers. In the novel, Ikem, Chris, Beatrice and Emmanuel, all make daring efforts to bridge the gap between the poor, illiterate and peasant class and the well off, educated and Westernized elite. That is why Ikem marries Elewa, and his "prospective mother-in-law sells tie-die cloths in Glegele market" (*Anthills* 156-7). Beatrice learns to be nice, not merely to Elewa, but also to Elewa's mother and hard-drinking uncle. By making such shifts in values many of the present day issues could be resolved because after all "this world belongs to the people of the world not any little caucus, no matter how talented" (*Anthills* 232). In this direction also Beatrice joins hands with Ikem and she gives shelter to Emmanuel, the student leader, Braimoh the taxi driver, and Adamna, the nurse at her home. It also exemplifies a union between intellect class and working class which was essential at that point of time to bring about the most positive change in contemporary Nigeria. By taking a strong stand for the cause of common people Beatrice becomes a symbol of the "triumph of the people's struggle, in spite of failed leadership and betrayed hopes" (*Anthills* 220).

Beatrice was of the belief that women should be given due recognition in the society as against the roles traditional institutions rendered to them. In this dimension also she dares to disobey patriarchy which permits conducting such rituals as the naming ceremony of new born to males only and performs the naming ceremony of baby born to Elewa, Ikem's girlfriend, after his death. She finds flaw in the traditional naming ceremony, pointing out that it "wrongly privileges masculine knowledge over maternal knowledge" (Parker77). The baby girl is baptized by Beatrice and is named, "Amaechina: May the-path-never-close" (*Anthills* 222). The name has got deep ramifications because it is significant of the never ending path of struggle. And the remaining characters in the novel are her fathers and mothers. In the naming ceremony for Amaechina, Beatrice brings together conventional values and the present conviction. She adopts the primeval practice to modern post independent Nigerian conditions, thus paving the way for a new hybridized situation that shares equal footing for both present and past and which could provide better greeting for the future. It is to the credit of Beatrice that the present generation could hope for such a future where the best out of the practices of past and future is trimmed to graft a new set-up of living. Through such acts of her she becomes Achebe's symbol of present-day womanhood.

Throughout the novel, Beatrice enjoys a very positive image because of her daring spirit and her leadership qualities. Also she asserted the feminine cause and does things which only men were supposed to enjoy. Her emancipation lies not only in attempting to turn out to be like a man by being highly ambitious and giving more importance to her career but also by making herself free from patriarchal values and mental subjugation of women. So the novel "embodies [through Beatrice] Achebe's most positive image of the modern woman" (Carroll 177).

Beatrice is projected as a character whose vision is more candid, balanced and objective. With such a vision she could figure out the intricacies of contemporary situation more meaningfully than any other character in the novel. Of the four protagonists, Beatrice, alone continues to exist and carry on the mission left behind by both Ikem and Chris who sacrifice their lives for the cause of the people and the nation. She is a brilliant presentation by Achebe who comes to give a new name to selfhood and womanhood as in opposition to what conventional value system has offered to women. She has the ability to exercise assertiveness and to make a paradigmatic change, and moreover she is self assured and self-initiated. All these qualities in her make her a figure worth reckoning with the label of the new woman.

Works Cited

Achebe, Chinua. *Anthills of the Savannah.* Ibadan: Heinemann, 1987. Print.

_______. *Arrow of God.* London: Heinemaan, 1964. Print.

_______. *No Longer at Ease.* London: Heinemaan, 1962. Print.

_______. *Things Fall Apart.* London: Heinemaan, 1962. Print.

Carroll, David. *Chinua Achebe: Novelist, Poet, Critic.* London: Macmillan, 1980. Print.

Dhawan, R. K., ed. *African Literature Today.* New Delhi: Prestige Books, 1989. Print.

Fonchingong, Charles C. "Unbending Gender Narrative in African Literature." *Journal of International Women's Studies* 8.1 (2006): 135-147. Print.

Laudry, Donna and Gerald Maclean. *Materialist Feminism.* Oxford: Blackwell, 1993. Print.

Parker, Michael and Roger Starkey, eds. *Post-Colonial Literatures.* London: Macmillan, 1995. Print.

13

Paving the Way to Selfhood: Anita Desai's *Clear Light of Day*

Kiran Thakur

Literature is replete with authors delving into issues of selfhood through varying contexts. In a society where most of the women feel marginalized, the women writers' quest for individuality becomes obvious. Questioning the notion of self as a pre-given, primordial and purposive entity, this paper explores the gamut of modes in which identities are produced, circulated and assumed. The present study endeavours to explore the theme of emerging social, economic, and emotional selfhood as traced in the Anita Desai's undeniable imprint of her individuality, i.e., Bim in *Clear Light of Day*.

As a great social visionary, Anita Desai has made bold attempts to explore the position of women in contemporary society. She has depicted a lively picture of the deprived and dispossessed class of women in her novels. Her novels are noted for profound probing into the inner life and feeling of women, bounded by the manacles of the middle class. Her writings are the explorations of the family problems, which perhaps are the chief cause behind the estrangement of the women from their family, and her autobiographical presentation *Clear Light of Day* is a pretty true reflection of that.

What makes Desai a figure cut apart is her digging deep into the interior world of human psyche and to bring the hidden innermost recesses to the surface. Thus with a recurrent play of web of thoughts and feelings the protagonists do not remain glued to the image of static creatures accepting life in whatever form and shape it comes to them rather they come to outshine every situation with an illuminating vision which they come to possess after a series of self introspection and self evaluation. This is what happens with Bim also who once at the pinnacle of self actualization, and envisioned with an illuminating vent of mind and open heart, she comes to accept everything around with an open embrace and the scattered chords of her personality get into a single whole and in a moment of self discovery she realizes that "I am larger, better than I thought; I did not know I had so much goodness" (Whitman 205).

Desai has assumed a lead role in penetrating closer to the Indian women consciousness through the character of Bim and has mirrored the images of women who are neither stars nor martyrs in the feminist cause. They are the voices of women leading their everyday lives, nursing their joys and sorrows and Desai has monitored the numbness, pain and anguish of their psyches. As a matter of fact, she has plumbed into the female psyche so well hitherto proving the fact that literature mirrors the society in true image to be true. In a quest at being a satisfied and meaningful existence, the characters like Bim have to travel a long way external reality to internal reality.

The very fact of self is inevitable to our existence because "Life that just happens in and for itself is not real; it is only real when it is known" (Jung 81). So one arrives at a clear understanding of self only when it comes to represent wholeness between the inner self and the world which accounts for sprouting of individual perception after a long course of action of self perception and self introspection that enlightens our mind. The novel explicates the complex journey of Bim from basic feminine to transformed feminine. But the journey from self ignorance to self actualization was indeed challenging one.

Bim, the protagonist in *Clear Light of Day* decides to face life's challenges alone and while doing this, even though she encounters an identity crisis, her strong will-power and determination come to her help. The novel is predominantly noteworthy for its enunciation of psychological scrutiny, and recounts the tale of Das family, in old Delhi that gives shelter to four siblings, i.e., Raja, Bimla (referred to as Bim), Tara, and Baba. The four siblings, i.e., Raja, Bim, Tara, and Baba are the victims of noxious, bare and bleak feeling of childhood. Their parents are too preoccupied with maintaining their refined image in the social circles and they spend most of their time in playing Bridge and visiting with varied personas from various social strata in the Roshnara Club every now and then in Old Delhi and hence they fail as parents in providing a secure environment to their children. Rather they bring Mira Masi, a widow at the age of 15 from their distant relationship to take care of them. Consequently the children feel like growing in an unwholesome, empty, hopeless ambiance of early days. The children are the quiet observers of such an intercourse of the life of their parents' life so they cannot feel the warmth and security of parental love and affection. Such an unhappy situation creates unequivocal uncertainty full of fright, insecurity, distrust and anxiety among the children as they grow up. And eventually two of them, i.e., Bim and Tara, being elders learn to take care of themselves and in turn provided support to younger ones Tara and Baba also. In the absence of their mother Aunt Mira used to look after them and hence becomes their surrogate mother.

After the death of their parents and Aunt Mira Bim comes to play the role of a mother, a protector looking after mentally retarded Baba and taking care of Raja when he suffered with tuberculosis. So Bim along with her siblings has gone through traumatic experiences at two levels, at personal level and at social level. At the personal level they have to face parental neglect and at the social level, they have to by stand the havoc following the India's struggle for freedom.

The main characters of the novel are Bim, Raja and Tara. Bim is an unattached history teacher; Tara lives in America with her diplomat husband, and their elder brother Raja who has given up his aspiration to become a poet, lives as a rich businessman in Hyderabad. Having long been estranged from her once beloved brother, Bim continues to live in Delhi and take care of her autistic brother, Baba. She feels very painful about the uncaring approach of Raja. Tara also goes in hunt for a better living with her husband. After the death of both the parents, Mira Masi also dies, thus everyone leaves Bim and Raja behind at Delhi to survive. In spite of these poignant setbacks Bim continues to look life with guts and fortitude. So at all stages, the novelist has made an attempt to present the moods and persistent states of mind or psyche of its heroine. So Desai's protagonists are usually sensitive women who, haunted by a peculiar sense of doom, withdraw into a secluded world of their own like Bim does.

Bim feels very angry about the insensitive outlook of Raja. Having long been estranged from her once beloved brother, she continues to live in Delhi and take care of her autistic brother, Baba. In spite of these emotional shocks she continues to face life with courage and determination. Her spirit of self-sacrifice gives her an unconscious feeling of superiority over the others. So at all stages, the novelist has made an attempt to present the moods and persistent states of mind or psyche of its heroine. Her protagonists are usually sensitive women who, haunted by a peculiar sense of disaster, withdraw into a secluded world of their own like Bim does but simultaneously they keep their spirits high and eventually are able to overcome the feelings of despair and emerge as resurrected beings envisioning the vicinity of their existence with fresh and enlarged perspectives.

Bim is very candid in her perceptions as to what she has got to do with her life. With her pragmatic and realistic approach she embraces each and every moment with an open mind and continues to carry the course of her life forward with the responsibility of her mentally retarded brother and of the complete household on her shoulders. And the endurances of the emotional traumas and acceptance of errands cultivate a spirit of independence in her and of course leadership qualities she has had since her childhood.

In her quest for individuation she ultimately rises above the average and accepts whatever is true. It is out of her that knowledge that she comes to realize that there is nobody to take care of her autistic brother Baba and only she has to nurture him as long as she lives, a promise that she makes to herself. It is out of that pledge only that she conforms to the mother image which otherwise is not an ordinary thing for any woman with average values and beliefs. She manages with some extraordinary alchemy to turn the misfortune into great fortunes for the whole family. It is out of that resolution only that she remains spinster and cultivates a feeling disdain for all those who are desperate in getting married. She says: "I don't know why they're in such a hurry to get married. Why don't they go to college instead?" (*Clear Light of Day* 220). To reaffirm and reassure her conviction she states: "I shall never leave Baba and Raja and Mira-*masi*" (*Clear Light of Day* 221), whereas Tara, Bim's sister always expected "to find treasure, to make her fortune, discover herself a princess" (*Clear Light of Day* 102). Her great sense of devotion and commitment for her family makes her most appealing and apt figure to be chosen for the proposed study.

The individuation process that gets started in Bim and by which she lifts from narrow and confined edge to a broader and open self, harnesses many fruitful outcomes to her. She accepts the truth that as a responsible member of her family she cannot shun her existential commitments. And with strong determination she holds on to her decision: "I shall earn my own living and look after Mira Masi and Baba and be independent" (*Clear Light of Day* 140). And she resolves to extend a helping and supporting hand to all those whose obligation hardly anyone would have liked to bear.

As Bim grows up into a young woman, the innate leadership qualities in her help her to face the hard realities of life. Early in life, she has decided to be independent in life by pursuing education and by deciding not to marry. While asserting her individuality, she has to defy certain traditional norms and taboos. And first of all she has to defy the institution of marriage. By showing disregard and disbelief in matrimony she starts off with her first step on her way to self emancipation. In the absence of any burden of hierarchical and patriarchic bondages she routes her way towards an independent and individual existence. Acting on these lines she represents the women who while going against the traditional and conservative web of inhibitions show a way out not only to themselves but thousands of other women aspiring to break away from societal taboos.

Having been blessed with rare virtues and extraordinary vent of mind Bim realizes that her potential and aptitude for learning and education could at its best be utilized by imparting the knowledge that she has so far accumulated in the form of education. And she opts for a career in teaching and becomes a teacher of history, though she has to go away from some of the preconditions of society imposed upon women in opting for a career because at that point of time permission was not rendered so easily to women to try their hand in such ventures of pursuing career. Even this choice of being a career girl avails her many benefits. First and foremost being that it tailored for her a ground where she could assert her freedom and independence. Besides it equipped her with sufficient sources to be a doer of the family and in serving her family she can experience fatherhood also. She comes to play the role of a father, a role that otherwise her brother Raja was supposed to play after the death of their parents. Being a professional also helped her in retaining the cool of her mind and maintaining her good sense. Her contribution in teaching in the college, nourishment of Baba at home enable her to "end all the storm of emotions in which she had been dragged back and forth . . . to what she did best, most efficiently, with least expanse of spirit – the keeping to a schedule, the following of a time table, the application of the mind of facts, figures, rules and analyses" (*Clear Light of Day* 169). Thus she seeks compensation in her profession that helps her to be the whole being. Her urge for a career was not solely out of a longing to satisfy her intellectual instincts; rather her career consciousness was guided by a need to secure means for the survival of her autistic brother Baba. She comes to learn that "being with others is a more primordial structure of human existence than being-for-one-self" (Macquarrie 102-3). And in a quest to be along with others she has to be self assertive.

In a bid to abide by the commitment for her siblings Bim goes unconventional firstly by getting into teaching profession and secondly showing her disbelief in the institution of marriage She chooses an independent life by remaining a spinster. "I think of hundreds of things to do instead. I won't marry" (*Clear Light of Day* 140) shows her urge to rise and go beyond the average. Her sense of commitment for her family is also acknowledged by Dr. Biswas, a family doctor of Das family who attends upon the ailing Raja and the alcoholic Mira Masi when he states, "Now I understand why you [Bim] do not wish to marry. You have dedicated your life to others – to your sick brother and your aged aunt and your little brother who will be dependent on you all his life. You have sacrificed your own life for them" (*Clear Light of Day* 97). This statement about the disposition of Bim provides a dual candid perception about her that firstly she is a woman for whom her blood relations reigns supreme and it is for the sake of the happiness of her family, especially for the sake of her younger brother Baba that she has sacrificed her own happiness. Secondly by defying matrimony she emerges totally unconventional, untraditional and moreover a liberal woman who would not keep herself at the mercy of patriarchy. She undoubtedly succeeds in paving the way to selfhood by railing against the shackles of patriarchy.

Through the character of Bim, Desai points to a kind of "feminist emancipation that lies in not limiting women to their traditional roles but in expanding and awakening them to several other possibilities. This kind of life, apart from being invigorating, also frees them from dependence on men" (Ghosh 252). Bim portrays herself as a purely enlightened woman by refusing to play the traditional role of a typical woman who is treated as an object of satisfying the sexual instincts of males. Yet by remaining unmarried also she plays the most demanding and challenging role that is traditionally assigned to all females that is to be a mother. Though she doesn't give birth to any child throughout her life, still she plays the role of a mother with utmost care, devotion and sagacity. She is the doer, a giver and a caretaker of her whole family who nourishes almost every member especially Baba like a mother and could be entitled as the "Archetype of the Eternal feminine" (Parmar 157). She nurses Baba like a mother, takes care of Raja when he was down with tuberculosis and attends upon Mira Masi when she falls ill with great care. Even Tara admits to Bim that "you looked so like Mama from a distance. . ." (*Clear Light of Day* 2). She also extends a helping hand and provides guidance to her students in various matters. So she finds new ways of seeing her existence and being a mother figure was perhaps the most beautiful way of looking at her individual existence.

The drifting away of Raja and Tara shatters Bim a lot and she experiences resentment and split of relationships. And she does experience identity confusion even though she is pretending to take effects calmly but towards the end of the novel, in her mood of introspection, she finds her own flaws and inadequacies in her own behaviour with her siblings. She finally realizes the seriousness of her situation and she now wants to get herself out of this ill-timed condition. This realization is a good sign in her and it gives the answers to the questions that have been recurring in her mind for many years.

Out of that process of self discovery and self realization Bim experiences a downpour of love intensifying in her heart for Raja and Tara. She realizes "how she loved them, loved Raja and Tara and all of them who had lived in that house with her" (*Clear Light of Day* 165). In a moment of self discovery she happens to send a message of forgiveness and acceptance to Raja which greatly raises her in our esteem. With forgiveness the self stands transfigured as apparent in the ending of the novel, where it is stated that "with her inner eye she saw her own house and its particular history linked and contained her as well as her whole family. . . . It was where her deepest self lived, and the deepest selves of her sister and brother and all those who shared that time with her" (*Clear Light of Day* 182). With the renewal of her 'self' she recollects the scattered flowers of the wreath in which all the brothers and sister were woven together. Thus the narrative gives shape to separateness and connectedness that emerge from a family saga. At the end of all time comes to play the role in resurrecting and preserving the unity and well being of the family. Time has at last unchained Bim from the hold of dread of being alone and she is the self-sufficient self over again prepared to continue her journey all the way through life.

Bim plays a vital role in getting all the family members back in their roots and making them believe in the power of familial ties and bonds of blood. With her emerging sense of selfhood the protagonist travels a long way from self alienation to self identification.

Works Cited

Desai, Anita. *Clear Light of the Day*. New Delhi: Allied Publishers, 1980. Print.

Ghosh, Anita. "Woman on Top: A Study of Feminist Consciousness of Modern Indian Women novelists." *New Lights on Indian Women Novelists in English*. Ed. Amarnath Prasad. New Delhi: Sarup and Sons, 2004. 250-265. Print.

Jung, C. G. *Psychology and Alchemy*. London: Routledge, 1980. Print.

Macquarrie, John. *Existentialism*. UK: Penguin Books, 1976. Print.

Parmar, Virender. *Women in the Novels of Anita Desai.* Jalandhar: ABS Publications, 2000. Print.

Whitman, Walt. *The Portable Walt Whitman.* New York: The Viking Press, 1945. Print.

14

Representing Immigration through the Logic of Transformation: Bharati Mukherjee's *Jasmine*

Lata Mishra

Jasmine is a novel of emigration and assimilation, both on physical and psychological levels. In this novel, Bharati Mukherjee fictionalizes the process of Americanization by tracing a young Indian woman's experiences of trauma and triumph in her attempt to forge a new identity for herself. The work *Jasmine* is characterized by a tendency in which feeling of being displaced is overcome by a desire to settle down, and find a new home. As Martin Heidegger puts it, "A boundary is not that at which something stops but, as the Greeks recognized, the boundary is that from which something begins its presencing" (Heidegger 154). The nostalgia for the past is balanced by a desire to capture the present; the loss of identity caused through the process of displacement is mended by gaining a new one.

Jasmine, the protagonist of the novel metamorphoses her selves constantly, ferrying between these multiple identities in different spaces and at different times. *Jasmine* shows the most predictable crusade towards Americanization and its obvious mutability of an Americanized cultural identity. Jasmine never feels exasperated by cultural incongruities. She survives to make a new start in the host country, ignorant of the deterrents from her native past.

Geographically, the story begins in India and takes off from Europe to America, where it bounces back and forth from Florida through New York to proceed to Iowa, then finally lands in California. The novelist deliberately transports her in time and space again and again so as to bring in a sense of instability into the novel. However, her displacement of culture is ended with "a set of fluid identities to be celebrated." These identities are changeable, unfinished and at the same time have scope of innumerable prospects (Mukherjee, *Darkness* 3). In the novel journey is a metaphor that advocates the ever-moving, regenerating process of life itself. In India, as Jyoti, Jasmine is seen against the backdrop of the rigid and patriarchal Indian society. In America, her self-awareness is reflected in her relationships with Bud, Taylor, and Du. However, her first husband Prakash initiates her transformation from Jyoti to Jane.

Born 18 years after partition, Jasmine's family moved from Lahore, where they had aristocratic connections to Hasnapur. Here they had to lead life of simple peasants. Having inherited a tradition of exile and migration from her family Jyoti is considered the most beautiful and intelligent in her family. Her life, as happens in patriarchal societies, is controlled and dominated by her father and brothers, "Village girls are like cattle, whichever way you lead them, that is the way they will go" (Mukherjee, *Jasmine* 46). Jyoti is "the fifth daughter, seventh of the nine children" (Mukherjee, *Jasmine* 39). Her worried mother wants to kill her in order to spare her the pain of a bride without dowry and diminish her future distress for a happy life. Although the killing is violent, for Jyoti belonging to a poor family it symbolizes relief from would - be restraints and afflictions. Thus in the beginning itself the writer throws light on patriarchal violence directed towards women.

Jasmine is found on the receiving end. The political disputes in the country, such at the Partition Riots and the rebel movements which affects Jasmine's family also depict the violence. However, Jyoti finds a US-based modern-thinking man, Prakash as her husband. Prakash encourages Jyoti to study English, and renames her Jasmine. Prakash prohibits her from having children at an early age and encourages her to read his manuals to improve herself and to cherish a better future for them both, in America. "Pygmalion wasn't a play I'd seen or read then, but I realize now, how much of Professor Higgins there was in my husband. He wanted to break down the Jyoti I'd been in Hasnapur and made me a new kind of city woman" (Mukherjee, *Jasmine* 77).

However, tragedy befalls her. Her husband dies and she returns to her family. She has to decide between the life of the rigid traditions of her family and perform sati, or to continue to live the life of Jasmine in America. Jasmine sets off for America as an illegal immigrant to Florida, Her illegal transmigration begins with the thoughts:

> We are the outcasts and deportees, strange pilgrims visiting outlandish shrines, landing at the end of tarmacs, ferried in old army trucks where we are roughly handled and taken to roped-off corners of waiting rooms where surly barely wakened customs guards await their bribe. We are dressed in shreds of national costumes, out of season, the wilted plumage of intercontinental vagabondage. We ask only one thing, to be allowed to land: to pass through: to continue.
>
> (Mukherjee, *Jasmine* 101)

Thus begins her journey of transformations, displacement, and a search for identity. She undergoes her first transformation from a dutiful traditional Indian wife when she meets the intellectual Taylor who calls her Jase, and then moves on to become Bud's "Jane." But before that she burns Prakash's suit in the hotel to put her past away by her informal sati. "Around her there were rusty metal trash bins punched with holes for better ventilation. I laid the suitcase inside one and lit it from bottom. It sputtered and flared. The outside melted, and then the cotton and wool ignited" (Mukherjee, *Jasmine* 120).

Sati for Jasmine is more like to discard the past and begin a new present. She represents her resistance to Indian restrictions, and her desire to new life. With her New York identity as Jase, a sweet, happy "day mummy," Jasmine discovers the joys of consumerism. Finally, she becomes Jane Ripplemeyer, an Iowan banker's beloved. It seems likely that as Jasmine leaves for California with Taylor and Duff, her identity will continue to transform. In New York, Jasmine explicitly recognizes her ability to adapt: "I wanted to become the person they thought they saw: humorous, intelligent, refined, affectionate. Not illegal, not murderer, not widowed, raped, destitute, fearful" (Mukherjee, *Jasmine* 171). The abilities to adjust to the requirements of a changing environment and to cut the past loose are Jasmine's survival skills. They allow her to deal with the transience and culture shock of time-space compression. Bharati Mukherjee ends the book on a novel note, and re-emphasizes the complex and alternating nature of identity of a woman in exile: "Then there is nothing I can do. Time will tell if I am a tornado, rubble-maker, arising from nowhere and disappearing into a cloud. I am out the door and in the potholed and rutted driveway, scrambling ahead of Taylor, greedy with wants and reckless from hope" (Mukherjee, *Jasmine* 241).

There are a number of sad incidents of "between-ness" in the novel. In India, between the identities of Jyoti and Jasmine, Jasmine feels hovering between the traditional and the modern world offered by her Indian husband, Prakash: between controlled and independent love (Mukherjee, *Jasmine* 69). In the United States, she often confronts situations that are "in between," highlighting the concept of "two." When she leaves Taylor, he is between marriage and separation with his wife who is also between her lover and husband (Mukherjee, *Jasmine* 175). In Iowa, she happens to hear "two" farmers talk about the difference between "horsepower" and "whorepower" (Mukherjee, *Jasmine* 179). Bud, her lover, knocks one of them, because those remarks were intended to her. This kind of between-ness with "two" issues leads her into distress.

The phenomenon of displacement in the novel can be traced by focusing on a demonstration of the rhetoric of loss and gain at work in the novel. Jasmine intense desire to build a home away from her native land and to rebuild her identity helps her to survive. The novelist seems to be absolutely reluctant in the preservation of cultures, the glorification of traditions and being indebted to the past. Mukherjee seems to advocate the violence that accompanies cross-cultural revision and personal change. Jasmine says: "There are no harmless, compassionate ways to remake ourselves. We murder who we were so we can rebirth ourselves in the image of dreams" (Mukherjee, *Jasmine* 25). Jasmine herself is an agent of violence as she kills the mad dog, and more significantly, the man who raped her.

> I extended my tongue, and sliced it. Hot blood dripped immediately . . . . My mouth had filled with blood . . . . I wanted that moment when he saw me above him as he had last seen me, naked, but now with my mouth open, pouring blood, my red tongue out.... blood, ribbons of bright blood, rushed between his fingers . . . . [I] began stabbing wildly through the cloth, as the human form beneath it got smaller and smaller.
>
> (Mukherjee, *Jasmine* 106)

It is the eagerness of Jasmine to kill her past self that permits her to dynamically proceed into alien but reassuring futures. The futures into which she propels herself toward are not guaranteed to be successful, but do have the potential for personal, material and spiritual success. Though Jasmine uproots herself from her native culture and transforms herself in accordance to a new culture she contradicts her own desires: on the one hand she appears to be in a state of constant change, "How many more shapes are in me, how many more selves, how many more husbands" (Mukherjee, *Jasmine* 215). On the other hand, she feels her roots penetrating foreign soil. "Taylor, Wylie, and Duff were family. America may be fluid and built on flimsy, invisible lines of weak gravity, but I was a dense object, I had landed and was getting rooted. I had controlled my spending and now sat on an account that was rapidly growing (Mukherjee, *Jasmine* 179).

For Jasmine, history is the commotion and fissure as a result, the self becomes multiple and opposing. Her survival depends upon a flexible strategy of appropriation and transformation. It is her idea of disconnected history that admits her to subdue the restraining structure of memory in her endeavour at re-inventing herself. In her self-structuring, she does not destroy or dispose of the past, but puts it to a process of excision: a simultaneous negation and preservation of the past. The past is counter-balanced in terms of its power of constraint and paralysis but well-kept as a means of re-creating identity within the framework of an in-subordinated reasoning. The obvious non-existence of any sign of bereavement, wistfulness, or pensiveness in *Jasmine* is quite noteworthy. At one place she weeps over photographs of migrant workers, though she is not related to it personally but she somehow associates herself to it. She then controls herself and decides never to mourn over Hasnapur ever again. "I remembered Kate's book of photographs of migrant workers that Lilian, the proud mother, had shown off to me back in Fowlers Key. That book had brought back such sharp memories of Hasnapur that I'd cried. It was now only a few months later, but I didn't think I could cry over Hasnapur, ever again" (Mukherjee, *Jasmine* 160).

There is a temporal ambiguity in this passage: it is not clear whether she promises herself not to bemoan again as if bemoaning is an intentional act, or she is surprised by the event of lamenting in which the subject is taken over by the intensity of memory. Memory usually forces a person to cry over the loss of the object of desire such as familial bonds, friends and homeland, Jermone Beaty and Paul Hunter in their book, New Worlds of Literature, say: Thinking of home is often accompanied by nostalgia the absence or loss of loved ones, the remoteness of the home place we are cut off from our childhood home are Exiles. And the rest of us can perhaps understand, that we are all "exiles" from our past, our childhood, that universal "home" (Beaty 1).

But in *Jasmine*, the novelist replaces the task of the memory to cry over the lost and gone by well calculated and manipulative memory that helps the subject in its crusade for identity formation as well as transformation. Jasmine therefore confesses: "I *have* memory." She never says: "I am in the grip of memory." Jasmine represents herself as being in control of her own destiny, or her own memory, "I rip myself free of the past" (Mukherjee, *Jasmine* 208), or even when to change and when not to: "I changed because I wanted to. To bunker inside nostalgia, to sheathe the heart in a bulletproof vest, was to be a coward. On Claremont Avenue, in the Hayeses' big, clean, brightly lit apartment, I bloomed from a diffident alien with forged documents into adventurous Jase" (Mukherjee, *Jasmine* 185).

Adorno describes this distinction in his short note on Jean Paul in *Minima Moralia*:

> The pronouncements, probably by Jean Paul, that memories are the only possessions which no-one can take from us, belongs in the storehouse of impotently sentimental consolations that the subject, resignedly withdrawing into inwardness, would like to believe the very fulfillment that he has given up. In setting up his own archives, the subject seizes his own stock of experience as property, so making it something wholly external to himself. Past inner life is turned into furniture just as, conversely, every Biedermeier piece was memory made wood. The interior where the soul accommodates its collection of memoirs and curios is derelict. Memories cannot be conserved in drawers and pigeon-holes; in them the past is indissolubly woven into the present. No one has them at his disposal in the free and voluntary way that is praised in Jean Paul's fulsome sentences. Precisely where they become controllable and objectifies, where the subject believes himself entirely sure of them, memories fade like delicate wallpapers in bright sunlight. (166)

Jasmine sees memory from a utilitarian point of view. She makes a rational use of her memory. She uses it to expand herself. It appears that she goes on assimilating memories of lost bonds, places and events. Though this psychological process where the subject goes on replicating in itself behaviors, attributes or other fragments of the surrounding world, especially of other subjects seems to be improbable but it does seem convincing that Jasmine has amalgamated her earlier beaten and raped self within her in a interior, but, by the same keepsake, outside it, external to the interior. Violence affects Jasmine; it results in a transformation. In Jasmine, violence results in a change in circumstances and mindset.

The continual apparition of death is a hint that Jasmine feels the need to kill her former identities simply because they cannot be articulated or used to augment the expansion of the subject. If she would have really assimilated memories of lost ones within her there would have been no need to kill the former selves. Jasmine's earlier memories or identities form an enigmatic territory. Because of this the figure of death dominates Jasmine's narrative. These dark terrains contain images of an earlier brutalized Self, which remains preserved as an alien body excluded from the Self: "What the crypt commemorates, as the incorporated object's 'monument' or 'tomb,' is not the object itself, but its exclusion, the exclusion of a specific desire from the introjection itself" (Derrida xvii). Jasmine tries to convince the readers that she has overcome the past by assimilating it but actually her past constantly lurks into her present. As Jane at the present time of the novel Jasmine juxtaposes in her memory each of her identities—as Jyoti, Jasmine, Jazzy, Jase and kali implying that she evokes and revises her past in articulating her identities. The author depicts this transformation and transition as a positive and an optimistic journey. Jasmine creates a new world consisting of new ideas and values, constantly unmasking her past. She tries to establish a new cultural identity by integrating new desires, skills, and habits. This transition is defined not only in the changes in her attitude, but more significantly in her relationship with men.

In case of an average person the supposed coherency would have been dislocated after having endured a shocking experience of the deprivation of her objects of love and aspirations. But

Jasmine rises above ordinary lives by transforming all her sufferings to something more positive: Jasmine, being in control of what puts her outside herself, is the epitome of an ideal capitalist, a pragmatically-oriented individual and an American heroine who faces the frontier (Mukherjee, *Jasmine* 240) and who can change and rebuild herself quite deliberately. Cultural fusion in the novel is thus a placing of the protagonist as a subject in control and as an agent of the re-building of the self. The protagonist is not affixed to any fixed or single identity since she discovers no fixed roots to cling to. Instead of anchoring to a final selfhood she cannot help but shuttle among temporary identities in different spaces in different times, one after another. Jasmine sways between the past and the present attempting to come to terms with the two worlds, one of "nativity" and the other as an "immigrant." Edward Said, in his essay "Reflections on Exile" says, "Exile is the unhealable rift between a human being and a native place, between the self and the true home: its essential sadness can never be surmounted the achievements of exile are permanently undermined by the loss of something left behind forever" (101).

Works Cited

Adorno, Theodor. *Minima Moralia: Reflections from Damaged Life*. Trans. E. F. N. Jephcott. New York: Verso, 2002. Print.

Beaty, Jermone and Paul Hunter. *New Worlds of Literature: Writings from America's Many Cultures* W. W. Norton & Company; 1994. Print.

Bhabha, Homi. *The Location of Culture*. London: Routledge, 1994. Print.

Derrida, Jacques. "Fors: The Anglish Words of Nicholas Abraham and Maria Torok." *The Wolf Man's Magic Word: A Cryptonomy*. By Nicholas Abraham and Maria Torok. Trans. Richard Rand. Minneapolis: U of Minnesota P, 1986. Print.

Heidegger, Martin. "Building Dwelling Thinking." *Poetry, Language, Thought*. Trans. Alfred Hofstadter, New York: Harper and Row, 1971. Print.

Mukherjee, Bharati. *Darkness*. Markham, Ontario: Penguin, 1985. Print.

_______. *Jasmine*. New York: Grove Press, 1989. Print.

Said, Edward. *Reflections on Exile and Other Essays*. Harvard: Harvard University Press, 2002. Print.

15

Alienated Self of Woman in Namita Gokhale's *Paro: Dreams of Passion*

Manoj Kumar

We live in a world where technological achievements unimaginable in previous societies are within our grasp: this is the age of space travel, of the Internet, of genetic engineering. Yet never before have we felt so helpless in the face of the forces we ourselves have created. Never before have the fruits of our labour threatened our very existence: this is also the age of nuclear disasters, global warming, and the arms race. For the first time in history we can produce enough to satisfy the needs of everyone on the planet. Yet millions of lives are stunted by poverty and destroyed by disease. Despite our power to control the natural world, our society is dominated by insecurity, as economic recession and military conflict devastate lives with the apparently irresistible power of natural disasters. The more densely populated our cities become, the more our lives are characterised by feelings of isolation or loneliness or alienation.

The term 'alienation' in common parlance, means turning away, or keeping away from one's immediate surroundings. According to the *Oxford Dictionary*, 'alienation' means "The action of estranging or state of estrangement in feeling of affection." According to *Encyclopedia Britannica* 'alienation' is "a term used with various meanings in philosophy, theology, and psychology and the social sciences, usually with emphasis on personal powerlessness, meaninglessness, cultural estrangement, social isolation, or self estrangement."

As far as *Paro: Dreams of Passion* is concerned, it is the first novel of Namita Gokhale. Namita Gokhale has believed in forging her own path, whether by marrying when she was barely eighteen, or by the sexual candour of her first novel *Paro* which took Indian literary circles by storm and pioneered the genre which made Shobha De famous. According to her, "Sexuality and sexual mores are an extremely vulnerable area of human identity. It isn't only the biology and animal instincts that are at work in the sexual arena social conditioning, the structure of the family, gender attitudes, all come into operation" ("Savaging the Civilised").

Priya Sharma, the speaker of the novel, is a socially, culturally alienated character of Namita Gokhale. Her father is no more. She has one younger brother who is studying to become a doctor. She is the only earning member of the family "Anyway, those emotions were rarely directed at me. In actual fact I barely existed for her. Family circumstance had more or less forced me to take up a secretarial course rather complete college; all our family savings went into making my brother a doctor" (*Paro* 8). She loves B.R. very much but she does not get her love. B.R.'s sight disturbs her even when she attends his marriages. "At the sight of B.R. my heart, my stomach, my legs, all turned to unset jelly" (*Paro* 11). After the arrival of Paro in B.R.'s life she feels like Paro herself.

> I could picture him slowly undressing her; my breath would quicken as he held each firm white breast in his long brutal fingers; I could see the glazed look in his eyes as he sat astride her. Somewhere, our roles would be transposed and I would become her, and feel a triumphant power in his climax, and arrive myself at heaven's gates, to the feverish clutch of my index finger. (*Paro* 14)

Once she goes to B.R.'s house to hand over some papers. Paro asks her, "Aren't you the girl who wore the red flower in her hair, that day?" She feels ashamed and uncomfortable in the situation.

'Yes,' I answered shamefacedly, wishing the earth would swallow me up, and swallow my white sandals and my white home-starched Lucknowi sari too" (*Paro* 17). She has to arrange the marriage. Her marriage is also not very special. "My marriage was a middle-class one, much as any other. We did not have many relatives, and so it was uneventful, even a little boring. My husband was a virgin, and does not seem to notice that I was not" (*Paro* 20). In the beginning, her life seems good. "Now that I was his wife, he wanted to ensure for me every possible happiness that he could provide. He even told me that I was beautiful" (*Paro* 21). But she does not forget B.R. The memories of love between them haunts her mind. "Sometimes, I would think of B.R. and any heart would sigh. But my head told me that I had not got such a bad deal after all" (*Paro* 21). When she visits Bombay she finds her mother in a bad condition and there is no one who can take after her. "My mother was still the same, except that she had developed a filmy mother's wracking cough; at although my brother was studying medicine he seemed quite unconcerned about it" (*Paro* 23). She dies four years later. She was suffering from T.B. and it was diagnosed only after her death.

There is also an important point about the Gokhalian heroine that they want to do different, that's why they feel alienated. Priya also wants to look different from the Indian woman. "I tried to take up smoking, but Suresh would have none of it, and even tried to restrain me from wearing anything but saris. I quickly retreated back into my Indian wife image, but I was watching and learning" (*Paro* 23-24). It is the learning from the higher class. She with her husband starts hosting regular informal get together at home. But all seems useless as she remembers the old days: "So it is that I am sitting here, many years later, still grappling with these visitations from the past. I am still trying to lay their ghosts, banish their tyrannical mythologies; it is to be a therapeutic experience, an old-fashioned catharsis, an enema. I shall vomit out my malice and envy and adoration" (*Paro* 25).

B.R. marries with Bubbles on the rebound just six months after Paro leaves him and already he is flaunting his mistresses through Bombay's cloistered social circles. Once Priya, Suresh, B.R, and his wife Bubbles are sitting at the Harbour Bar in the Bombay Taj. At the same time the insistent pressure of B.R.'s foot reaches Priya. She also responds him cautiously and remains hopeful. Soon after, he calls her directly to his flat for dinner. Suresh is already backing in Delhi and Bubbles has gone to Poona to her parents. But it is not dinner that she is going to take at his flat. It is something else.

> We moved to the bed, and he entered me. He lavished so much tenderness upon me that I was overwhelmed with gratitude. I wouldn't have minded dying in those moments of perfect bliss.
>
> Just then there was a loud bang. The air-conditioner had fused. We continued, but the room became unbearably warm. 'Let's shift to the guest room,' he said. (*Paro* 37-38)

It is love for Suresh and hatred feelings towards her arranges marriage, which forces her to do such work. Now it continues for an uncertain time. Priya does not want to go back Delhi. She tells her husband that she wants to spend another month in Bombay. She starts to meet B.R. almost every evening and has dinner with him, with wine, candlelight, roses and all other trappings of a covert romance. She considers, "It was a second youth, a middle-aged revival of dreams. I had indeed never even dreamt of such passion, and I kept delaying the inevitable return to Delhi and Suresh's clumsy hateful arms" (*Paro* 39). She is getting love through this relationship but that is not a matter of love for B.R. It is the way of enjoying sex. B.R. Priya describes his nature.

> Sex had become, to him, more than a sport, it was a duty, a vocation, a calling. I sensed that it was with sex alone that he reached out to the world, and it was with sex that he shut out thought, emotion and feeling. Women could, perhaps, sense this immense sexual generosity, and came to him for succor and

> healing. And he allowed himself to be used as a lamp-post, or as a letterbox for women to send messages to their husbands through. I do not think he ever refused a woman; it was as though he were bound, by his code of honour, to ravish every female that he encountered. I think in a curious way he needed me. The habit of servility was of course ingrained in me, and B.R. had of course been my boss. It was not long, nevertheless, before our adultery ran its course. (*Paro* 40)

Her love life with B.R. is soon ended by herself when she finds another beautiful woman at his house. On the same day she finds out her with B.R. in a restaurant. This is the end of her life of love with B.R. She returns to Delhi. Suresh behaves in an awkward way because he has heard some gossip about her and B.R. Even after that he trusts her: "I trust you absolutely. But even then it is not good for women from good families to be talked about" (*Paro* 44). Priya is a very alienated character. Sometimes it is difficult for her to identify herself:

> I napped lightly for a while, and then I began to masturbate. I did not fantasise, but sometimes I became Paro, and sometimes I was myself. Sometimes I was B.R. devouring Paro, and then B.R. tenderly loving Priya, and then Paro with Suresh copulating with Priya who was actually Paro. I was all these people fragments of their thoughts, feelings, terrors passed through my writhing body. It was as if the basically voyeuristic nature of my life had been forever laid bare. I was possessed. (*Paro* 95)

Priya is unusual here. After satisfactory sexual relationships with her husband she masturbates. After all this, she becomes pregnant. Suresh is very happy because he is going to have a baby after all. But on her husband's birthday night she loses her baby. Suresh is deeply hurt. He gets busier and busier in his law work. Priya consults a psychiatrist. At last her wound heals but the feeling for the lost baby frequently appears in her life.

> The intimacy of our early married years, where we shared, if nothing else, the thrill of social battle, had quite disappeared. Then we had that brief interlude of happiness which was shattered by

> my abortion. Now we were two separate people; we knew each other's habits intimately but losing the baby had left painful, indelible scares on both of us, and we shared only our silences. (*Paro* 95)

Priya finds Paro in herself. That becomes clear when Priya mumbles the name Bubu in Suresh's ear when he is going to make sexual advances. Paro lovingly called B.R. as Bubu but it is not noticed by Suresh. He is earning enough to serve his family. But it is the feeling of alienation which forces Priya to a small bookshop for a part-time job. "But I was unmoved for that job represented escape from my empty home" (*Paro* 100). This is the place where she comes in contact with B.R. After all she is ready to fly again in the sky of love. It is the feeling of alienation which forces her in her old love life again. "I bunked the shop and disappeared downstairs to the beauty parlour for a quick hair set; I was, if I say so myself, quite well preserved for my thirty-odd years. A quick dab of lipstick and blush on, and I was quite ready to take on the world" (*Paro* 103).

Her bookshop is in Oberoi Hotel. B.R. is also staying there. She feels safe, cherished and beloved in his presence. She tells him that she is living a loveless life. Suresh is getting busier and busier. He has several juniors working with him in his chambers now. He is so busy that he has no time to talk to his wife.

> We saw less and less of each other, and met at weekend dinner parties, or across the silent dining table, at breakfast and dinnertime at home. I couldn't sleep well, somehow, and whenever I awoke at night. To drink water or go to the bathroom, the rhythmic complacent music of his snores would awaken in me an almost murderous irritation. (*Paro* 116)

This is the important aspect of Gokhalian heroine hat they considers themselves alone. From the beginning to the end of the novel we find them alone. It is their lonelinesses which makes them alienated. Priya's mother dies soon after priya's marriage. Now she feels loneliness even with Suresh. On the other hand the formalness of other relation makes her alienated. In spite of Paro we do not find her with another friend.

> I realized suddenly that I was quite alone in the world. I had nobody, but nobody, who loved me, liked me, or even cared for me. I had a host of acquaintances—my kitty party friends, all of whom despised me with the same intensity with which they disliked each other; Atul Bhaiyya, whose wife didn't like me in the least, and who wrote me a token cheque every Rakshabandhan; Lenin, who had sent me a postcard once from Paris; and B.R. who, paired with Paro, still figured as one of the twin divinities in my private mythology. And, of course, Paro herself, friendly, deceptively normal, enacting scenes from a cosy family life with Bucky—Paro, whose very existence made mine seem duller. (*Paro* 117-18)

Even in the bookshop she is feeling bored. She considers to Suresh be indifferent as he never listens to anything she ever says. His mouth, his stinking yellow teeth and his red cavernous tongue are so bad according to Priya that she does not ever want to kiss it. She hates his hairy nostrils and his constricted constipated sphincter. At last she decides to write down everything about their lives. Paro and Suresh find everything that she has written their lives. Suresh becomes aware about her relationship with B.R. "Writing about us like this is something, which, to my mind, a Hindu housewife would ever do. And I must say, you don't seem to like us overmuch. In fact you have made fun of me. And as for your relationship with B.R." (*Paro* 124).

It is unbearable for Suresh. He decides to live apart. After that Priya leaves his house and goes to Bombay to her brother's house. Now she feels real loneliness at the departing time. "I felt alone, and not at all confident. Actually, I felt nothing, only numbed, and trusting only to memories of instincts and responses to get me through" (*Paro* 131). Priya's sister-in-law Dolly thinks that Priya is spoiling the children, so her brother suggests to her to shift to the Andheri flat. Again she becomes alone when she shifts to the Andheri flat. The feeling of affection haunts her when she leaves home. "I felt terrible at leaving the children, for I had grown fond of them, and needed the warmth of my nephew's trusting body to get me through the lonely nights. They were at school when I left; and I am sure that they missed me for a while" (*Paro* 136).

Here she realizes that she should call her husband. When she calls surprisingly it is Paro who attends her call. She puts down the phone without saying anything. She decides to end her life. After two days of starvation she takes 30 Calmposes to end her life. But it does not work. She goes near the sea to end her life. But when she enters the sea, she feels a sharp bite on her ankle. She turns back towards the shore. The pain is unbearable. She wants to go to the station. At last she reaches B.R. house. She again finds her love life.

> 'Ek whisky water and ek whisky neat ki darkhast hai', he commanded. Miraculously, the drinks appeared. With sure deft hands, he began massaging my legs with alcohol; the pain persisted, and I swooned, but not with pain alone. He handed me the other whisky to drink. Slowly, the pain subsided, or perhaps I just got used to it. Still he stroked my legs. His gentle fingers found their way upwards, and soon I found myself murmuring words of love. His lips sought mine, and the ecstasy of my love for him overtook me. Somewhere along the way I succumbed to the cumulative effect of the tranquillizers, the pain and the whisky; I awoke to find my self still in B.R.'s arms. (*Paro* 142)

She calles Suresh from B.R.'s telephone. Suresh allows her to come back to his home. Her life is calm now. As they do not have a baby, they decide to adopt a child. They also visit an orphanage. But they do not adopt anyone. At the end Paro kills herself. Paro, the so-called friend of Priya, is dead now. Although Paro cannot be mean to Priya anymore, yet Paro's absence haunts Priya's mind, which alienates her from the whole world.

> Paro was dead. I couldn't imagine a world without her. I sad and thought for a long time, but no thoughts came. I got up, and emptied the ashtrays, and remembered Paro in the hospital, many

> years ago, with bandaged wrists, but she had survived. There were dark stains on the carpet, and my sari pallav was torn. She couldn't breathe, she couldn't move, she couldn't be mean to me any more. I looked at the empty chair. She hadn't meant to die; I was sure about that. It was just a silly accident, a tantrum. But then, she had looked so despairing, staring out of the window, her hair falling about her face- and now she was dead. (*Paro* 167)

We can say that *Paro: Dreams of Passion* is a satire about Delhi upper class and it deals with the upper crust of contemporary Indian society in metropolitan towns. The novels of Namita Gokhale mostly pursue the themes of relationship between two hearts under different situations. *Paro: Dreams of Passion* is a fine example of many relations on the basis of physical and mental too. The loss of virginity is an important aspect of Gokhalian heroine which makes them alienated. Gokhalian heroines are always aloof, alone and alienated. They never have companions or friends to share their ups and downs of life. They always feel that nobody in the world understands them. However, they are ambitious and hopeful. They have the courage to stand alone and find their own ways to live. Sometimes, they choose wrong paths that lead to their destruction.

Works Cited

"Alienation." *Encyclopedia Britannica.* Vol. I. 1973 Edition. Print.

"Alienation." *The Oxford English Dictionary.* 1933 Edition. Print.

Gokhale, Namita. *Paro: Dreams of Passion.* New Delhi: Penguin Publication, 1984. Print.

"Savaging the Civilised: Namita Gokhale." *Expression India. Online.Netscape*: 17 Oct. 2007. <http://www.expressionindia.com/ie/daily/20000510/Savaging the Civilised.html>.

16

Silence and Voice of Indian Woman in *The Dark Abode*

K.P. Prameela

The Dark Abode is a realistic novel by Sarojini Sahoo with the latest encumbrances and discussions of this time in which we live. Its popularity and bombardment with translations in different languages are proving the timely intervention of the novel. It is a story of an unseen but profound relationship between an Indian, specifically Oriyan housewife Kuki and her Pakistani counterpart, painter Safiq. They are connected through the net, physically very far but emotionally very near. They exchange their hopes, hugs, day-to-day affairs, likes and dislikes, preferences and quarrels, philosophy and humanity in full spirit. There is nothing to hide between them, as the relationship is purely personal. It is spontaneous, going beyond all barriers stipulated by the system.

Kuki is wedded to an engineer and has two kids. She is the same middle class Indian trophy wife, with daily chores and stipulated schedules. Being educated, she is a little bit upset over her transformation as a normal housewife. She loves her husband and he does everything to her. When she finds a friend, in her lonely days time, she is happy to talk. Slowly his enquiries and indicted remarks make them fall in love. He persuades her to join him for a free life for which she is preparing. But the man is a Pakistani, Muslim and someone who does his work with a free mind. He is indicted and caught by the military regime for his connections and gets punished. At the same time, Kuki's husband,

Aniket, is also sent to a foreign company by his employers. She is alone and perplexed. In moments of crisis, Kuki realizes that her love and solace of life are falling apart in two countries, sexes, religions and systems. Being in the middle, she can only maintain a silence with a sigh. The story speaks loud and sends it message around through a seemingly silent protagonist.

The novel is centred around Kuki, her middle-class ideas, perceptions of life and living style. Like, any other Indian woman, she possesses a family, children, husband and their small world. When she drives herself into a new love, the family suffers a lot. But it is essential for her since she is caught in between patriarchal settings and lover-turned-husband. Whenever misogynous characteristics pull her back, instinct for freedom drives her towards the computer through which she enjoys the multitudinous love. All her outer-layered conflicts and difficulties are driven by the ambitious nature of any middle-class housewife. When she finds a parallel and safer inner world, she drives alone into it with utmost care. Indeed, the novelist outstandingly correlates a number of socio-political and international issues in the fabric of its main story-line, like terrorism, anarchism of the military regimes, freedom of expression in art, problems of polygamy in Islam, plurality of gods in Hindu culture, communalism, huge divide between rich and poor, rural and urban, Hindu and Muslim, hostility between neighbouring countries, distressing work-pressure on youth in the present corporate culture etc. to enrich the dimensions of the literary piece. These accessories make the story profoundly convincing and thought-provoking. The most appealing factor is that the all the problems are knit into a well-narrated love story of an ordinary woman.

Indian village women are traditional. They are slowly getting urbanized, semi-educated, partly Westernized. They believe in freedom, but not on the cost of home and its given protection. Duality between thoughts and practices is the main thing they face everyday. She neither objects to the older systems nor accepts the newer ones totally, even though both have partial goodnesses and faults in them. She rightly needs freedom and self-reliance within the family, which she feels, not possible in the patriarchal set-up. She is the real representative of Indian, Hindu woman, who values her relationships, but aspires for a democratic approach in it—a villager turned semi-urban, a lover turned wife and mother, an educated turned unemployed housewife, who always dreams of free movements and economic self-reliance. She is not at all boisterous in explaining herself: "When you see me and touch me, you will realize that I am an ordinary human being with my own sorrows and grief, doubts and dissatisfactions, I am no goddess; I possess no divine powers. I hunger, I thirst, I crave for sex; I have my own aspirations and ambitions. I also pretend; I also lie; I also betray Aniket and live my life behind a mask . . . " (Sahoo 54)

Sahoo put forward the followings incentive thoughts for the reader through the portrayal of Kuki in *The Dark Abode.* She tries to explain sexuality in her own view.

1. Sex is just a game for him. I am yet to discover what orgasm is. You will be astonished to know that I have not been kissed for last fourteen yeas. I know it probably seems very unnatural (Sahoo 57).

Women are bodily beings. Imperial, feudal values imposed on Indian woman, specifically Hindu woman always project them as objects. The caricatures in art and protagonists in the earlier texts depict them in men's view. During the age of woman writers, woman has started to talk about her body, slowly accepting her body and sexuality. Here Kuki opens up her mind. Sahoo could fill the psychic space of Kuki through each word and sentence of the novel. Writing emails and using ultra modern techniques to communicate make it more effective. Sahoo uses the possibilities of the cyber world, widely accused for its misuse and negative communication to create inter-connective surroundings for Kuki.

2. Women are fetching not only physical outfits but also emotional solace at home and she has a right to ask for it.

Rothblum Esther, Professor of Psychology, University of Vermont views that "Heterosexual couples fall into more traditional roles once they marry" (qtd. in Carlin Flora's column in *Psychology Today*, September-October 2004, p.27). On a larger view, household responsibilities are not very easy, but always unpaid, unnoticed, under-valued to which housewives get acquainted during the long years of marriage. Couples adjust to accommodate each other, but with always men in the dominant position. Men rarely try to note that the individual wishes of their wifes. The custom prevailing in our country always says that a wife is happy with her husband. She has no separate individual wishes. Thus, he also believes that food, clothes, shelter and children are her happiness. Aniket often breaks this perception while Kuki rightly finds it contradictory to her choices and interests: "After marriage, I discovered that Aniket was not very sensitive or open to understanding female psychology" (Sahoo 57). Bhabha and Spivak have deliberated this state of Indian woman: "Indigenous patriarchal tradition is a burden on Indian Hindu women and this manipulate voice of Indian women accordingly" (Moore-Gilbert 454). Here, the women writer conveys Kuki's mindset through her body language. But her partner, Aniket, is not capable enough to understand his better half's mind-blowing changes! Gender sensitivity is an essential matter in some occasions in anyone's life, but always considering woman as 'the other' or 'inferior' is drastic which will ruin the mutual respect needed for a long life.

Here the author breaks the age-old beliefs imposed on Indian womanhood. She questions the whole concept of patriarchal family headed by men and asks for new initiatives to maintain a more democratic, emotionally attached and gender-free union of its members concerned.

3. Human relationship is at par and beyond gender, sex, caste and creed. Women are trying to assert unconditional love from men.

Open and wide relationship is indeed a dream for both men and women. An Indian traditional husband cannot apologize before his wife, only because he is a man! He cannot show any respect towards his wife openly. He is supposed to behave like a master and the wife as his unconditional slave. But when it comes to the lover, equal deliberations and comments are possible. For the society, lovers have no authentication. In our set-up, only arranged or a legal marriage has approval. Any other type of union of opposite or same sex cannot be said or defined as a 'family'. Safiq can easily apologise to Kuki and touch her feet, express his respect in any number of words while her husband Aniket cannot. If he does so, it will be against the practice of his so-called manliness, practised in Indian households.

The difference between lover and lover-turned-husband is horrible and heartbreaking for any woman. So Kuki keeps quiet, accepts silently, when Safiq says: "My love for you is purer, more intense and eternal than Aniket's" (Sahoo 50). At the same time, she believes in their husband-wife relationships, tries to fulfil her traditional roles, but never finds herself enjoying the same. She always feels like a missing soul in her routines, like Dr. G.R. Madan found it more sensitive and appropriate, "The wife today faces the major confusion in status and role, not because of any temperamental weakness or genic incapacity, but because her behavior has changed more drastically that of man" (Madan 365). The whole conversation between the lovers breaks the age-old hypothesis of man-woman relationship and exposes what is missing inside the Indian homes. Self-doubt and helplessness are the main characteristics of Indian girls inside the home. Here Kuki is no exception!

For a secular mind, there is no caste or creed in life. Her/ his mind would not like to see a person in terms of his religious identity. Attraction towards the opposite sex is merely going beyond all barriers set by tradition. The irony is that in the age of international marriages accepted all over the world, our regional newspapers fill up their columns with the news of honour killing happening in Indian villages! Again, it is easy to believe the newspaper reports, which says that more than 50 per cent of love marriages breakup soon after marriages take place. According to statistics aired in the regional channels, an average number of 50 divorce cases are registered daily in the family courts in Kerala state only.

4. Women would do anything like men if there is a scope for doing it.

Women enjoy secret love, but like men, are hypocritical in accepting it. More specifically, our society never accepts love relations! This is accepted and said by Kuki many times on the computer! Inadvertently, she experiences that something is lacking inside her relationship inside the family. She has no way to communicate this to anyone. She helps herself by communicating and sharing her sorrows to someone very far. Again and again she remembers the lines rendered by her lover: "You are my beautiful widow and I am the skeleton of your husband" (Sahoo 135). This line echoes inside the human souls without any hindrances and barriers. This proves that lovemaking is essential, eternal and integral in human life. It is an interactive activity, which can be happened anywhere, anytime in life.

But for a wife, it is essential to love her husband even though he is a bastard. Men have not bounded to follow these stipulations. It is women who should be responsible to maintain the 'morals' of the family and the society. Housewives are known as 'devis'. There is no such big name given to any man! So woman is supposed to keep quiet even when she is put on the pyre with her dead husband. Time has changed a lot. But, even in the age of free sex in the parks and roads, there is no scope for fair and free conversation between husband and wife. Aniket is supposed to behave like a husband and Kuki should follow his words in all affairs. Slowly she gets used to being silent when he shouts at her: "Am I a watchman, employed to watch over you twenty-four hours a day?" (Sahoo 149).

Lacking emotional attachment inside the home, Kuki wanders in the possible world of Internet. Slowly she finds herself enjoying, changing, wonderful, writing poetry, singing songs, feeling occasionally someone is calling her and getting energetic while thinking so. She is slightly doubtful about her free conversation with a stranger. So she never books Aniket's wrong deeds in front of that 'stranger'. Being a 'Bharathiya nari' she tries to swallow the burden of family values. Practically, she has no better option! When Safiq questions her about her perverted long life, she dares to thunder back, "I am fine with my perverted life; you can carry on living in your world. Who are you to insult me repeatedly like this? Who gave you the right to dictate my life?" (Sahoo 61). Here she proves herself to be a reliant being with self-respect. But the agony is that she cannot argue this one with her husband in the same tone with an open mind.

5. Kuki is a representative of this world/gender discrimination is a worldwide phenomenon.

Sahoo always tackles the regional form of feministic scholarship in her writings. She never blindly accepts what Western feminists argue. Radical forms of actions and practices never to appeal to her. Asking for equality does not mean to women that they become like men in anyway. She posits her desire of emancipation as a right, to have equal living conditions for all, in which women will be living with their biological peculiarities and priorities. Opportunities and attitudes will be there to handle any form of domination. Gender discrimination and isolation of women is a universal fact, prevalent inside and outside family. She adjudicates Virginia Wolf's words through Kuki: "As a woman, I have no country. As a woman, my country is the whole world" (Sahoo 12).

6. Problems of middle-class mindset in men, need for feminism

As in the case of any middle-class family man, Aniket is ambitious, always compares himself with other colleagues. Instead of his higher education and established set-up, his possessive mentality often turns into the privatization of womanhood/wifehood. He believes that kids love Kuki more and expresses frustration obout it. He needs to be the 'Master' of the family, never go for any companionship inside. He controls his love towards his children! This master nature in Indian men often gives way to wife battering for small reasons. Thus the sole bread-winner of the family becomes emotionally alienated in the family. Moreover they have their ego problems and official pressure which there excercise on their wife and children. Here in this novel, Sahoo indicts this conventional psychology through Aniket: "Aniket had a notion that women lose their softness and simplicity if they worked" (Sahoo 64).

Preparing men to accept the fact that women-empowerment, liberation and human freedom are essential for the well being the family and society is very important. Indeed redefining women means re-defining men along with the changing time and space. Without it, our struggle for freedom will be reduced merely to a political game. Ms Sahoo essentially conveys this social message. She has elaborated the feminist social responsibility to re-define men, as explained by Nancy Duncan that "Feminism also began to argue that what needed to be done was not simply to study women, but to study men in a new way, such that gender roles and sexual relation would be problematized, in order t explore new gender systems are constructed and to question the naturalness of gender itself as a binary position" (20).

7. Questions dual standards stipulated for men and women.

Women are always been men's property. Properties cannot speak. They have no sexuality. Their bodies are for the enjoyments of men. So they cannot show any interests in their body. This state of slavishness was known as a process of *cultural mummification of the individual thinking* by Franz fanon (Fanon 44). Gayathri Chakravaorthy Spivak rightly explained this situation in her well-known essay 'Can Sabaltern speak?' (Baba 66-111). In this row, Deborah Cameron has also explained that "Speech and silence have been powerful metaphors in feminist discourse" (83). After some years, when literary items depicting subaltern realities have emerged and made their presence in the social arena, Spivak had to accept that "If the subaltern speak, then thank God, the subaltern is not a subaltern anymore" (Harasym 158). Through Kuki, the feminist author has proved that the middle class Indian woman is no more a subaltern. She is not fully free in her life, owing social and familial customs and practices, but she is able to understand her situations in her own view. This helps her to proceed ahead and live a hopeful life within the parameters of the land in which she lives. Sarogini Sahoo proves herself as a represented Indian womanist writer over here, narrated by Layli Phillips the editor of *The Womanist Reader:* "To be a womanist, one must identify one's cultural roots and experience oneself as a cultural or ethnic being rather than a racial being, but one must also be able to see oneself and one's people as part of a larger global body defined by common humanness" (xxxvi). She never tries to mimic or copy the life of a Western woman in the depiction of Kuki. Here we find the changing psychic facets of the Indian woman, who finds herself transformed through these times.

Many women writers have tried to portray the battle between women and the familial system in which they live in. The system is becoming more powerful and destructive with ultramodern equipments. Each time, being in the second position and less equipped, women got injured, but they cannot give up their struggle for their human rights. A woman likes to maintain all kinds of relationships with men. She has started to demand love, life and equal status in life. In the story line, the novel ends in a tragic mood, but the hopes and dreams of a womanist writer cannot end like that. She has to protect her sense and sensitivity with utmost care. So she concludes the story: "She would wait for the voice that once charmed her ears and echoed with a subtle resonance in her soul, a voice she had never told anyone about, then or ever since" (Sahoo 174). Kuki must be waiting for that positive voice which will resonate with her voice.

Without any doubt, we can say that this novel and the protagonist Kuki are the recent literary interventions of the Third World women, by an Indian woman, for all women of all times. Since there is no man's world, without women, all men in all times have been inexplicably interwoven within this female world. This fact is underlined in the novel. The aesthetics of opposite love, another positive contribution of this novel, which demands a separate look.

The novel easily conveys the issues and struggles of middle-class Indian housewife—to live like a human being, with all her distinctive human emotions. As Saroj Iyyer precisely said, "What does a woman do for a family?" Instead we have to ask, "What does the family do for a woman?" (84). This is the symbolic act extended by this novel. The whole essence of the novel can be termed as 'freeing the spirit' experience for all readers, especially women, who believe in human freedom. There is no artificiality in the portrayal of characters. Kuki speaks inside her soul, slowly and carefully nourishes her aspirations, not jump into any speedy conclusions! So the readers can very well keep pace with her and endeavour a dialogic relationship with Kuki. She inspires them to keep their soul alive and act accordingly.

Works Cited

Bhabha, Homi K. & G.C. Spivak. *A Companion to Post Colonial Studies.* Eds. Bar Moore-Gilbert, Henry Schwarz & Sangeetha Ray. London: Routledge, 2000. Print.

Duncan, Nancy. "Body Space." *The Feminist Critique of Language—A Reader.* Deborah Cameron, ed. London: Routledge, 1998. Print.

Fanon, Frantz. *Racism and Culture—Forward the African Revolution,* London: Pelican, 1970. Print.

Harasym, Sarah, ed. *The Post-Colonial Critic: Interviews, Strategies, Dialogues*, London: Routledge, 2002. Print.

Iyyer, Saroj. *The Sruggle to be Human*. Bangalore: Book for Change, 1999. Print.

Madan, G.R. *Indian Social Problems*. Volume 1. 5th Edition, New Delhi: Allied Publications Limited, 1993. Print.

Philip, E. & Celia Wolf-Devine. *Sex and Gender: A Spectrum of Views*. Canada: Wadsworth, Thomspon Leaning, 2003. Print.

Phillips, Laylli, ed. *The Womanist Reader*. Newyork: Routledge, 2006. Print.

Sahoo, Sarojini. *The Dark Abode* Trans. Mahendra Kumar Dash. Indian Age Communication, 2008. Print.

Williams & Chrisman, ed. *Colonial Discourse and Post Colonial Theory*. Wheatsheaf: Harvester, 1993. Print.

17

Routing Relationships through Diaspora: Exploring the Short Fiction of Jhumpa Lahiri

Priyanka Tripathi and H.S. Komalesha

In the parlance of postcolonial Indian writing in English, Jhumpa Lahiri has often been read, sometimes exclusively, within the framework of diaspora (See Noella Brada Williams; N. Sharda Iyer; Suman Bala; Basavaraj S. Naikar; Anurag Chauhan). Her status as a diasporic writer more describes the diasporic and immigrant issues she deals with in her writings than her own condition of being an Indian diasporic citizen in the United States. In this paper an attempt has been made to examine the seminal role diaspora plays in building as well as breaking human relationships in the backdrop of Jhumpa Lahiri's short fiction.

Nandini Sahu, while writing about the nostalgic note in Lahiri's short stories mentions her inevitable status as the writer of the Indian diaspora. She states: "through Lahiri's stories, we learn bits and pieces about Indian life in diaspora and how Indians fit into their lives in America" (Sahu 171). Lahiri concentrates on the dilemma of complex human relationships in the modern situation, diasporic relationships or non-diasporic relationships. Looking at her short stories from close quarters, one may find that the best portion of her writing deals with the understanding of human beings, their life and relationships that can cut across national lines. In the context of Lahiri's portrayal of human relationships, Nandini Sahu mentions R.K. Kaul, who comments: "The author has narrative skill, which captures the reader's attention immediately . . . . Whether the setting is in Bengal or in the US, she creates a probable world where human relations are all that matter" (Sahu 168).

The basic theme of her writing thus appears to be human relationships in all their varied and variegated shades. As Saloni Prasad says, Lahiri's stories are all about the inner psyche of the characters: "the relationship between parent and child, siblings, lovers, husband and wife and even simply between the residents of the same building" (Prasad 261). Even Ashutosh Dubey while discussing *Interpreter of Maladies* says that Jhumpa's stories are more about the need for understanding, communication and faltering marriage than about the encounter between an Indian and Indian Americans (Sharma 23-24). This remark by Ashutosh Dubey as quoted in Roshan Lal Sharma's article applies to *Unaccustomed Earth* as well. This paper argues on these grounds and looks at Jhumpa Lahiri as a writer of human relationships and in the process also examines how diaspora builds up tensions which eventually can manage or damage both conventional and unconventional human relationships.

Before this paper elaborates on different types of relationships that one comes across while reading the short stories of Jhumpa Lahiri, it may be necessary to clarify what conventional and unconventional relationships are. By conventional relationships, this paper means the relationships formed keeping marriage and family at the centre, such as conjugal, parental, sibling relationships etc. Unconventional relationships refer particularly here to those relationships that are formed outside the institution called marriage.

To begin with conjugal relationships: "A Temporary Matter," the first story in *Interpreter of Maladies*, deals with fissures and indifference that generally creep in and affect connubial relationships. In the context of this short story, a young couple slowly drift apart after their baby is stillborn. They become so indifferent to each other that they rarely meet though they live in the same flat and even when they cross each other's path they barely speak. There is nothing much said between the couple but those unsaid act like slow poison and can potentially kill their relationship. Noella Brada Williams in an article observes the reasons behind this couple's indifference to each other: ". . . the sheer number of these small failures to provide care helps to define the depths of Shobha and Shukumar's common yet isolated experience of grief for their lost child as well as their waning care and love for each other" (Williams 457).

From the very beginning, the kind of equation Lahiri portrays between them is that of discomfort. The relationship they share has lost its essential warmth and they are more like housemates and less like husband-wife. To quote from the short story: "They weren't like this before. Now he had to struggle to say something that interested her, something that made her look up from her plate, or from her proofreading files. Eventually he gave up trying to amuse her. He learnt not to mind the silences" (*Interpreter of Maladies* 12). Their life is a mix of odd elements and they have failed to add life and vigour in their relationship which existed between them before Shobha gave birth to the dead child. Lahiri finds a situation in day-to-day life where there may be a scope for rejuvenating their ties. The notice stating that there will be a power cut for an hour for five days may symbolise the temporary darkness in their life. When Shobha says: "We can light candles" it could be suggestive of a ray of hope that marriages can work all over again if the couple put in their efforts to come out of their dark times. Thus, the darkness in the story is utilized to stimulate nostalgia, confront fears, confess guilt, build trust and strengthen relationship between the couple.

Similarities can be drawn between "A Temporary Matter" in *Interpreter of Maladies* and "A Choice of Accommodations" in *Unaccustomed Earth*. In the short story, "A Choice of Accommodations", Amit and Megan have two daughters. They are happily married but somewhere boredom has crept into their relation. They plan to attend Pam's wedding, not just for the sake of attending the wedding but also to spend some time together. During this trip, they find moments to regain the lacking warmth of their relationship. In both the stories, the void in relationship is filled finally with the intimate physical relationship they forge. Both the stories end on a strong note where strong biological drive to consummate leads to rejuvenating an equally strong and warm emotional bonding, thus bridging the gap between the couple. Concluding lines of both the stories can be quoted for further illustration:

> Shobha had turned the lights off. She came back to the table and sat down, and after a moment, Sukumar joined her. They wept together, for the things they now knew.
>
> (*Interpreter of Maladies* 22)

> Megan's eyes were on his face, an arm stretched in front of her and a hand pressed to his chest, as if to prevent him, now that they were finished, from collapsing on top of her again. But he hoped that he was forgiven, and for a few moments, they remained together on the narrow bed in the little room, his heart beating rapidly, vigorously, plainly striking the skin of her palm.
>
> (*Unaccustomed Earth* 127)

Thus both the short stories hinge on re-exploring cold conjugal relationship through making love, through coming together in unison. As D.H. Lawrence says in a different context, the true secret of a successful marriage is in the long, slow, enduring things and not in the occasional spasm of any sort: "Little by little, living together, two people fall into a sort of unison; they vibrate so intricately to one another. That's the real secret of marriage, not sex; or at least not the simple function of sex . . . the great relationship for humanity will always be the relation between man and woman" (Lawrence 54). Apart from conjugal relationships, Jhumpa Lahiri also brings out equations between parents and their relationship with children.

"Unaccustomed Earth", the first story in her second collection poignantly deals with Ruma's relationship with her father in particular and her parents in general. Here, Ruma, a young mother settled in a new city, is visited by her father. During his stay with her, he spends much of his time in digging the earth for garden and in the process forges an intimate bond with his grandson. However, Ruma cannot cling to her father as her son has been able to. Her relationship with her father is marked by a lot of tensions. After her mother died and her father is left alone, she thinks many times before asking her father to stay with her in her house. She is not sure whether her father, who is a product of a different set of values and relationships can understand the equation she has with her husband. She also thinks that he might interfere in her way of life; as a result, staying together might prove to be a disastrous experience. Thus, Jhumpa brings out the tensions in the relationship between a youngster who has successfully accustomed herself with the American way of life and her father who finds it difficult to adapt himself to the new culture in which he struggles to live.

The first generation immigrants, who have been living in the new society and reaping the economic benefits of that society, desperately try not to get influenced by the culture of the new land. They try to avoid their children from embracing American lifestyle. It is perhaps easier for their parents to maintain the 'sanctity' of their 'culture' but for the children, who are born and brought up in the foreign land; it is quite difficult to maintain the cultural insularity their parents have adapted in the foreign land. These dilemmas between two different generations groping to live in the migrated land mark the essence of "Unaccustomed Earth".

In the same short story, Ruma's father fondly thinks of the past when Ruma was so much dependent on him. He is still very protective about her as if her well-being is also part of his and not hers alone. To quote from the short story:

> He remembered his children coming home from college, impatient with him and his wife, enamored of their newfound independence,

> always wanting to leave. It had tormented his wife and, though he never admitted it, had pained him as well. He couldn't help thinking, on those occasions, how young they'd once been, how helpless in his nervous arms, needing him for their survival, knowing no one else. He and his wife were their whole world. But eventually that need dissipated, dwindled to something amorphous, tenuous, something that threatened at times to snap. That loss was in store for Ruma, too; her children would become strangers, avoiding her. And because she was his child he wanted to protect her from that, as he had tried throughout his life to protect her from so many things.
>
> (*Unaccustomed Earth* 54)

This problem in parent-children relationship is again very neatly captured in the "Interpreter of Maladies." The central characters of the title story of *Interpreter of Maladies*, Mr. Das and Mrs. Das are born and brought up in USA. They are very much 'products of America'. They feel a sense of 'liability' towards their children and that may be one of the reasons Jhumpa Lahiri begins this story, with the initial bickering of the couple about the trivial issue of who should take their young daughter to the toilet. Some may justify it as an act of sharing responsibilities of a child but any work as part of child's upbringing cannot be so finely classified between husband and wife. In fact the couple more behaved like always bickering siblings and less like mature couple taking care of their children.

As observed in the short story: "They were all like siblings, Mr.Kapasi thought as they passed a row of date trees. Mr. & Mrs. Das behaved like an older brother and sister, not parents. It seemed that they were in charge of the children only for the day; it was hard to believe that they were regularly responsible for anything other than themselves (*Interpreter of Maladies* 49).

If we move from parent-children relationship in Jhumpa Lahiri's short fiction to the relationship between siblings, then we come across the story "Only Goodness" in *Unaccustomed Earth*. Generally, the sibling relationships are considered to be the closest in most people's life. In a certain sense, it is closer than the relationship between parents and children.

Using a span of about five years, Lahiri in the short story describes the gradual progress of the relationship between a brother and his sister. Rahul is Sudha's brother and she is very fond of him. As he grows up the fondness increases as both of them find a friend in each other: "She felt a new bond with her brother, a sense, after years of regarding him just as a kid, that they were finally friends (*Unaccustomed Earth* 129). Unfortunately, the warmth in their relationship gradually weakens in the due course of time. Sudha had introduced alcohol to Rahul just for fun as part of the life of youth in America. However, it becomes an addiction to Rahul. Even after several sessions at rehabilitation centre, he could not restrain himself from drinking alcohol. During his visit to his sisters' place, he drinks alcohol and leaves her son unattended in the bathtub without the plastic ring. This carelessness by him could have resulted in tragedy. This offends his sister to the extent that she asks him to leave the house the next day. The emotional trauma Sudha undergoes while asking her brother to leave her house makes the scene poignant. The short story ends on a sad note but gives the reader various shades of the relationship between a brother and sister.

While dealing with conventional relationships, Lahiri also sketches out some of the traits that do not fit into the frame of conventional relationship. Especially mentioned here are relationships outside the institution of marriage. Though these relationships are often termed as extra-marital or illicit relationship, Jhumpa knows for sure that they have been formed out of a particular emotional or physical necessity, but are not graced by society. For Jhumpa, as Sanghvi addresses, these relationships are not only a matter of ethical decision, but also are of adventure, replete with vivifying ironies that render the task difficult but ultimately worthwhile.

In the story "Hell–Heaven" in *Unaccustomed Earth,* Usha in the later stage of her life thinks of her mother's past wherein she believes that her mother was in love with Pranab Kaku and not with her father. Though there is no physical relationship between them, the warmth works at a different level. As Usha observes in the short story: "He brought to my mother the first and, I suspect the only pure happiness she ever felt. I don't think even my birth made her as happy. I was evidence of her marriage to my father, an assumed consequence of the life she had been raised to lead. But Pranab Kaku was different. He was the one totally unanticipated pleasure in her life" (*Unaccustomed Earth* 67).

Similarly, in *Interpreter of Maladies* Mr. Kapasi in the short story "Interpreter of Maladies" feels fascinated towards Mrs. Das. He discovers the element of passionate romance in a relationship with Mrs. Das, which is lacking in his own marriage. Seeing her bare legs, he gets excited. He thinks of the monotonous relationship he shares with his wife:

> Even when they had made love she kept the panels of her blouse hooked together, the string of her petticoat knotted around her waist. He had never admired the backs of his wife's legs the way he now admired those of Mrs. Das, walking as if for his benefit alone. He had of course seen plenty of bare limbs before, belonging to the American and European ladies who took his tours. But Mrs. Das was different. Unlike the other women, who had an interest only in the temple, and kept their noses buried in a guidebook, or their eyes behind the lens of the camera, Mrs. Das had taken interest in him.
>
> (*Interpreter of Maladies* 58)

Mr. Kapasi finds Mrs Das charming because he has, for the first time in his career, come across a woman who has taken interest in him and has found his translator job interesting. Added to this, she confesses him about her second son who was born out of a fling she had with a Punjabi friend of her husband. However, his interest in her soon turns into a disappointment as he learns that her confession is more to purge herself of her guilt than with any interest in him as an individual. When he cannot offer her any cure or solace, he asks her "is it really pain you feel, Mrs Das or is it guilt?", she responds with a withering glare that "crushed him; he knew at that moment that he was not even important enough to be properly insulted" (*Interpreter of Maladies* 66). Thus, in the short story though the sexual attraction outside marriage is not just clearly expressed, it is boldly acknowledged.

Of course, there are some short stories in Lahiri's collections where the sexual relationship outside marriage is boldly dealt with. Dev in "Sexy" satisfies his physical desires and emotional needs in Miranda while his wife is away. In each of these situations, Lahiri tries to portray emotional and psychological responses of a person in a particular situation. In an interview with Arun Aguiar for a magazine, she states: "Relationships do not preclude issues of morality. . . . When I sit down to write, I don't think about writing about an idea or a given message. I just try to write a story (which is hard enough). And there's obviously a message, or a moral, or something (smiles). I think that's good—but it's not something I actively think about, to be honest with you" (Aguiar online).

In the process of silhouetting human relationships, Lahiri subtly discusses the concept of marriage with all its nuances. Indira Nityanandam while analysing the theme of marriage in *Interpreter of Maladies* states, "The concept of marriage vows being sacrosanct is a part of the expatriate's native culture, but when these people come into contact with the alien culture, everything changes" (Nityanandam 67). Marriage, especially in the Indian context is like a 'bond', a 'lifetime commitment'. Even if love evaporates and there is no physical charm left, they continue with marriage if not for their own sake, at least for the sake of their children. It becomes a stigma if either of the two walks out of marriage to seek separation or divorce. It is considered that the chastity of marriage is at question if such practices come in vogue.

In the short story, "Sexy" in *Interpreter of Maladies* Laxmi's cousin even after being aware of her husband's affair, waits for him to return to her. She patiently undergoes the pain and suffering of tolerating her husband with some other woman, which is "a wife's worst nightmare" (Lahiri 83) just for the sake of her child. The bond of marriage is such that neither wife nor husband can simply break it, no matter what their priorities are. Though Usha's mother was strongly attracted towards Pranab Kaku, it was beyond question for her to think of walking out of marriage. In addition, Dev comes back to his shell in the short story "Sexy". It is a general opinion that marriage is not just coming together of two individuals, it also brings with it, significant past, culture, ideas etc. Being part of the same culture may bring in with the couple the same values towards the institution of marriage. This may perhaps help them in bonding well within their marriage. As Morris quotes McGoldrick observation:

> . . . becoming a couple is one of the most complex and difficult transitions of the family-life cycle even though it is often perceived as the least complicated and most joyous. This romanticized view of the transition to marriage may contribute to a couple's lack of adequate preparation and subsequent difficulty and distress during the transition. Many people consider marriage as the unimpeded, blissful joining of two individuals. However, Carter and McGoldrick (1989) have suggested that marriage really represents the merger of two entire systems combining in developing a new, third family system. (Morris 2)

Lahiri also discusses these aspects in the stories "A Temporary Matter," "This Blessed House," "The Third and Final Continent" in *Interpreter of Maladies* and the triptych entitled "Hema and Kaushik" in *Unaccustomed Earth*. Her characters share similar background many times and different backgrounds at other times. Ruma and Adam in "Unaccustomed Earth" and Amit and Megan in "A Choice of Accommodations" in *Unaccustomed Earth* share different cultural set up in their upbringing. For Lahiri, they may not be just different cultural backgrounds. Rather, they may be two different situations for her. She attempts to distinguish between these situations to portray the best of both situations. Her characters explore more of their inner self than their cultural background. Siddharth Dhanvant Sanghvi, while attempting to understand Jhumpa Lahiri, writes:

> The characters in *Unaccustomed Earth* are not as lightly drawn as in *The Interpreter of Maladies*, and their true displacement is not of geography but of self. She unleashes people caught in states of emotional flux, having migrated from what is conventionally considered morally right (as in the case of "Hell-Heaven") or emotionally appropriate (see Hema and Kaushik). Dithering on the borders of self and society, the private and the public, these characters are exiled from the state of being at ease with who they are, and not culturally but internally, and intuitively.
>
> (Sanghvi *TOI*)

In fact, the brilliance with which Lahiri gets into the inner psyche of the characters taking care of their intellectual and emotional make-up is highly suggestive of the way in which relationships occupy a central place in her writing. In a way, her characters embark on a unique quest to find and seek meaning in relationships that are splitting apart due to their divided immigrant experience. What is noteworthy in Jhumpa's characters is that they are, for various reasons, unable to strike a meaningful relationship either with their partners or parents, siblings, friends, etc. This is perhaps because when individuals lose their sense of community, inherent in them that connects them with the surrounding world, they fail to foster any kind of strong and sustained relationships either with themselves or with others. In fact, even conjugal relationships in India are contingent upon other relationships and hence it is commonly said that marriages in India are more between two families than between two individuals. Since these contingent and supporting relationships are absent in the immigrated land, a kind of vacuum develops between individuals in a relationship, which unless understood and acted upon in time can snowball into creating big gaps. This point is evident in stories such as "A Temporary Matter," "Doors," "Mrs Sen," "Blessed House," "A Choice of Accommodations," etc. In all these stories the tension in relationships between characters is because there is a dialectics between family-centred culture and career-centred culture. People, who are products of a collectivist culture, find themselves at odds in an individual-centred society such as the one prevalent in the US. Moving between values of collectivist and individualist cultures these characters are perfectly equipped to deal between the universal and the individual relationships. But they find the homogenising forces of globalization and the mechanized living of the Western world as a serious threat to their cultural identity. From this perspective, in all her portrayal of relationships we find diaspora playing a decisive role in defining human relationships.

Works Cited

Aguiar, Arun. "Interview with Jhumpa Lahiri." *Pif Magazine.* 28 July 1999. Web. 15 August 2008. *<http://www.pifmagazine.com/SID/598/>.*

Bala, Suman. Ed. *Jhumpa Lahiri: The Master Story Teller.* New Delhi: Khosla Publishing House, 2002. Print.

Chauhan, Anurag. "Incomplete Compromises in Jhumpa Lahiri's *Interpreter of Maladies.*" *New Lights on Indian Women Novelists-Vol. 1.* Ed. Amar Nath Prasad. New Delhi: Sarup and Sons, 2003. 204-211. Print.

Iyer, N. Sharda. "*Interpreter of Maladies-* A Saga of Asian Immigrants." *New Lights on Indian Women Novelists in English- Vol. -2.* Ed.Amar Nath Prasad. New Delhi: Sarup & Sons, 2004. 219-226. Print.

Lahiri, Jhumpa. *Interpreter of Maladies.* New Delhi: Harper Collins, 1999. Print.

______. *Unaccustomed Earth.* New Delhi: Random House, 2008. Print.

Lawrence, D. H. *Lady Chatterley's Lover.* Mumbai: Jaico Publishing House, 2000. 54. First Published by Jaico in 1960. Print.

Morris, Michael Lane. "Transition to Marriage: A Literature Review." *Journal of Family & Consumer Sciences Education* 17.1 (1999): 1-21. Web. 2 July 2008 *<http://www.natefacs.org/JFCSE/v17no1/v17no1Morris.pdf>.*

Naikar, Basavaraj S., ed. *Indian English Literature.* New Delhi: Atlantic Publishers and Distributors Ltd., 2007. Print.

Nityanandam, Indira. "Marriage in *Interpreter of Maladies.*" *Jhumpa Lahiri—The Tale of the Diaspora.* New Delhi: Creative Books, 2005. 66-69. Print.

Prasad, Saloni. "Probing the Inner Self: Jhumpa Lahiri." *Indian English Poetry and Fiction: Critical Elucidations.* Ed. Rajiv K. Mallik & Amar Nath Prasad. New Delhi: Sarup and Sons, 2007. 261. Print.

Sahu, Nandini. "The Nostalgic Note in their Flute: A Reading of Arundhati Roy and Jhumpa Lahiri." *Indian Women's Short Fiction.* Ed. Joel Kuortti & Rajeshwar Mittapalli. New Delhi: Atlantic Publishers, 2007. 168-171. Print.

Sanghvi, Siddharth Dhanvant. "The Betrayal Artist." *The Times of India.* 21 April 2008, Kolkata. Print.

Sharma, Roshan Lal. "Interpreting Maladies in Jhumpa Lahiri's Title Story." *Mapping Migrations.* Ed. Charu Sharma. New Delhi: Book Plus, 2006. 23-24. Print.

Williams, Noella Brada. "Reading Jhumpa Lahiri's *Interpreter of Maladies* as a Short Story Cycle." *MELUS* 29.3/4 (Fall/Winter 2004): 451-464. Print.

18

Language, Literature and Society—The Paradoxical Psyche of an Archetypal Indian Woman: Sita in Anita Desai's *Where Shall We Go This Summer?*

V. Ramesh

The foundation of all literature lies in the intrinsic human passion to communicate the theatre of human experience. It had been this aspiration which gave rise to the oral chronicling convention across the earth. With the growing elegance of the written avenue, the same bent found a more intricate, judicious and absolute representation in formal literature. The ripeness of the Indian English novel provides a fascinating instance of how this urge to get across has taken a genre quietly from the earliest segment of imitation through an intermediary period of absorption to reach a phase of the bona fide self expression.

The study of a novel is the study of the society or the changing tradition of the society. It is the society which rears or feeds the individuality. It is, in fact, an invention of the modern education which is revolutionizing Indian economy. Whenever the writers are faced with a preference, they turn to the bygone customs of their own country. This entrench them in Indian tradition and also account for their verve.

Intolerance is instinctive to human nature and Sita of Anita Desai's *Where Shall We Go This Summer?* is no exception. A hypersensitive and out of ordinary character, she symbolizes a distinct dimension to the image of woman in family and society. To empathize or appreciate her delineation, a study of woman's position in society through historical standpoint is desirable.

Feminism and feminist movements are neither novel nor exceptional. "It (Feminism) emerged to be a worldwide cultural movement to secure a complete equality of women with men in the enjoyment of all human rights – moral, religious, social, political, educational, legal, economic and so on" (Barche 9). And literary texts lend authenticity in creating awareness or making a powerful analysis of the society's working against the interests of women. But the positive exposition of women's plight and struggle can bring about a radical transformation in public attitude towards man-woman relationship and boost their self esteem and lend credence to their just and long-pending demands. The evolution of the 'New Woman', signifying a new realization of her duties and responsibilities in family and society, is mainly aimed at the assertion of her rights as a human being and her determination to attain gender equity with man.

A silent sufferer, a showpiece of Indian culture and a cog in the family wheel and without an identity of her own to accomplish self-gratification and self-fulfilment, the ethnic Indian woman is depicted in a multiplicity of roles—mother, wife, daughter and sister. A monument of endurance and loyalty, she takes pride in service and self-sacrifice and enjoyed an enviable status during Vedic age. Manu lays down the rule: "Where women are honoured, there gods are pleased; but when they are not honoured, no sacred rites yield rewards". *Rig Veda* decorates woman with compliments like *jaya, jani* and *patni.* But slowly, the woman's position lost its significance and charm. The *Maitrayani Samhita* equates women with dice and drinks and daughters became encumbrances. But there were people who stood for the cause of women. Some among them are Swami Vivekananda ("Educate your women first and leave them to themselves") and Annie Besant ("The rising of India as a nation depends on the education of Indian women").

The adoption of the new Indian Constitution brought enfranchisement to all women. The University Grants Commission advocated that "there cannot be educated people without educated women". The slow but steady changes in cultural, social and economic patterns of life have expanded and altered the nature of actuality for women.

The spotlight and stress on women and their struggle for survival in the current conglomeration of standards in society stem from the legality of gender equality, the new found freedom through constitutional rights, the empowerment and discernment attained through education and the strong tide of unity realized through organizations and forums serving their cause. But the modern Indian woman is torn between two extremes of emotions – the traditional submissive role and the modern 'liberated' independent status.

An analysis of the above factors narrows down the deliberation on women's quests as the exploration for identity and defining the self. The voluminous feminist literature has assorted tones and standing—placid, leading and voluble. The confrontational issues are male chauvinism, sexist bias, psychological and physical exploitation, hegemonistic inclinations of not only male but also even some female sections of society and the neglect and disdain for the woman's psychological, cultural, familial and spiritual quests. Some of the remedies suggested for the resolution of these issues are: recording the protest in the mildest form, searching for a compromise through mediation or moderation, love and persuasion or burying oneself in a self-made exclusive environment, mostly escapist in style.

Any dialogue or investigation of feminism is inconclusive without a corresponding scrutiny of the 'paradox' of feminism. The clarion call that the 'new', 'enlightened' and 'modern' woman is intellectually on a par with man and economically independent, discarding all fetters and pulls off appreciable status in society on the levels of security, dignity and freedom is an understatement.

Expectations and specifics of truth diametrically differ. For instance, the gender factor wields a greater pull to the inconvenience of women.

A study conducted in the Indian subcontinent shows the existing predicament of women, being pulled down below the poverty line in stead of achieving economic parity with men, as 'poverty within poverty'. The modern woman is not guaranteed of emancipation from male dominance even if she attains economic independence. Ajita Garg dubs it "enslavement on two fronts – domestic and employment" (25). This justifies the Communist Manifesto that 'the bourgeois sees in his wife a mere instrument of production, echoed glumly in bride burning and dowry deaths'.

Even outside the family, she is reduced to the level of an article of trade, exploiting her flesh obsessively in advertisement and sales promotion and thereby taking away the last shreds of the dignity of her person. Engels declares: "The social status of the lady of civilization, surrounded by sham homage and estranged from all real work, is socially infinitely lower than that of the hard-working woman of barbarism" (495).

Indo Anglian fiction falls easily into two conspicuous segments—the pre-and-post independence group of writers. The pre-independence Indian writing in English mainly stimulated the native literature and also signalled the fusion of the highest ideas of the East and West. Pioneer men novelists of the India in transition like K.S. Venkataramani, Mulk Raj Anand, R.K. Narayanan and K.A. Abbas dealt with questions relating to socioeconomic and political truths in their novels. After independence, women novelists of significance emerged elevating the genre with their centre of attention on the real predicament of women in the male chauvinistic society. Chief among them include Kamala Markandaya, Ruth Prawer Jhabvala, Nayantara Sahgal, Santha Rama Rau and Anita Desai.

Among them, Anita Desai stands apart with her emphasis on the exploration of the troubled sensibility of woman. This is a neo-concept and a typical neo-Indian phenomenon. For instance, in Jhabvala's work, social background has remarkable attention whereas Kamala Markandaya is bifocal in presentation—characters and also themes relating to financial, political, social and cultural. Hariprasanna has this to say about Anita Desai's novels: "Her novel is concerned with the emotional world of women, revealing a rare, imaginative awareness of various deeper forces at work and a profound understanding of feminine sensibility" (81).

The poignant race of women in Anita Desai's novels pictures the uncommunicative miseries and vulnerability of millions of married women, tortured and tormented by existentialist problems and dilemmas. "The journey within" her characters, the psychological discernment, reveal the trauma of existence in a hostile milieu, the conservative, strait-jacket and taboo-ridden society.

The deep-seated ideas of Anita Desai's *Where Shall We Go This Summer?*, as also in most other novels of her, are the irreconcilable inner and outer worlds, the imponderable gulf between expectation and reality, leading to the anguish of the sensitive soul. Sita's articulated problems represent those of the inarticulate middle class people— universal and eternal. Some of the paradoxical philosophical mysteries encapsulated in the novel are: the meaning or value versus vulgarity or monotony of life and prospects or unfeasibility of escape from the bondage of procreation for a woman. Anita Desai endeavours to offer her own solutions to these apparently unanswerable questions in a persuasive way.

Sita is a middle class married woman in her forties. She is the mother of four children and pregnant for the fifth time. She lives in a Bombay flat and her husband Raman is an upper middle class factory owner. By all standards, she has a comfortable and even unperturbed lifestyle, dotingly yearned by women of her age and status. But her calibre is different. Her totally alienated and incongruous inner self, incompatible with the world outside, desires that the child should be 'kept' in her womb for ever and she could never even imagine of aborting it, as Raman misjudges her thoughts. This results in her hysterical outburst: "Mad", she gasped, "you're quite mad. Kill the baby? It's all I want ..... I mean I want to keep it. I don't want it to be born" (35).

This idea is really a phantasmagoria and clearly inconceivable in reality. Women have been traditionally brought up to esteem motherhood as the highest fulfilment of womanhood. Sita distrusts this notion. She frankly tells Raman "children only mean anxiety, concern, pessimism, not happiness" (20). Sita is stubborn. In the world in which her husband and children live, the one in which cruelty and inhuman tendencies form the core, creation is totally an aberration. Shanta Rangaswamy succinctly states: "She wonders whether she has gone insane or the world around her" (240).

Raman and Sita live on different planes. Raman could never fathom her mind's depth and its unusual and unilateral projections. They are temperamentally incompatible since Raman is pragmatic and outspoken while Sita is an introvert with a sensitive soul and heightened imagination. For instance, Raman sees no meaning in Sita trying desperately to save a wounded eagle from the crows: "They have made a good job of your eagle ...... look at the feathers sticking out of that crow's beak." " 'Perhaps it flew away', she cried, knowing it had not" (41). When Sita is psychologically affected by her life in Bombay, Raman could not decode her sensitive reactions to the happenings around: "But you're not leaving for such small incidents, Sita? They occur in everyone's life, all the time. If you're an adult, you know how to cope with them – they are only small incidents" (37).

It is only Raman who rushes to the rescue of Sita, takes her away from the island, educates her and naturally marries her. But

Sita's inner conflict, the boiling cauldron of emotions, misconstrues this as a resultant act of pity and lust. She strongly feels that she is forcibly evacuated from the theatrical era of her life (may be a ruined one) and violently led into the 'ordinary', 'empty', 'meaningless' and mundane married life, offering her no contentment.

But, sometimes, she becomes compassionate and genuinely anxious about her husband's troubles: "His boys at home must have worried him, while he was at work in the factory which was not without its problems either" (138). But she is inept, perhaps, disinclined to express her concerns and warmth: "It simply did not exist for her and should not make it exist. So she did not speak any words of love or reassurance to him. She looked away . . . " (41).

The discord and cavity between the mother and children are also paradoxical and full of dissonance: "All that mattered to her, they discarded" (137). Sita is attracted towards art but Menaka chooses science, especially medicine. "There are no dead-ends, now, in art. There is something, Menaka, and alive and creative". Menaka is for a life of "order, logic and sense" and averse to her mother's "disorder and nonsense" (116). The chasm is apparent: "Menaka lost interest – she had heard that argument too often. Arguments with her mother always ended in this kind of haze of obscurity and nonsense that her trim and practical self loathed instinctively" (69).

Distressing impact of her son's cry on her heart is rendered in the following words: "Each time it tore a fresh gash in her. It made her wild, it made her run" (141). The laceration of the mother's psyche is very true. Her father is both grand and mysterious. "He had been ugly, grotesquely so as to arouse first notice, then pity and finally regard – a hypnotized kind of notice and regard" (66). He was a practical activist and self-educated in jails. "He looked very much like a saint, a mini Gandhi" (67). Thus Sita's father was more a man of the community than an affectionate father to his children. He was busy with his public activities as a social reformer. His children grew up with the crowd of people around him for ever. In fact, Sita is puzzled by her father's magic, miracles, cures and clinic. She admires, respects and adores him but cannot treat him as her father. She could not understand the mystery at all.

But Anita Desai is subtle in her suggestion that Sita's father's life was the illustration of the magnifying quality of faith which made life ultimately meaningless. Sita had to face her dying father alone, because Jeevan had left the island a few days earlier and Rekha, within minutes of his death: "It was Sita, alone, who bewildered and confused, was left on the island for someone to arrange the funeral"(61).

Rekha, Sita's elder sister, is spiritually and devotedly closest to her father and helps him fulfil his devotional desire through hymns passionately sung in the large gatherings as she has the voice of a 'goddess'. But Sita is a small fly because she is not endowed in any exceptional way. Rekha leaves the dying father in search of greener pastures and Sita is left alone to seek her own way of life. Even the description of her physical appearance such as dragging jaw, round shoulders and drooping eyelids liken her with down-to-earth personality, closest to the unexceptional and run of the mill person that everyone comes across in life. But Sita is a stubborn romantic dreamer trying to escape procreation, a very normal human phenomenon.

Sita's perplexing behaviour has another groundwork – her mother deserting them. Sita foolishly imagines that she is without a mother. She is greatly frustrated and becomes disjointed when she learns through her brother Jeevan that their mother has forsaken them and run off to Benares and is leading there a widow's life. She makes resolute attempts to trace her whereabouts but is unsuccessful as she neither knows her name nor remembers her face nor even in possession of a photograph to assist her in her search. This deprivation of motherly care and affection leaves a deep blemish and profound negative impact throughout: "Why had she left her husband whom they called the second Gandhi?"(6).

The intention of her visit to the village, Manori, is built on her repulsion with her immediate environment, her family and the deep abrasions made by the life in the city of Bombay. Her views of the merchant class flow like this: "They are nothing—nothing but appetite and sex. Only food, sex and money matter. Animals . . ." and again,

It's all a madness—the boys acting out that scene from the film they saw, fighting each other on the floor; Menaka and her magazines and the way she's torn all those drawings of hers I'd kept so carefully; the ayah taking Karan to that—that roadside dump where all the ayahs sit and gossip and fight; the way you (Raman) laughed because I tried to keep the bird alive; the people here all around us, living here, all round (36). The merchant ladies are reminiscent of "elephants, she thought, eating grass, shifting from foot to foot, swaying their trunks, small-eyed, eating" (49). Incidents such as Menaka's destruction of new buds in a potted plant nauseate her.

R.S. Sharma brands Sita as an escapist: "Sita seeks to escape essentially from the cannibalism that is operative, unseen and unobserved, in contemporary city life" (95). Her flight from the mundane reality of her existence is to discover succour and serenity in her childhood home - a place of escape, a sort of dreamland, a place of freedom and relief to the psyche of Sita buffeted by the complications of modern life—in the island of Manori. But that is not to be so. The atmosphere there of miracle, magic and spell has evaporated and Sita becomes cynical to the core.

Even the sea as a symbol of life represents adversity and the island is an escape from it. The unendurable and horrendous life is reflected in the feelings towards sea: "There's just the sea—it drowns us or strands us on the sandbar - and there's the island.

That's all" (149). The rustling of the leaves of the palm trees, "the sound of battle and the sound of distress" (141), exemplify Sita's own offended and agonizing self, inconsistent between illusion and reality.

The very house, which has been once the seat of miracles, human service, cure of diseases, source of all relief to the despondent, the very temple of God, in the island of paradise, is now 'a waste of ashes', 'the cold remains of the bonfire' her father had blazed', and 'ashes white and waste'. The house is full of 'spider webs' and 'skeletal palm leaves', with the 'odour of bats and mildew' (28) like undersea cave and discarded shell.

An analysis of Anita Desai's women characters, especially the protagonists, show their vigorous and fervent endeavours at setting sights on spiritual accomplishment which are made obvious through various metaphors—in the case of Sita, it is the metaphor of violence. The episodes or activities or essentials remain as backgrounds but the reactions of these protagonists—moral, spiritual and emotional—find more emphasis. They meddle with the idea as to whether it is possible to reconstruct the social order based on the psyche of women. Sharad Srivatsava is succinct in the assessment that ". . . in this regard, her novels are, in themselves, a metaphor of deconstruction, for in deconstruction, reconstruction is inherent" (21).

Sita and Maya in *Cry, The Peacock* rummage around for a life of gratification which they are unable to accomplish in the marital context. For them, this realization implies approval of their tender, delicate feelings and emotions and a throbbing life of consciousness and as such what they demand is an insightful approach in others towards them. Sita's retraction is exploratory of her great need for love, the kind of free and absolute love that would encase her.

To Sita, her identifiable ephemeral vision of perfect harmony between a man and woman is uncovered in her recounting to Raman a scene that she has observed of a young woman dying of tuberculosis and being earnestly attended to by a person who loves her. This kind of love transcends the self and makes no claims. It is a love in the face of death, the ultimate human certainty. This kind of communiqué is totally missing between Raman and Sita which stimulates her to retort thus: "What a farce marriage was, all human relationships" (105).

Her ineffective struggles to straighten out the two levels of her survival induce her to have the unrealistic longing of 'keeping' the baby in her womb for ever. At one level, she is a wife and mother. But she is also a person and woman. She discovers that in the structure of citation established by the society, she cannot be a wife and mother without conceding her existence as a person and as a woman.

Sita's return to Bombay after the 'escape' to Manori is not to be miscomprehended as symptomatic of her collapse and dismal surrender. She, in fact, returns with a new perspicacity, a new insight. The visual symbol is highly appealing: "The wind jumped up and buffeted her so that she could not stand still and she began to trail after him, knowing she would follow him, trail of foot prints he had laid out for her" (150).

Sita has become mellow, enduring and animated to cope with the trials and tribulations in life with all its ups and downs. Her tussle is investigative of the "intelligent and sensitive woman's revolt against the male smugness and philistinism trampling all finer values in marital life" (66).

Scrutinized from a feminist thrust of stance, Sita conquers 'personhood' but does not renounce family or society. She has traversed the "female phase" in life which is a phase of self-discovery, a turning inward freed from the dependency of opposition, a search for identity. She has now come to new terms with the family—"new terms with love and with work" (13).

There is categorically no swap or amendment in her assessment of her husband and society. Her return can never be connected with that of prodigal son's return - a return with the ardent entreaty to be 'accepted'. Sita never conjures up the vision that such an acceptance is meaningful to a woman. Sita's lesson from her experience tells every woman that, in spite of the posture of the society, the new woman must not flee from it.

Anuradha Roy declares, "Novels, however great they are, cannot change or destroy repressive social structures: but by posing questions, by suggesting re-assessment and re-definition, they can help in formulating a consciousness which can, perhaps, ultimately, bring about a constructive change (145).

Thus Anita Desai undeniably divulges a commendable grasp of the quandary and dilemmas of woman and portrays her own vision of a variegated facet of woman in modern India and her fully stimulated feminine sensibility.

To conclude, Srinivasa Iyengar's prophetic words about Anita Desai's facility and its impact on readers is conspicuous through its manifestation in her works: "Anita Desai's is an original talent that has the courage to go its own way" (465).

Works Cited

Asnani, Shyam. "New Morality in the Modern Indo-English Novel." *Indian Women Novelists*. Ed. R. K. Dhawan New Delhi: Sterling, 1990. Print.

Barche, G.D. "Facets of Feminism in Indian English Fiction." *Indian Women Novelists* Set 3: Vol .1 Ed. R.K. Dhawan. New Delhi: Prestige Books, 1995. Print.

Desai, Anita. *Where Shall We Go This Summer?* Delhi: Orient Paperbacks, 1982. Print.

Engels, Marx et al. "The Origin of Family, Private Property and State." *Selected Works*. Moscow: Progress Publishers, 1982. Print.

Friedman, Betty. *The Second Stage*. New York: Summit Books, 1981. Print.

Garg, Ajita. "Women Doubly Enslaved." *Social Welfare (M)*. Aug 1988. Print.

Hariprasanna, A. "An Expression of Feminine Sensibility: Anita Desai's *Bye Bye Blackbird*." *The Indian Journal of English Studies*. Vol.33:1994-95. Print.

Iyengar, K. R. Srinivasa. *Indian Writing in English*. New Delhi: Sterling Publishers, 1972. Print.

Krishnaswamy, Shanta. "Anita Desai: The Sexist Nature of Sanity." *The Women in Indian Fiction in English*. New Delhi: Ashish Publishing House, 1984. Print.

Roy, Anuradha. *Patterns of Feminist Consciousness in Indian Women Writers*. New Delhi: Prestige Books, 1991. Print.

Sharma, R. S. *Anita Desai*. Liverpool: Lucas Publishers, 1988. Print.

Srivastava, Sharad. *The New Woman in Indian English Fiction: A Study of Kamala Markandaya, Anita Desai, Namita Gokhale and Shoba De*. New Delhi: Creative Books, 1996. Print.

19

Kamala Markandaya's Indian Women—The Principles and the Principals: A Feministic Elucidation

V. Ramesh

Even a perfunctory version of the significant creative production of the postcolonial novels in English brings out the evolutionary formula clearly discernable in the Indian society and its women conclusively epitomize in the classic shift of the women characters from "feminine" to "female." This is an overtone of the theory expounded by Elaine Showalter regarding assorted phases of the twentieth century women liberation movement (13). The first segment involves imitation of the current crushing tradition and internalizing its ideas and concepts. In the next stage, women begin protesting these crunching shackles and begin advocating for their autonomy. In the last and concluding phase, a turning-inward phase, the phase of self-discovery, women search their own minds seeking identity of their own.

K.R. Srinivasa Iyengar's axiomatic expression is quite curt and justifiably authenticated: "Women are natural story tellers even when they don't write or publish" (435). The first cohort of Indian women writers in English dwelt on specialties, with explosive indulgences, such as the co-existence of post colonial reminiscence, the neocolonial perception and also the post modernist revivalism. The succeeding age band of women novelists has adjusted their voices to the altered psychological pragmatism of Indian life after independence. Hence the examination of the post modern Indian women novelists impinge on the feminine insight of the women characters, their progression towards a stirred consciousness that leads to fortification of their inner self in a male dominated society. This self introspection leading to self-judgment leads to their conception of the implicit inner potency. This vigor protracts them throughout when they adorn different dimensional roles in society—mother, sister, wife, daughter, etc. They are rendered as cultural backbones of the family. Such an attitude and analysis leads these writers to conceive protagonists who belong to one of the following clusters: women of the first brand are hyper sensitive individuals inept to cope with the environment around them and the tussle and the mismatch drag them to the inevitable catastrophe—entry into the blind and the no-return path of neurosis. Women of the second set are mute victims and their throbbing transforms them into idealists. Women belonging to the third breed are adept in identifying and admitting the new and important knowledge about themselves as a consequence of their suffering and this awareness or realization make them 'sober' in outlook and thus they reach a kind of 'fulfilment' in their relationship with the planet. These women could fine-tune well within and outside their bounds by developing value systems of their own and moreover, their inner resources empower them to defy the irrational social system.

Kamala Markandaya's novels are in search of affirmative resolution for unenthusiastic state of affairs. It is true that she pictures the negative or gloomy facets in Indian women's lives, but there are positive signals that togetherness and mutual understanding could work wonders in making a meaningful existence.

Rukmani's character in *Nectar in a Sieve* is intended in such a way that there is a gradual emergence from the plane of innocence to experience and in other words, from mutiny to concurrence. When Rukmani reaches her husband's place, she can see only a mud hut: "Rukmani wanted to cry. Merely a mud hut and nothing else . . . and she sank down" (Markandaya, *Nectar in a Sieve* 50). But better sense prevails upon her when she learns that the hut was built by Nathan himself with his own hands and began to admire him. She had the maturity to say, "A woman, they say, always remembers her wedding night . . . but for me there are other night . . . when I went to my husband matured in mind as well in body" (Markandaya, *Nectar in a Sieve* 66) she was also a prudent and sensible housewife. Her friends Kali and Janaki have taught her and made her well versed in all chores relating to a peasant's wife. Nathan is surprised enough to admire the vision of Rukmani when she produces so much store of money, rice and dhal for Ira's marriage. A true helpmate, she assists her husband on the field. Rukmani's audacity, fortitude, ingenuity and the serene tolerance of her lot are well exploited.

Regarding the scarcity of food, she says: "Want is our companion from birth to death, varying only in degree. What profit to bewail that which has always been and cannot change?" (Markandaya, *Nectar in a Sieve* 113). Even at the greatest moment of physical and emotional crisis, Rukmani has the determination to console her husband: "Have we not been happy to-gether? Always, dear, always" (Markandaya, *Nectar in a Sieve* 110).

Time is a great healer and with the passing of time, Rukmani could review her life, "...with calm of mind with all passion spent" (Markandaya, *Nectar in a Sieve* 135).

R.A. Singh writes, "Rukmani's spiritual stamina, heroic impulse, love-like simplicity, love for her children, tolerance and respect for traditional values make her an outstanding character" (6). She is an archetypal figure figurative of the anguished soul of India through the ages. She is the accomplishment of India's consecrated convention and as A.V. Krishna Rao puts it, "the real truth of the novel is the spiritual stamina of Rukmani" (6). Thus Rukmani is an admirable picture of stoicism and resilience. Ira, the daughter of Rukmani, has also the reverberation of grit: "... to-night and to-morrow and every night; so long as there is need. I will not hunger any more" (Markandaya, *Nectar in a Sieve* 137). Rukmani corroborates her: "She was no longer a child, to be cowed or forced into submission, but a grown woman with a definite purpose and an invincible determination" (Markandaya, *Nectar in a Sieve* 138).

Mira, the upper middle class woman, is torn between passion and India's independence in *Some Inner Fury*. Though relatively free, when she grows rapidly, several boundaries are forced on her—not allowed to travel alone, cannot swim with Kit and Richard and cannot stay with Roshan alone. But she smashes them down and engrosses herself in many social dealings. But the unregulated independence could give her only a sense of restiveness. The aspiration for perspicuity makes her cross the bounds of the family and she now grasps the perils of rampant freedom: "It was out; the uncertainty, one's helplessness, the fear, the despair, never allowed into the consciousness but always existing there" (Markandaya, *Some Inner Fury* 165).

The deep-rooted forces of convention check her from trespassing. Markandaya's memorandum is clear—no roots, no survival. Thus the impermanence of negative freedom drags her back to the roots, a show of matured thinking: "To keep our peace we would have to go back then to the world from which we came, to which we could always return because it is a part of us even as the earth was of those others who stayed" (Markandaya, *Some Inner Fury* 192). Roshan is all in one—forthright, erudite, endowed and progressive. Her conception of freedom is universal—national and global—and thus a role model for other women. Mira is so much refreshing to Roshan, "She gave me a chance to go and I took it ... I uncovered at last the gateway to the freedom of the mind, and gazed entranced upon the vista of endless extensions of which the spirit is capable" (Markandaya, *Some Inner Fury* 49). Premala champions the traditional Indian woman who fails to transmute her entreaty for brazenness into her daily life. A culturally nonconformist woman, she is an indecisive character.

In the words Shanta Krishnaswamy:

> In Premala, the author shows the insecurity, isolation, bewilderment and vulnerability that the traditionally brought up Indian woman feels, when she has to adjust to western norms of living, when she has to accommodate to tastes and values of a culture in flux...she tries to be an ideal wife and companion to her husband. She ends up being a non-person and her death puts a stop to her desperate adjustments, to her soul shrinking compromises. (88)

Thus Premala is a woman of customary Indian model, Mira, a modern woman with an insightful penchant for Indian culture and Roshan is a pictogram of enlightened progressive womanhood. The continual motif is conformity of tradition and a judicious espousal of progressive modernity.

Sarojini of *A Silence of Desire* is a mainstream middle class orthodox Hindu housewife, having her own conventions of livelihood. The novel itself is about the longstanding dichotomy of head and heart, emotion and reason. Dandekar tries to wean Sarojini away from superstitions and sacraments, whereas she wants him to disregard western notions and see 'what lies beyond reason'. She is: ". . . good with her children, an excellent cook, an efficient manager of the household, a woman who still gave him pleasure after fifteen years of marriage...she did most things placidly...and from this calm proceeded the routine and regularity that met the neat and orderly needs or his nature" (Markandaya, *A Silence of Desire* 6). Her rendezvous with the Swamy seeking a cure for her illness is within the sanctions of the tradition and society in which she exists. Sarojini proclaims, "Without faith, I shall not be healed" (Markandaya, *A Silence of Desire* 82). Dandekar, her husband, becomes suspicious as regards her visits to Swamy, but at long last, while recuperating from his illness, realizes that he wants her because of a "spiritual ingrowing which made it impossible for him to be whole so long as any part of her was missing" (Markandaya, *A Silence of Desire* 115).

Sarojini, on her part, is happy to bring back together herself with the 'hard reality' of the family after she has recorded her voice of dissent against the repression unleashed by the institution of family. She becomes cognizant that within the ambit of society and tradition, she could voice her protests without shirking her duties and responsibilities. She is an emissary of the 'new and revolutionary' Indian women in the making.

In *Possession*, two women, Lady Caroline Bell and Anasuya, warrant our interest. Anasuya, the traditional Indian woman is uncommunicative, civilized, gifted, beneficial and spiritually informed and in the words of Shanta Krishnaswamy, "Anasuya is capable of a decent respectable existence as a woman of means ...in the ilk as Mira and Roshan, who prove that a decent existence is possible without a man...they have evolved a long way from the likes of Nalini and Rukmani" (103). Caroline, the English lady, is chilly, fanatical, egotistical and mercenary. Uma Parameswaran writes: "Lady Caroline Bell is an autocrat, typical of the British Raj in India" (115). These two embody clatter of not only persona but also customs.

Nalini of *A Handful of Rice* is a vulnerable prey and the grounds are multifold in nature – economic scarcity, traditional mooring and the compulsory choice between morality and success ethics. But she plays the sheet anchor role in the novel. She gives a personality to Ravi, the renegade vagrant, by marrying him. She buttresses and nourishes him in times of adversity as well as prosperity and also counsels rightly when Ravi is not in a position to make his choice between fidelity and ferocity i.e. veracity and success ethics. But being a woman of tradition and bound by the laws of custom and manners, she cannot break free and thus, has to bear the tortures and torments silently, "Nalini never complained...but he had never heard her complain. Neither of the ills of her pregnancy, nor of him." She would say, "We'll manage" (Markandaya, *A Handful of Rice* 165). For the sake of family and also its members, she favours forbearance and endurance.

K.S. Narayana Rao says, "Markandaya's novels ....reveal a spectrum of moral attitudes on the part of the characters...which include the traditionally moral, immoral and the amoral attitudes...And her women characters...are, in fact, better drawn than their male counterparts...it is usually the men who get away with their delinquent sexual conduct" (69-70). Hence Nalini's visible debility is actually her asset because she deems family bonds and personal relationships, more than anything else, to be absolute importance. This is also Kamala Markandaya's inflexible conviction.

Vasantha of *The Nowhere Man* is steadfastly fastened in Indian tradition. A staunch believer and disciple of Gandhi, she could pilot a modest life eschewing opulence even in an alien land, England. Her strong religious belief makes her cruise through successfully the turbulences that include racial prejudices in England, sociological changes and rough feelings emanating from generation gap and thus develop a strong faith in mankind. Though a little traumatized because her son, Laxman, marries an English girl, she stoically bears all physical and emotional smarting. About Vasantha, Markandaya verbalizes: "Vasantha was a Hindu, born and bred in a subtle religion, whose concepts, being on the cosmic scale, made no concessions to puny mankind; a religion that postulated one God, infinite, resplendent, with a thousand different aspects but one: God the Creator, preserver, destroyer union with whom was the supreme purpose and bliss" (Markandaya, *The Nowhere Man* 17). Her concept of happy life could generate in her contentment even in the last instant: "It has been a happy marriage" (Markandaya, *The Nowhere Man* 35). That's why, Srinivas, becomes stranded and 'nothingness' creeps into him after Vasantha's death to transmute him crestfallen.

Amma, Aunt Alamelu and Saroja of *Two Virgins* hang about on one side demonstrating the dictum that while acknowledging the shifting social codes due to the contract of western ideals of life, it is only decent to linger ingrained in compliance to tradition. The moral codes and the individual conduct should never be sacrificed in the misconceived notion of modernization. But Lalitha is an atypical, inclined towards a western way of life. Her mind set that the traditional society is asphyxiating and her false ideas about modernity, coupled with obstinacy and fickle minded nature burst her bubble of misconstrued pride in her beauty, feminine desirability and sexual power. In fact, Saroja matures steadily from the bad practices and experiences of Lalitha and could only conclude that only the woman suffers more and has a greater share in bearing the burden of social evils but men remain as ever scot free, completely unconcerned and unaffected.

Markandaya records: "There is no escape for them (women); they had to stand where they were and take it" (Markandaya, *Two Virgins* 123). But Aunt Alamelu and Amma regard custom and social system above anything else. Margaret P. Joseph writes: "Aunt Alamelu is the rock of tradition, the norm of moral behaviour" (147). They are opposed to anything called liberal as typified by their strong censure of Lalitha's western education at Miss Mendoza's school.

Kamala Markandaya's communication is patent – in the search for liberation, women should never be advocated to adopt unlimited and unfettered conduct by throwing to winds the social structure and principles of practice of tradition or convention. They need to be sensible and measure up to the ideals of the tradition bound society.

Queen Manjula and Shanta Devi of *The Golden Honeycomb* are moulded in the same principles but with a few minor diversities. Queen Manjula is gallant, advanced and mercilessly revolutionary in outlook. She is compassionate to her natives unlike the king, her husband. When he becomes incapacitated, she poisons him and against tradition, watches the funeral pyre. She advises her son, the young prince, to have relationship with a common girl, Mohini, to produce a male heir to the throne. But Shanta Devi, her daughter-in-law is unforthcoming and timid and cannot fight against Manjula, when Mohini is thrust into her life. But, Mohini, even though a commoner, is not taken in by the riches of the royal style and does not surrender her autonomous existence by refusing to marry the prince: "I don't want to be your queen: I want to be free" (Markandaya, *The Golden Honeycomb* 32), She is thus a foil to Shanta Devi who has no freedom at all. By making use of history, Kamala Markandaya juxtaposes freedom and responsibility and also the slavish submission even in the higher echelons of society.

Kamala Markandaya, perhaps, wishes to suggest in *Pleasure City* that by being strong, the problems of life could be faced challengingly and also overcome by women. Timidity and passivity, the negative traits of most women, need to be replaced with fuel and nurturance in all women. These women are capable of even creating vacuum in their men; Cyrus Contractor missing Zavera and others like Sitaraman, Hablekar and Tully comforting themselves by staring the photographs of their women.

Feminism is yet to attain the eminence of a resilient faction in India despite the increase in the number of urban working women. If feminism has the aim of achieving responsible status in society, in a limited measure, it is a success. But as a fight to achieve equality with men, it is too far away from success, at least in this sub continent.

Kamala Markandaya exposés the tribulations, eccentricities and attitudes that victimize Indian womanhood. But the defeat is not total in their struggle for existence or against the inequalities in the social order. The empathy and surrender are their vital components of strength. The two extremes, abject surrender on the one hand and the absolute apathy to death or separation may seem paradoxical. Yet these qualities underscore their inner stamina. Markandaya proclaims that the Indian woman is the pillar with endurance and stoic sense, showcasing a better future through preserving the tradition and guarding the culture. But mere conformity to traditions or a passionate following of modernity are incoherent or treacherous. Kunthi and Lalitha become victims by crossing the bounds of freedom but Mira, at the right moment, checks herself without straying too far. Kamala Markandaya suggests that freedom is to be necessarily tempered with responsibility to achieve advancement and evolution. Her women are branded, though not for making a comprehensive depiction but for offering an in-depth study of the human psyche enmeshed in the values of different hues – social, traditional and spiritual. A.V. Krishna Rao is candid, "Markandaya's contribution to the Indo Anglian fiction lies essentially in her capacity to explore…vital formative areas of individual consciousness that project the images of cultural change and in her uncanny gift of inhabiting the shifting landscapes of an outer reality with human beings whose sensibility becomes a sensitive measure of the inner reality as it responds to the stimulus of change" (67).

Works Cited

Beauvoir, Simone De. *The Second Sex*. Harmondsworth: Penguin, 1952.

Dasan, A.S. "The Indic Tradition of the Novel as a Social Act." *The Rains and The Roots: The Indian English Novel Then and Now*. Mysore: Sahrdayata, 2006.

Iyengar, K.R. Srinivasa. *Indian Writing in English*. New Delhi: Sterling, 1990.

Joseph, Margaret P. *Kamala Markandaya*. New Delhi: Arnold Heinamann, 1980.

Krishnaswamy, Shanta. *The Woman in Indian Fiction in English*. New Delhi: Ashish Publishing House, 1984.

Lerner, Gerda. "The Challenge of Women's History." *The Majority Finds Its Past: Placing Women in History*. New York: Oxford University Press, 1979.

Mackimon, Catherine and. "Feminism, Marxism, Method and the State: An Agenda for Theory," *Signs* 7:3.

Markandaya, Kamala. *The Golden Honeycomb*. New Delhi: B.I. Publications, 1977.

_______. *A Handful of Rice*. New Delhi: Orient Paperbacks, 1967.

_______. *Nectar in a Sieve*. Bombay: Jaico, 1965.

_______. *The Nowhere Man*. New Delhi: Orient Paperbacks, 1975.

_______. *A Silence of Desire*. New Delhi: Hind Pocket Books, 1965.

_______. *Some Inner Fury*. Bombay: Jaico, 1971.

_______. *Two Virgins*. New Delhi: Vikas Publishing House, 1975.

Myles, Anita. "Introduction" *Feminism and the Post Modern Indian Women Novelists in English*. New Delhi: Swarup and Sons, 2006.

Parameswaran, Uma. *Kamala Markandaya*. Jaipur: Rawat Publications, 2000.

Rao, A.V. Krishna. "Continuity and Change in the Novels of Kamala Markandaya." *Perspectives on Kamala Markandaya*. Ed. Madhusudhan Prasad. Ghaziabad: Vimal Prakashan, 1984.

_______. *The Indo-Anglian Novel and The Changing Tradition*. Mysore: Rao and Raghavan, 1972.

Rao, K. S. Narayana. "Kamala Markandaya." *Osmania Journal of English Studies* 10:1 (1973).

Showalter, Elaine. *A Literature of their Own: British Women Novelists from Bronte to Lessing*. New Jersey: Princeton University Press, 1977.

Singh, I.A. *Indian Women: The Power Trapped*. New Delhi: Galaxy, 1991.

Singh, R.A. *Women's Writing in India: New Perspectives*. Ed. K.V. Surendran. Delhi: Sarup and Sons, 2002.

20

The Dravidian Aesthetics in Anita Desai: A Feminist Perspective

V. Ramesh

Literature is the finest and the most resourceful approach of manifestation, illuminating or sustaining or resuscitating the various social movements. Srinivasa Iyengar quotes Gandhiji as regards the use of English by the Indian writers to convey their message to the readers: "The purpose of writing is to communicate, isn't it? If so, say your say in any language that comes to hand" (Iyengar iv). But the Indian literature comprises many literatures—Tamil, Telugu, Kannada, Malayalam, Hindi, and Bengali and so on. But ideologically, it is Indian in thought and feeling and emotion and experience.

The portrayal of society in Indian literature is anything but candid and forthright. Indian novel, in particular, is an end product of the Indian renaissance; it came into vogue as an upshot of the bearing of the west on Indian life and literature. It records the constant commotion and the ensuing fruition and reconstruction in society. The transition may take different forms – status of life, ethnicity, bearings and ethics of men as well as the behaviourial paradigm. "Basically social change implies first, internal differentiation or multiplication of forms of roles and relationships within a social structure and secondly, replacement of older structures by new structures" (Bisaria 28). "The Indian English novel to-day has bloomed and blossomed into variegated tapestries, tastes and sensibilities offering a variety fair to the reader in India and abroad" (Dasan 10).

The mien of the contemporary Indian novelists also expounds an unambiguous and conspicuous divergence from the post modernist 'nihilism' thanks to the Indian roots, Indian aesthetics, creative imagination and compassionate posture. "Indic art imitates life as all arts do. Imitation is a two-dimensional process—gathering of knowledge of life that is fragmentary and distilling and discerning the knowledge that is poignant with eternal verities . . . Indian literary aesthetics has a tradition of celebrating compassionate humanism without any precondition and superimposing agenda" (Dasan 15).

Thus the novel as a social act presages that there are positive alternatives to the smothering negatives in life. The same is the watchword of the Dravidian culture that attempts radical adaptations at the familial and societal strata to increment and supplement the excellence and elegance of living towards the emancipation of women.

The state of women in Indian society is subjected to considerable change. Earlier women were stripped of social status and veracity. Now their clout in social and cultural set up is seen in these arrays, "the constitutional right to equality of opportunity and status before law, right against discrimination, right to property, reservation of seats in legislative bodies at different levels, right of choice in marriage and numerous other rights and privileges" (Sorot 77). Vimala Patil has this to affirm on this premise: "Women in India have changed at a faster rate than women anywhere else in the world and their 'attitude' has changed the very face of our society" (Patil iii).

But in spite of all these vociferous avocations broadcasted through various literary genres, the post colonial Indian society depicts a dissimilar impression. In fact, the Indian women writers in English were branded 'sub-altern' by the male dominated Indian literature, thus prevailing upon their sustaining and indisputable roles. But shunning the protests and braving the challenges, this select band of writers unveil the status and context of modern women in all their facets—the fall, the rise, the fall-rise and the rise-fall. In the guise of tradition, man humiliates woman, keeping her under permanent crunching shackles, physically and mentally.

Anita Desai's strong suit is chiefly human relationship—reminiscent of the Dravidian thoughts. "Her women characters herald a new morality which is not confined to physical chastity. It demands accommodation of individual longing for self-fulfilment" (*Kakatiya Journal* 2). Desai's role in sensitizing readers about the Indian views of feminine sense and sensibility against cultural imperialism and tradition-bound outlook, sacraments and institutions that means subjugation of women has been breathtaking indeed. Her fiction stands as a collective metaphor for her ways of celebrating womanhood in the midst of conflicting ideologies, human bondages and phallo-centric notions of womanhood.

Most of her fictional female characters are existential characters jittery in asserting against suppression and voicelessness. Her aesthetic rootedness in Indian culture in no way contradicts her value stances against the ill-treatment of women.

". . . *Fasting, Feasting* is a most beautiful novel, very moving, very funny, terribly illustrative of what happens to women in different parts of the world" (Kaufmann ii). In general many modern critics are susceptible to flout stylistic and structural excellences of innovative works, riveted more on thematic explications. But this novel is all in one—gripping, sparkling and neurotic—a scrutiny of the conundrum of feminine existentialism not only in the post independent India but in the more progressive socio cultural landscape also.

Fasting, Feasting has two clear cut apportionments—the comparative investigation between Indian family machinations, socio-cultural and spiritual, and the familial existentialism in

America. The former is tradition-bound and the latter is altruistic and acquisitive, the unifying facet being the female characters.

The Indian state of affairs is populated by Uma, Aruna, Arun, Anamika and Mira Masi. The seemingly close-knit structure of the family is pictured in Anita Desai's words: "It was hard to believe they had ever had separate existences, that they had been separate entities and not MamaPapa in one breath" (Desai, *Fasting, Feasting* 9). But, but for Uma, others effortlessly and clandestinely indulge in surreptitious activities. Docility is Uma. A succession of happenings sounds the death-knell leading to Uma's regression. The birth of Arun, the long-awaited heir of the family, strikes down her academic career. Uma needs to be educated in domestic chores of house work or baby sitting. Her show of reluctance is doused with bullying galore: "Uma tried to protest when the order began to come thick and fast. This made Mama look stern again. 'You know we can't leave the baby to the servant" (Desai, *Fasting, Feasting* 97).

As soon as she attains puberty, Uma's parents make vigorous and frenzied efforts, as if panic-stricken, to 'celebrate' her marriage. The first proposer is enamoured of her coquettish younger sister, Aruna, just 13 years old. The second proposal also does not mature into a success, failing at the betrothal stage and not before the swindling of a sizable sum as dowry. Such catastrophes leading to melancholy is made more poignant with the remarks of Aruna: ". . . a certain mockery was creeping into her behaviour, a kind of goading, like that a sprightly little dog will subject a large dull ox to when it wants a little action" (Desai, *Fasting, Feasting* 97).

Anita Desai's seeming scepticism and irresolution of the familial environment are reiterated in the following articulation: "The tightly knit fabric of family that had seemed so stifling and confining now revealed holes and gaps that were frightening – perhaps the fabric would not hold, perhaps it would not protect after all" (Desai, *Fasting, Feasting* 142). Mira Masi, the good old widow and aunt of Uma, perhaps, is the only reserve of reassurance and succor after the mortifying calamities of the arranged marriages of the 'ill-fated' Uma. Mira Masi pacifies: "She is blessed by the Lord. The Lord has rejected the men you chose for her because He has chosen her for Himself" (Desai, *Fasting, Feasting* 61).

Anita Desai frames Uma's state of mind: "that of an outcaste from the world of marriage ....retreating to her room, she sank down on the floor, against the wall and put her arms around her knees and wondered what it would have been like to have the Lord Shiva for a husband, have Him put His arms around her" (Desai, *Fasting, Feasting* 101). The desolate and estranged Uma was permitted to visit neither her neighbours nor the convent nearby as her parents had the inherent mistrust that she would embrace Christianity. Her contemplation of getaway from this murky survival in the shape of a career, endorsed in the words of Dr.Dutt, "... a young woman with no employment, who has been running the house for her parents for long. I feel sure you would be right for the job," (Desai, *Fasting, Feasting* 101) is frowned upon by Papa. Her dream remains unconsummated and she is holed up in her mind-numbing subsistence.

Anita Desai has a representative style of making her internally chaotic central characters find communication by affiliation with exterior ambiance: "At night, she lay quietly on her mat, listening to the ashram dogs bark...then other dogs....barked back—gradually the barks drowned. Then it was silence. That was what Uma felt her own life to have been – full of barks, howls, messages and now silence" (Desai, Fasting, Feasting 131).

Aruna, the tenacious younger sister of Uma, goes against everything traditional. The wedding is unalike: "This was to be an event so chic and untraditional – as had never been witnessed before in the town, at least by their relatives" (Desai, *Fasting, Feasting* 86). Aruna herself becomes a changed personality: "...

every trace of her provincial roots . . . obliterated and overlaid by the bright sheen of metropolis" (Desai, *Fasting, Feasting* 86). Ultimately, Aruna becomes a quarry of her own preferences with her westernized lifestyle, leading her to a point of no return. By flaking her own conformist role of a typical Indian wife, mother and daughter-in-law and faking an eccentric, contrived and unfeasible neo-colonial lifestyle, she remains 'aloof' in the socio-cultural milieu, not only losing the benefaction but also earning the scorn and the censure of the parents and relatives. Her phobic consciousness and the ensuing claustrophobic schizophrenia alter her into an android.

Anamika, Uma's cousin, is another demonstration of the tragic fiasco in marriage. Her parents' wish insinuates a deep-seated rampant evil prevalent in the traditional Indian society. Disregarding Anamika's pleasant demeanour and short entity, her parents 'drown' her in a 'good' family. The groom is "much older than Anamika, so grim-faced and conscious of his own superiority . . . insufferably proud and kept everyone at a distance...he barely seemed to notice Anamika . . . impervious to Anamika's beauty, grace and superiority" (Desai, *Fasting, Feasting* 69). Anamika's wrapping up is that she "...was simply an interloper, someone brought in because she would, by marrying him, enhance his superiority to other men. So they had to tolerate her" (Desai, *Fasting, Feasting* 10). At home, her dismal predicament is implausible – receiving regular blows from her mother-in-law with her husband standing as a mute witness, endless cooking schedules to satisfy the insatiable hunger of all and sundry in the family, massaging the feet of her mother-in-law or tidying the heap of clothes, no outings except the occasional brief ones to the temple, that too, in the company of other women and unfortunate enough in not having sanctioned private company of her husband. In spite of all these, she managed to conceive but the unvarying beatings of her mother-in-law leads to miscarriage and irreversible disability. Even her self-immolation and the subsequent death do not perturb her parents who could just dismiss the episode by throwing the blame on fate –"that it was fate, God had willed it and it was Anamika's destiny."(151) Thus Anamika was relinquished at the altar of marriage.

Mira Masi is the only woman in the novel who feels emancipated. Her sparse needs a bland diet of uncooked food, austere lifestyle, compromise with family rituals – make her a courageous individual capable of coping with the unnatural and crooked world outside. She could blend judiciously the inner and outer worlds without relegating either to the background. She does not detach herself from the outside world: she, in fact, relishes gossiping and carries tales from one family to another. She could renounce her material comforts and ignore its snares. As such, she could achieve inner freedom and comfort and remain a source of retreat for comfort for others.

In Part II of the novel, two more female characters materialize, Mrs.Pattons and Melaine, asphyxiated individuals by the modern impersonal and appealingly free western life style. Mrs.Pattons, an obsessive compulsive eater, stocks edibles in large measures. Her bulimic daughter, Melaine, is a 'loner' and she exhibits the gloomy lonely feeling of the affluent: " ...dressed in denim shorts and a faded pink T-shirt, holding a party-sized bag of salted peanuts...she sits in the gloom of the unlit staircase, munching the nuts with mulish obstinacy...she looks sullen rather than tearful. It is her habitual expression" (Desai, *Fasting, Feasting* 164). The overdose of freedom and the resultant repulsion transform the environment into a stifling and phlegmatic one.

Thus whereas the women of the East could not detach themselves free from the crunching shackles of the burdensome tradition, the western women feel humiliated by the excesses of their own society. As a matter of fact, both Uma and Melaine represent two women belonging to two entirely dissimilar cultures reacting to the superfluous social customs in their own styles. But they are meek victims bereft of will power to fight against the vicious might of the existing benchmarks.

History does not tell us that the discrimination of sexes subsisted in the days of Adam and Eve. "From being the very incarnation of power (Shakthi) and knowledge (Gnyan), women came to be held only as child-bearing machines and their horizons have been supposed to be confined only to their familial role" (Choubey 195).

Girls are not only less preferred but also more laden with more odd jobs. The disgrace suffered by Uma through failed marriages invalidates Simone De Beauvoir's account: "Feminists say that marriage is the destiny traditionally offered to women by society" (Beauvoir 445). Jana Matson Everett underscores the point that "in India, a woman is considered to be an embodiment of sacrifice, silent suffering, humility, faith and knoledge."(Everett, 76) Even the parents forget that Uma is not just a body but a soul as well. Mira-masi is the prototype of an Indian widow: "..quite alone, safe in her widow's white garments, visiting one place of pilgrimage after another like an obsessed tourist of the spirit" (Desai, *Fasting, Feasting* 165).

In India, Mama parades taciturn submission to Papa and follows all his whims and idiosyncrasy meekly and in Massachusetts, Mrs. Patton is identically servile while Melaine Patton is a victim of parental indifference.

Thus *Fasting, Feasting* is an arraignment against men who believe in holding their women in their vice like clutch, it is an avowal against women who are conceited of their servility and an impeachment against men who trade in marriages as means of mounting money and power. Thus the novel is multicultural in outlook with tirades against male-bigotry, lackadaisical attitude of females and also their disinclination.

Any society in a whirlpool of change breeds many negative feelings in the oppressed, women—alienation, anxiety, insecurity, fear etc. These women pine for adjustment and readjustment. But, while tussling with problems and refusing to accept the life of repression, the positive compromising attitude, they settle on living life in their own way. This awakening of the consciousness and not making any attempt to arrive at a straight forward solution are their potency in their ceaseless battle to trounce the stronghold of male ascendancy. This faculty to endure the domestic injustice and the institutionalized tyranny unseat the myths of feminity, motherhood and marriage. This is also what the Dravidian culture is all about. It is highly pertinent to recall the ire of Periyar E.V. Ramasamy at this juncture: "We recommend that women should stop delivering children altogether because conception stands in the way of women enjoying personal freedom" (45).

Works Cited

Beauvoir, Simone de. *The Second Sex*. Trans. H. M. Parshley. Hammondsworth: Penguin, 1983.

Bisaria, Sarojini and Dinesh Sharma. *Social Change*. New Delhi: NCERT, 1982.

Choubey, Asha. "Thorn in The Flesh: Male Chauvinism and Female Apathy in Anita Desai's Fasting, Feasting." *Indian English Literature* Vol. IV. New Delhi: Atlantic Publishers and Distributors, 2003.

Dasan, A.S. "The Heritage of Rootedness." *The Rains and the Roots: The Indian English Novel Then and Now*. Mysore: Sahdayata, 2006.

Desai, Anita. *Fasting, Feasting*. London: Chatto and Windus, 1999.

———. *Kakatiya Journal of English Studies*. 3.1. (1978).

Everett, Jana Mattson. *Women and Social Change in India*. New Delhi: Heritage, 1981.

Iyengar, K.R. Srinivasa. "Preface." *Indian Writing In English*. New Delhi: Sterling, 1984.

Kaufmann, Gerald. "Preface." *Fasting, Feasting*. London: Chatto and Windus, 1999.

Patil, Vimala. "Empowered by Fresh Attitudes." *The Tribune*. Chandigarh. 21 July 2002, Sunday Spectrum.

Ramasamy, E.V. *Periyar on Women's Rights*. Madras: Emerald, 1989.

Sorot, Balram S. "Transition, Transformation, Transmigration : Society in the Indian Novel in English." *Spectrum of Indian Writing in English*. Ed. K.A. Agarwal. Jaipur: Book Enclave, 2004.

21

The Indomitable Spirit of the Suffering Woman as Portrayed in Mulk Raj Anand's Short Fiction "Lajwanti"

Sangeeta Sharma

The pathetic story "Lajwanti" is written by the Sahitya Academi, the World Peace Council Prize, and the Padma Bhushan, award-winner Mulk Raj Anand. The 22 stories published in *Selected Short Stories of Mulk Raj Anand* are divided into five groups from the thematic point of view. This heart-rending story "Lajwanti" is included in the second group of five stories entitled 'The Tears at the Heart of Things'.

It revolves around the character of a young, recently-married girl Lajwanti who is hit by her cruel fate and circumstances. In this story, Anand has attempted to evoke pathos in the reader for the plight of men and women crushed by forces too strong for them to bear. Overtones of social criticism can also be noted.

Lajwanti, the central character, is shown to be fleeing from her in-laws' house situated in Hauz-Khas, Delhi, in the midst of May month *loo*, holding the cage of her *maina*. Her husband Balwant is away studying his B.A. at a college and still has one more year to return to his wife. Disgusted by the unwanted attentions of her elder brother-in-law, Jaswant, she decides to flee and thus starts afoot to Pataudi, Gurgaon, her parents' house. The story is narrated in the third-person narration by the author. The girl works on the same family land where Jaswant works. Jaswant, on the ploy of goading her to work, keeps attempting to draw her attention towards him. She has, till now, resisted the advances of Jaswant but while trudging on foot towards Gurgaon, she gets the augury that Jaswant would be hot on her trail. At this premonition, she starts feeling guilty for not surrendering to Jaswant's carnal desire. On rethinking, she feels that had she given herself up to Jaswant, it would not have mattered much, considering her husband's absence, her father-in-law's benevolence and mother-in-law's intense desire to have her grandson. She could have just closed her eyes.

After giving Jaswant a hot chase, Lajwanti reaches a confectioner's shop where she had hoped to receive the support of the menfolk who would have saved her from the clutches of Jaswant. Unfortunately, Jaswant reaches there at the same instant and persuades her to accompany him back home. Meanwhile, the menfolk there just watch nonchalantly. When Lajwanti neither yields to Jaswant's barks nor to his false persuasion, he becomes physically violent. The plight of a solitary, helpless woman in an effort to protect her virtuosity is at the centre of the story.

At that time, like angels, Engineer Din Dayal and his wife arrive in their jeep and halt at some distance. Shrimati Dayal, seemingly a woman activist, rescues her. When she learns that this victim of violence has already walked ten miles from Delhi, she tells her husband that she will not leave the woman on the road to die of heatstroke but would take her along in the jeep to their residence. She gets Lajwanti released from the grip of Jaswant and takes her to her house. As they reach home, Shrimati Dayal provides some cool lime water to them and simple water for Lajwanti's maina. The duo try to settle the matter in the presence of Jaswant and ask for Lajwanti's desire. She makes it clear in no unequivocal terms that she wants to go to her father's house and never wants to set her foot on her in-laws' threshold. The Dayals see the girl board the bus to Pataudi, her father's place. When Lajwanti reaches her father's house, her frail father who is going out to bathe his buffalo, cannot believe his eyes. For an illiterate person like him, it is inauspicious for daughters to return to their father's home, uninvited. Despite the shock, he does not question her. herself is not very happy to cause trouble to her frail, old father by her sudden arrival. She is well-aware of the poor condition of his father who has survived all these years under the grinding pressures of life.

On his return, her father in a few words communicates to her that he will take her back to her in-laws' house lest people start calling ugly names for her. Lajwanti meekly obeys. In the very next scene, her father is shown to be asking forgiveness for his daughter from Lajwanti's father-in-law, Chaudhri Taj Singh, by placing his turban on his feet. Though the latter is polite, he takes long to forgive. Lajwanti, till that time, gets absorbed in a dialogue with her maina and with a fluttering heart prays for the father-in-law's approval to come fast before the arrival of her mother-in-law or Jaswant. But, at that point itself, the mother-in-law returns from the well carrying pitchers of water.

The woman starts casting aspersions on Lajwanti and paints her to be a woman of a loose character. Her father is able to understand her situation very well but as per the prevailing custom, he doesn't want to take her back. He just wants the in-laws to accept her back and for that he also allows Jaswant to hit and kick Lajwanti.

For Lajwanti, her humiliation is complete. The plight of the Indian uneducated, rural woman of the 1960s-70s is displayed in this heart-rending story where she cannot act in an autonomous manner. Crushing her feelings and self-dignity, she is forced to uphold the old customs and bear physical and mental torture. Left with no better option, Lajwanti, sitting on the ledge of the well, starts contemplating suicide by drowning herself in the well, where she has gone to fetch water. The maina is her only friend with whom she converses now and again in the story and the readers comprehend all her inner feelings through their conversation. Notwithstanding the inner conflict, she finally takes a slight tilt and drowns herself into the well. Still in two minds, she keeps herself afloat for a few moments but as she hears the mother-in-law calling her out, the little possibility of her coming back also wanes. She tweaks her nostrils and finally ducks within the water. But before she can lose her consciousness, she gets the feeling that she is being laid in the slush near the well. Her belly is pressed and water oozes out from her nostrils and mouth in spurts. She has, at last, with a tormented heart, accepted her destiny. She has survived the suicide attempt and she is condemned to live.

Her fleeing from her marital home to her parental home shows her indomitable spirit to fight against the odds of her life and to live. After the failure of her suicide attempt, she realizes that there are no escape routes for such women who, by the cultural norms of a feudalistic society have got only one role that of a married person in such a society. They are denied the 'personhood.' The chances of their individual growth are nil and the emotional, financial, legal and familial support system are inadequate. The role of a middle-class Indian woman still continues to be that of a dependent, she is subject to the vagaries of patriarchy and the mood-swings of her husband.

Even in the year 2011, the Indian woman is denied full autonomy as a person. Her subjectivity is shaped up by the feudal and capitalistic mores of a developing society. Although the story ends at a very ambiguous note, the message is very clear for an alert reader that women like Lajwanti have no honourable exits available to them and they have to accept this cruel system and operate within it. They have to find their own survival strategies in such a callous society. She is denied even a chance to drown herself into the well and gets rescued by men. Her own family disowns her and marital home looks down upon her. She is reduced to the status of a slave with no freedom and very vulnerable to the male gaze. Anand, through this short fiction, creates a masterpiece that holds up a mirror to the Indian society.

He, most artistically, exposes the hypocrisy of Indian marriage and joint family system.

Mulk Raj Anand, through his gritty realism, gives us an honest and no-frills picture of independent country. The setting is Delhi, the capital of the country, and the story reveals how women like Lajwanti have to suffer the cruelties of their social positions in a country slowly coming out of the euphoria and idealism that attended the birth of a nation. That mood is exhausted; so are the values of the countrymen. It is a bleak landscape of an emerging independent nation where the women are no longer treated as *devi* but as sex-objects, domestic slaves and dumb creatures with no voice and rights. Her only place is the marital home where she is supposed to suffer all her indignities and die because she cannot return to her parental home and society will not support her in any way.

By destabilising and deconstructing the notion of the happy married woman in a country where women are venerated, Mulk Raj Anand thoroughly critiques this system of patriarchy and in a subtle way censures this value system that denies full autonomy, legal rights and financial support for the female members. This is a bleak picture that has not changed in the last 65 years. Dowry deaths, female foeticide and infanticide, bride-burning, acid attacks, sexual harassment and molestation cases all confirm that the daughters of Lajwanti have become more vulnerable and insecure in the India of the twenty-first century.

22

Manju Kapur's *Difficult Daughters:* Mission for Mental Thirst and Physical Lust

Satendra Kumar

It is an accepted fact that the women writers have added a new dimension to Indian-English fiction with their exquisite perception of men and matters. Their fiction constitutes a major segment of the contemporary writing in English. It provides insights, a wealth of understanding, a reservoir of meanings and a basis of discussion. Through women writers' eyes we can see a different world, with their assistance we can seek to realize the potential of human achievement. They have dealt with the place and position of women in Indian society and their problems and plights from time to time. While doing so, they have analyzed the socio-cultural modes and values that have given Indian women their role and image along with their efforts to achieve a harmonious relationship with their surroundings. In due course, they aimed at portraying realistically Indian women's sense of frustration and their alienation. Time and again we see the Indian women as displaced, alienated figures, ground in the mill of convention, domestic injustice and institutionalized tyranny, the victims of their time, of their society, of their own romantic illusions. When the woman awakens, she awakens to the absurdity of life which follows the disintegration of familiar reality.[1]

Amritsar born Manju Kapur who also authored *A Married Woman (2002), Home (2006),* writer and Professor of English at Miranda House in Delhi University, insists that the world she creates in her novels is not because of any personal analysis of the world in front of her. All her novels deal with the state of middle class women in Indian society. While *Difficult Daughters* (1998) depicts against the backdrop of India's partition. Her first novel is the result of five years of research and writing. She, a celebrated author of the prize-winning novel, has written as a seductive story of love, set at a time of political and religious upheaval. It stems the intellectual experience of her academic life. "I can analyze only because I am a teacher", revealed in one of the interview.[2] Having started her writing career late her 40s-middle-age angst had something to do with it—she realizes she cannot afford to take forever on one book. She is happy as she is passing her moment between college, home and writing. "Writers are not stars. They are not public figures', she believes. In one of the interviews she unlocks: 'I get both inspired and depressed. I wish I could write like that. Writing is a muscle that needs to be exercised all the time."[3]

The present paper entitled "Manju Kapur's *Difficult Daughters:* Mission for Mental Thirst and Physical Lust"[4] is the creative endeavor to seek the seed of courageous woman who fails before lustful and voluptuous Professor. In the novel woven from the fabric of the separation era, Kapur narrates the story of Virmati, the trials and tribulations of that age, the bloody battle waged between her loyalties to her family and her love. The Indian flavour is brought across beautifully and subtly so as not to mar the language. It reaches out to the readers across the barriers of time and place merging a bygone era into contemporary life.

Virmati's tale is one of a vicious circle of longing, hate, hesitant, hopes and innocent aspirations. In love with a Professor Harish Chandra who is already married with a wife having two kids, hers is a saga of revolt against deep rooted family tradition, self doubt, resolution and acceptance. The relationship parallels India's struggle for freedom, and eventually with the Independence along with the partition of country, Virmati becomes the Professor's second wife resulting in her ostracism from family.

The story is partially based on the love story of Kapur's own mother, Virmati. Manju Kapur was so moved by the love story of her parents set in partition times that she has tried to reintroduce it bit by bit, before it evaporates from her memory. It is not only about difficult daughters but also about difficult mothers, about mothers who do not understand their daughters, about daughters who want to break out into new paths. It starts very well and is quite gripping at the beginning with a daughter going on a quest to understand her mother, after the mother has died.

The novel, published in 1988 just after Arundhati Roy's *The God of Small Things* and recipient of the Commonwealth Writers' prize for the best first book, Eurasia region, depicts women of the three generations, focusing on Virmati, the daughter of the second generation. Belonging to a deeply traditional Punjabi family, Virmati grows up with the conditioning that the duty of every girl is 'to get married' and a woman's *shaan* is in performing her duties in her home and not in doing a job. She is already engaged to Inderjeet, a canal engineer. However, she secretly nurtures the desire of being independent and leading a life of her own. Defying the patriarchal notions that enforce a woman towards domesticity, she asserts her individuality and joins A. S. College 'the bastion of male learning'. It is here that she is caught in the whirlpool of misplaced passion towards the Oxford-returned and already married Professor Harish Chandra.

In spite of her illicit revolt against the family and firm stand against the Professor she succumbs to his implorations and gets involved in a useless love, doubtful marriage and unwed pregnancy. She is being used and the Professor enjoys the best of the two worlds. Even when he marries her reluctantly, she wilts under the implacable and hostile gaze of Ganga, her husband's first wife, and loses all sense of identity. She is given 'pariah's status and is forced to live in a cramped space. Professor's attitude towards her is patronizing and demeaning and all she does is 'adjust, compromise and adapt'.

Virmati's tale is seen through the eyes of her daughter Ida, going on a quest to understand her mother (Virmati) after her funeral who used to be a "...a silent, brisk, and bad-tempered" (2) mother. She decides that she "...must go to our birthplace, hers and mine, overrun with aunts and uncles still living in the ancestral home." The opening statement of the novel made by Ida, "The one thing I had wanted not to be like my mother" gives a jolt to the reader. It is possible to trace the feminism implicit in Ida's edginess towards her mother's weakness. Virmati's unwed pregnancy, its heartless termination, disregard for filial duties and the way she usurps Ganga's rights is unpalatable to Ida. Though Ida does not have the heart to reject Virmati as her mother but head rejects her as a woman after having an insight into her mother's past. Apparently educated and childless Ida leads to free life than her mother's external terms and succeeds in breaking out of an unsuccessful marriage and staying single. Yet inside her she feels some of the same anxieties as had plagued her mother. "I feel my existence as a single woman reverberate desolately", says Ida who has achieved more than her mother and much more than her grandmother but still she feels alienated from everything around her.

The story moves like pendulum to and fro sometime in Lahore and at the other times in Amritsar and in between L.G. Road. Suraj Praksh and Kasturi Devi had eleven children "Breeding like cats and dogs. Harvest time again" (12). The eldest daughter is Virmati, the chief protagonist around whom the whole story is webbed and framed. She has been engaged early with one engineer but Virmati does not want to marry, rather she lingeres on the marriage by dint of death in the family of her future husband as well as in her own family. "*Hai re!* What is the need to do a job? A woman's *shaan* is in her home. Now you have studied and worked enough."(13). "Studied means developing the mind for the benefit of the family", reveals Kasturi.

Shakuntala's visit to Dalhousie plants the seeds of aspiration in Virmati. It is solely by the word of Shakuntala pehnji that she gets a boost up, "Times are changing and women are moving out of the home, so why not you?" Why not, indeed, thinks Virmati, looking, at her almost breathless with admiration and love (16). She starts thinking, "It was useless looking for answers inside the home. One had to look outside. To education, freedom and the bight lights of Lahore colleges" (15)'. Her determination shows her assertive nature and the reader starts assuming that she will be successful in carving out a niche for herself. Shakuntala is M.Sc. in Chemistry and tastes the wine of freedom while Virmati has drunk only creamy milk in winter. Once she finishes VIII, she is sent to Stratford College. Anyhow she passes her F.A. exams and makes her entry in A.S College, "the bastion of male learning". It is here that she comes in the clutch of Oxford returned Professor Harish Chandra who makes her the toy of his physical lust in the name of mental thirst.

A new chapter openes in the life of Virmati that she has to develop illicit physical relationship with him only in pursuit of her studies consumed by the desire of standing on her own leg in the idle pursuit of quenching her mental thirst. A new arena is constructed of exchanging love letters which culminates in illegal and unwanted relationship. Again she is forced to marry by the family but she tries the suicide. As a result of that Indu, the second daughter of Kasturi, is married to Inderjeet (80).

Virmati shares with her lover that, "All I want is a change from my old life and chance to do something useful. I do not mean ever to marry" (101). As a result of that she is sent to RBSL College Lahore for further studies where she is anchored by her room-mates Swarnalata: "It is because of my father that I am here. My mother wanted me to marry" (107). At this junction Syed Husain, friend of the Professor, again paves the way for their romance in his guest house. "She could feel the pressure of the Professor' thigh against her own. At such moments the meaning of her life seemed perfectly plain. She just had to follow that memory upwards, to feel him thrusting inside her strong and large, as she moaned and arched with pleasure" (133). Many times Swarna advises her, "Men do take advantage of women" but she is too trapped to come back (138). The result is that she becomes pregnant and this is another crucial stage in her life that she has to bear and finally she has no option but abortion. After passing the exam she gets an opportunity to administrate a school where she performes her duty well. But see the stroke of fate the Professor does not leaves her there and sucks her body like a mango and as a result of that she is terminated from her service.

Now Virmati plans to go to Shantiniketan and while on the way there she halts at Delhi in the house of a poet, a friend of the Professor where after much hiccups her marriage with the Professor is launched and they got the licence to move freely. "As Virmati rubbed her eyes, watering from the smoke, she knew rather than felt that the burden of the past five years had lifted" (186).

Virmati comes to the house of the Professor where she has to reside just like a prisoner with Ganga, his first wife with two children and she thinks, "I should not have married him but it is too late" (195). Like Lady Macbeth she has murdered sleep and is the only one awake (149). She feels that "A woman's happiness lies in giving her husband happiness" (210). After marriage she visits her mother's house the first time where she gets the shock of her life: "It would have been better if you had drowned in the canal than live to disgrace us like this," says her mother. "You have destroyed our family, you *badmash*, you *randi*! You have blackened our face everywhere! For this I gave you birth". Virmati gets up and faces Kasturi. "I am going." Her heart is breaking but her voice is determined, "You will never see me again" (204). Meanwhile she gets a job in a nearby school. By Almighty's grace she also conceives but after three months there is a miscarriage. She thinks that "He (God) is punishing her for the first time" (227).

To remove the dullness of her deportment she is given an suggestion to do M.A. in Psychology and is sent to Lahore. It is a good idea for Ganga as she will get the full love of her lost husband. "Ganga rejoiced. He was sending her away. True, she was going to study...the house would be all hers. Just like it used to be. Poor Virmati. What woman would want to exchange a home for a classroom'? (228-89). With the passage of time Virmati again conceives and this time she gives birth to a girl who is given the name Ida, the daughter of third generation, which means "a new slate, and a blank beginning" (256). The novel ends with the words of Ida, "This book weaves a connection between my mother and me, each word a brick in a mansion I made with my head and my heart. Now live in it, Mama and leave me be. Do not haunt me any more" (259). She is shown as a radical modern woman of contemporary India. She is an issueless divorcee who succeeds in breaking out of an unsuccessful marriage and staying single, a phenomenon unheard of in her grandmother Kasturi's time. As she is not in good terms with her mother, after her death she delves into her mother's past in order to understand their relationship. She goes to Amritsar to their ancestral house to trace the history of her parents. Virmati never tells Ida to assert her identity and inheritance from her mother she, "Adjust, compromise and adapt" (236). Ida is tormented by the fact that she has never understood her mother, tries to create the space that her mother had carved for all her life as a way to make peace with her.

The story of Virmati is just like the swamp and marsh; the more efforts she makes, the more she goes down entrapped by her own sensuality as much as lured by the seductive promise of the Professor. Passion transforms her so much that she fails to see things in the light perspective. Trampling patriarchal norms, she defies societal expectations to assert her individuality and hopes to achieve self-fulfilment but what does she really get? Totally alienated from her own family she fails to create a space for herself for which she had been striving all along. What happens to Virmati is unfortunately the most representative destiny of the Indian woman even if she is highly educated. This is the irony of Manju Kapur's women.

There comes a transitional phase in their life and they tend to become different from a traditional woman, and want to break out into new paths. However, the chance is more of theoretical in nature, when it comes to offer boldness in reality. It is then she lacks courage and resumes to patriarchal hegemony.

We all know about women's emancipation today, but the day before yesterday things might have changed, but how much really? Even today, thousands of girls sit within the four walls of their houses and wonder why they don't have the right to choose their own lives, decide for themselves whether they want to be homemakers or more. Marriage is still the reason for their birth. When once asked if this examination of women's histories was a persistent theme, Kapur replied:

> One of the main occupations in all my books is how women manage to negotiate both the private and public spaces in their lives -what sacrifices do they have to make in order to keep the home fires burning-and at what cost to their personal lives do they find some kind of fulfillment outside the home. They have to do so many things, they have to play so many roles and there is a lot of stuff to say about women and it is also what I know. [5 & 6]

By her undying passion and thirst she is able to have a niche and slot in the heart of the readers. In order to determine a new meaning in life Virmati is led to either a false existence or else to death and destruction. Both ways, it is painful and she is penalized. This sense of the essential absurdity of life, of wilful waste of human potential, comes through the reading of the novel. One realizes that equality and liberation are operative words which can't be reconciled with the existing reality even if wealth, beauty, education and opportunity are used as means of tipping the balance in favour of woman.

Notes and References

1. Quoted in *Manusmarati* (3/56). Manu, the earliest of law givers had stated: "Where women are honoured, there the gods are pleased but where they are not honoured, no sacred rites yield rewards." It is further explicated in the following Sanskrit shloka:

   "Doomed to be destroyed is that house whose women, for not getting proper regards and respect, curses it to be destroyed." *Manusmarati* translated by Buhler, *Rising of Women,* Dharma. (Quoted by P. Thomas). The story of Satyavan-Savitri and Anusuya cannot be underestimated while sharing the history of women.
2. One of the interviews published in the *Hindustan Times* dated 16 April 2006.
3. Ibid.
4. John Donne, Metaphysical bard of 16th Century, reveals: "All love outside marriage is not lust just as all love within marriage is not love."
5. The predicament of Indian woman in *Difficult Daughters* can be summed up in the following words of Vidyapati (Early15th Century (A.D.):

   Let no one be born,
   But if one must
   Let no one be a girl.
   if one must be a girl
   then may she never fall in love,
   If she must fall in love
   Free her from her family.
6. Betty Friedan in her book *The Feminine Mystique* declares: " woman can find fulfillment only in a creative work of her own and today their creativity has unleashed many a novel. Kapur is one of those women authors like Shashi Deshpande, Arundhati Roy, Githa Hariharan or Shobha De on whom the image of the suffering but stoic woman eventually breaking traditional boundaries has had a significant impact. Virmati is the girl caught in the flux of tradition and modernity, custom and fashion. The novel reveals a saga of Indian woman's innocent aspirations, her rebellion against the tradition-bound society, self-doubt, resolution and acceptance."

23

"She Had Been Alone: A Moment of Private Triumph": Alienation in Anita Desai's *Fire on the Mountain*

Sophy Pereppadan

Loneliness and aloneness are two contrastive human experiences whose result is the individual's distancing from the normal and conventional social conditions. While the first one is an undesired and unwelcome situation, the second is a choice and a decision of the individual concerned. The tenuous line which demarcates these two situations as different is very delicate. This is why there is all chance for a lonely person to get accustomed to the situation by slowly accepting it, and to transform it into an experience of aloneness which is desired and enjoyable.

Similarly, at any moment aloneness can slip into loneliness depending upon the attitude of the person and the pressured circumstances in which the person is placed. Thus loneliness which is considered to be a social evil can become a positive individual virtue in a congenial situation. Both these conditions are the outcomes of either defective or constructive social interactions. A person might resort to aloneness as a way to vindicate her/his social deformity. Those who fail to defend their predicament get enmeshed in extreme forms of loneliness.

Anita Desai's novel *Fire on the Mountain* presents two major figures, both of whom prove themselves to be social misfits and hence are ostracized from the social mainstream. The novel unravels the tension in the characters' inability to become reconciled to reality. They manifest their adjustment problems variously: Nanda Kaul, the protagonist of the novel who lives in a make-belief world of her own fantasy, and Raka, her great granddaughter who escapes into the freedom of nature only to break away from the human world of entanglements.

Published in 1977—a time sufficiently distanced from India's freedom struggle and a period quite exact to evaluate India after gaining freedom—the novel *Fire on the Mountain* has very clear agendas to achieve, the most important among these being the focus on the chaos created by the Western dominance, even in the psyche of the Indians. Here Desai poignantly presents the real picture of the families of Indian postcolonial society. She presents the cultural and social changes that India had sustained under the influence of the foreigners. There is a radical change in the relationships between family members. Generally speaking, close family ties and love relationships have disappeared from society. We find Nanda at Carignano after completing her full course of the responsibilities towards her family. She wants to live in an isolated place for the remaining part of her life, after completing a long and busy time as the wife of a Vice Chancellor. After such a hectic life it is understandable that she needs some peace and rest. After the death of her husband, when she becomes free to have a peaceful life, she is simultaneously deserted by her sons and daughters. It is here that we find the first fissure in the family ties.

The novel sustains the tension within the novel by highlighting the contradictions in the nature of its characters. Once in an interview Desai claimed:

> I am interested in characters who are not average but have retreated, or been driven into despair and so turned against or made to stand against the general current. It is easy to flow with the current, it makes no demands; it costs no efforts. But those who cannot follow it, whose heart cries out 'the great no,' who fight the current and

> struggle against it, they know what their demands are and what it costs to meet them.
>
> (qtd. in Bande 19)

As estrangement from society becomes the best qualification to be a character in her novel, all female characters are social aliens in this novel. Thus the negative effects of the post independent and postcolonial India led the most vulnerable sectors of Indian society to wreck and ruin. As a result, woman who was once protected and taken care of in the families, is now carefully isolated from these familial comforts: she is an alien in her father's home (Raka), she is treated like a servant and stranger in her husband's home (Tara), and for her children she is a burden to be disposed with (Nanda Kaul); and finally in society she is no more a goddess than an object for pleasure (Ila Das). The reader is placed at a very precarious decision-making role regarding the mindset of these characters. The broader questions this study attempts to address are: Is their alienation real or contrived? Were they aliens or escapists? What is the role of society in general in their peculiar social positioning? Were they all lonely or alone? In an attempt to find answer to these questions, this study focuses on two major characters: Nanda Kaul and Raka.

The most distracted and confused character of the *Fire on the Mountain* is of course Nanda Kaul who after a long life of servitude to family, finally found solitude in her Himalayan home called Carignano. Hers has been an existence choked with activities—the multiple responsibilities of running a household, looking after her children, and maintaining the social status of her Vice-Chancellor husband. She is stifled with this crowded 'full house' where she has to be "at the hub of a small but intense and busy world" (*FOM* 29). The experience of her ennui and the tediousness of her existence at this place are qualified in her memory, as a place where everything is cluttered with "too many" and "so many":

> There had been *too many* trees in the garden . . . full of *too many* marauding parrots and squirrels and children . . . . There had been *too many* servants in the long row of whitewashed huts behind the kitchen . . . . There had been *too many* guests coming and going . . . . *Too many* trays of tea would have to be made and carried to her husband's study . . . . *Too many* meals, *too many* dishes on the table, *too much* to wash up after . . . . They had had *so many* children, they had gone to *so many* different schools and colleges at different times of the day, and had *so many* tutors . . . .
>
> (*FOM* 29-30; emphasis added)

More than in reality, it is in the mind of Nanda that these 'too many's' and 'so many's' creates a sort of pandemonium. Such vexation itself is sufficient to justify Nanda's desire to escape from all these exasperations into a lonely place.

Nanda Kaul's departure from the human world to Carignano is a symbol of the intense desire of an individual to withdraw to a deserted place, only to keep a distance between person and society. Out of her terrific sense of ennui she muses: "Have I not done enough and had enough? I want no more. I want nothing. Can I not be left with nothing?" (*FOM* 17). 'Nothing' itself becomes a virtue to be desired for, and Nanda leaves all humbug of life and get away to these barren and lonely hills of Carignano: "All she wanted was to be alone, to have Carignano to herself, in this period of her life when stillness and calm were all that she wished to entertain" (*FOM* 17). Finally, she finds and creates a 'space' which suits the dreams of an isolated woman. She can enjoy great relief for a brief spell of time as it is her own 'space' not like the earlier house which she calls "his house, never hers" (*FOM* 18). What she enjoys at Kasauli hills most is the barrenness and the starkness of the place: "she revelled in its barrenness, its emptiness" (*FOM* 31). Nanda's feelings and desires are disproportionate to the normal responses of a woman of her age and social status. She even wishes to disappear from the situation by metamorphosing into a pine tree and to stand among other pine trees: "To be a tree, no more and no less, was all she was prepared to undertake" (*FOM* 4). She wants to live in this place with the sound of the cicadas and with the pine trees because they are unsympathetic to react to her.

The only pastime—and to that matter the only digression—she has is *The Pillow Book of Sei Shonagon.* It has a particularly interesting passage with the title "When a Woman Lives Alone," which she finds as a description of her own mindscape as well:

> When a woman lives alone, her house should be extremely dilapidated, the mud wall should be falling to pieces, and if there is a pond, it should be overgrown with water plants. It is not essential that the garden be crowded with sage-brush, but weeds should be growing through the sand in patches, for this gives the place a poignantly desolate look.
>
> I greatly dislike a woman's house when it is clear she has scurried about with a knowing look on her face, arranging everything just as it should be, and when the gate is kept tightly shut. (*FOM* 27)

The confusion and disorder narrated in this passage fits well with the inner chaos of Nanda. We tend to regard Nanda as a formidable old woman who has snaps all ties and discardes everyone due to her rebelliously detached attitude and her desire to live in complete isolation. She finds her solitude and calm being raped by the postman first, entering the lonely hills of Carignano. She tries to convey her irritation at this intrusion of the postman "with a cold and piercing stare from the height of the ridge onto his honest bull back" (*FOM* 3). However much Nanda Kaul gets irritated with and resists the arrival of the postman, he comes and detaches one letter from the bundle and hands it over to her. Reluctantly she accepts the letter and is determined to say, "'No' to whatever demand or request it contained. No, no, no" (*FOM* 12).

Thus the first unwelcome intrusion into the peaceful existence of Nanda happens in the form of a letter. This is a request sent by her daughter Asha, whom she remembers as the one who is the "least loved" or "the most exasperating of her daughters" (*FOM* 14). This letter could be taken as the confirmation of a series of 'crimes and punishments' endured by all women in families through generations and it rakes up a kaleidoscopic view of the series of incidents in Nanda's life. The episodes begin with her bitter life at her 'husband's home' while taking care of 'his' children and serving his 'out-of-the-way' dealings silently. All these traumatic experiences in her life affects Asha's daughter Tara badly, and she also becomes a failure in her life. She needs some time for relaxed recuperation, after the several mental breakdowns due to her husband's ill-treatment to her. Besides, Asha wants her daughter to accompany her husband to Geneva, so that she can get their problems solved. Tara's sickly child, Raka, remains an obstacle for all these arrangements. She has a bad attack of typhoid; she is convalescing and hence needs a lot of care. Asha has a notion that the company of Raka would help to wipe out the loneliness of her mother Nanda too. Besides, she has to help with the confinement of her another daughter, Vina. So the final decision is that Raka should be sent to her great grandmother Nanda in the Kasuali hills. Nanda struggles to suppress her anger and her disappointment at her granddaughter's helplessness to keep Raka.

Normally anybody would expect that the presence of Raka should naturally uplift Nanda, and should have incited her spirits, but we find a resisting woman, never ready to reconcile with her changed condition. Here is a woman who is fed up with the routine life, who "had suffered from the nimiety, the disorder, the fluctuating and unpredictable excess" of such a predicament (*FOM* 30). Generally speaking, there is only one field in which women find themselves trapped, which is the monotonous, routine, boring housework—which traps women in the dull walls of the house leaving them seemingly unproductive. Nanda has been all her life a slave of her husband's family, discharging all responsibilities silently, though she is turbulent inside. She wants to escape such distressing and tormenting existence not just physically, but in her memory also.

Nanda has been to practising stillness and composure for years for an hour every afternoon. Everyone in the house has known that it is Nanda's hour of rest and so she is not to be disturbed. There is a craving in her mind searching for solitude. At night, after the badminton and after the departure of the guests, Nanda would walk in the garden and watch from the darkness her husband returning after driving his mistress back home. Suppressing all her feelings of dejection in her heart, she appears like an agitated bird which is distracted and disturbed by cruel men. She wants to hide herself from all gazes and to relish her state of aloneness. Desai's comment about this peculiar condition of Nanda's is very interesting: "That was one time she had been alone: a moment of private triumph, cold and proud" (*FOM* 26). In her husband's house she is able to get such moments of aloneness only temporarily.

Nanda has the hope that in Kasuali she would be able to stretch those moments to infinity. But even here her isolation is imperfect, because she is constantly distracted by letters and telephone calls. After she has read her daughter's letter, she attendes a telephone call from her childhood friend, Ila Das. "First Raka and then Ila Das erupt in to the cold, proud stillness in which Nanda Kaul had planned to live throughout her life" (Chellappan 172).

Nanda resists the encroachment and occupation of Raka into her life and solitude with all might and bitterness. She is a hated and failed mother and wife. The very sense of her uselessness in life has forced her to flee from her normal surroundings. She is a 'wishless' person who has done with all elaborations and expansions of her life such as: "bags and letters, messages and demands, requests, promises and queries"—all hurdles to the life of a recluse (*FOM* 3). She believes that by closing off all crossroads to her life such as these, she would be able to mark her own territory off with a 'no entry' board. Once she even wished to be like a 'tree' among the crowd of pines, unidentified and anonymous. Gradually her withdrawal syndrome intensifies and she is now ready even to negate life itself: "She would be a charred tree trunk in the forest, a broken pillar of marble in the desert, a lizard on a stone wall. A tree trunk could not harbour irritation, nor a pillar annoyance. She would imitate death, like a lizard. No one would dare rouse her" (*FOM* 23). Her irritation reaches the level of death wish. She yearns to have a complete resignation from life itself, rather than getting involved with the past cares once again.

But the very thought of the coming of Raka breaks all doors of her memories, and she is left totally defenceless. Her aloneness gradually gives way to loneliness. The vacuum of her mind is now being populated with the glorious memories of the past and she adorns them with the extravaganza of imagination too. It is in order to save her from self-berating, that she quickly builds around her a citadel of self-glorifying virtues. She is full of qualms that her great granddaughter's arrival would "mean the opening of that old, troublesome ledger again" (*FOM* 30). She has resolved that she is not going to be disturbed by any intrusion whatever it may be. She knows that "[s]he had come to Carignano to be alone. Stubbornly alone" (*FOM* 80). With the violence and intrusion into this sanctuary of aloneness, she finds herself exposed and unguarded. She will have to now re-play all those past tones once again shouldering the responsibility of a child. The novel sympathetically comments: "She could no more picture a child—a new, additional child—in this perfected natural setting . . . (*FOM* 31). However, Raka fastens together the links that Nanda wanted to break off permanently, and once again the past lives with her in all its force and vigour in this barren mountain. Nanda is a person who values love above all; but she is incapable of expressing this love to others. She has valid reasons for this. Her husband's infidelity, his disregard for her and her children's callousness are severe blows on her. In reality, she is not the queen of her home, but just an unloved woman, mother of *his* children, a social symbol of *his* respectability; she is also the servant and slave who has to be always in silks, standing at the table head, waiting for *his* guests. She is tired of caring for others and she needs some rest. She wants to be discharged, because she has already discharged all duties expected of her as a mother and wife.

Nanda is neither proud of nor triumphant in her aloneness; but she is bitter about it. Towards the end of the novel, she realizes that the stories fabricated by her, regarding the glory and grace of her past, are mere 'tranquillizers' to keep herself normal. She oscillates between two contradictory forces: withdrawal and involvement, detachment and attachment—she wants to withdraw from the world in order to be able to get involved with oneself. These two opposite attitudes pull her towards two opposite directions, creating a rift in her own personality. She finally appears to be an old woman, caught in the web of "self-contradictions." This is why aloneness is impossible for her. She has all necessary tranquillity and calmness in her surroundings but she is turbulent within.

The mail carrier who comes with a letter from her daughter first disturbs Nanda's quiet. This letter is not a singular and individualized instance meddling up with her peace, but it carries with it a succession of connected memories. The letter is not a request to allow Asha to send her granddaughter to Carignano hills, but it is a decision, and for that matter a violation into the territory of Nanda's peace and quiet. All her life she has been exploited by her husband first, then by her children. She is always considered an object, which does not have its own preferences. All her empathy towards the hostile world that renounces her is permanently suspended, and she decides to lead a life of indifference and apathy, since she has nothing to give it, or to expect from it. She does not even feel the need of a society and its contacts. Raka has suffered severely from her father's brutality and from her mother's nervous break-down. Her father made many attempts to 'socialize' her, and her mother invited children to tea on her birthday. Both these have been very painful to Raka, who secretly ever tries to escape all such dreadful circumstances.

In fact, it is her family background which compells her to love solitude and secrecy. She is a sickly child and a terrible presence for her parents, who are continuously fighting between them. Besides, "[s]he had not been asked to Carignano. Yet here she was, fitted in quietly and unobtrusively as an uninvited mouse or cricket" (*FOM* 80). Raka is unconcerned about her own existence here. It is as if she interprets the responses of the elders as a dismissal and elimination of her from the human world. This is why she becomes well accommodated in the company of nature. The novel observes: "Solitude never disturbed her. She was the only child Nanda Kaul had ever known who preferred to stand apart and go off and to disappear to being loved, cared for and made the centre of attention. The children Nanda Kaul had known had wanted only to be such centres: Raka alone did not" (*FOM* 79-80).

The most significant paradox lies in the attitude of these two individuals living under the same roof. Nanda is surprised to see the child's heedlessness and she "wondered if she at all realized how solitary she was" (*FOM* 79). Here is a child who is so naturally alone, and is never disturbed by either the presence or the absence of the interfering world of elders. This has a strong contrast to Nanda's own condition: Nanda who is here to enjoy solitude and aloneness is constantly disturbed not by outside intrusion; but by her own self. This paradoxical position of these two characters gets accentuated with the perception that Nanda who is at Carignano to be alone, and just for that, is not able to enjoy it; while Raka who is here to be taken care of is let and left alone.

Raka prefers aloneness and is opposed to all discipline and order. Like her own great grandmother, she dislikes friendships and such social relationships. She needs only one thing, 'to be left alone;' and pursues her own secret life in the hills. Even though Raka's arrival fills Nanda Kaul with a little bit of irritation, she is stunned by Raka's sense of independence, her instinct to be herself, and her tendency towards being solitary, her desire to be obstinately alone. The child presents herself to be very independent, because she "saw herself to bed each night, as no other child [Nanda] knew had done, silently, and slept alone" (*FOM* 80). Raka's total rejection of everything around her seems to Nanda so natural and effortless, when it is compared to her own planned and willful rejection of the child. "In contrast to her great grandmother, who lives as a recluse in her house in the mountains, Raka makes the surroundings and the uninvited landscape her home. She explores it, discovers it, and in the end she destroys it by setting fire to it" (Dengel-Janic 123). Thus Nanda's expectation about a weak and helpless child is turned out by the seemingly independent and self-sufficient Raka. The novel itself contrasts these two characters by stating: "If Nanda Kaul was a recluse out of vengeance for a long life of duty and obligation, her great grand daughter was a recluse by nature, by instinct. She had not arrived at this condition by a long route of rejection and sacrifice she was born to it, simply" (*FOM* 48).

Nanda discovers that Raka has an independent selfhood which she herself could not accomplish yet. Hence she is attracted towards Raka: she is a child who has a natural instinct to maintain an attitude of careless disregard for company. Moreover, Raka tries to neglect the desire for love, care and concern. She never wants to be the centre of attention. Nanda Kaul, on the contrary, "[a]ll her life makes sacrifices to get attention and love and is ready to engage once again in a period of dedication when Raka comes" though she was unwilling once again to rake up the past (Bande 171).

Nanda makes a futile attempt to get the child interested in ordinary things and patterns of life. She invites Raka for a walk with her to the hills, secretly attempting to know her better. Raka, a surreptitious child by nature, is always alert, searching out opportunities to disappear from human habitations into the loneliness of nature. It is a very difficult endeavour for these contradictory moves to meet on the same purpose: "They had never walked together before and made an awkward pair, now bumping into each other and politely apologizing, then wandering so far apart that they no longer seemed to belong to each other. Both walked stiffly, held themselves very upright, not letting themselves go with a natural stride" (*FOM* 56). This is the only time the child is seen in the company of elders after she had reaches Kasuali hills. Whenever they walk together, both of them are moving in parallel lines and it seems impossible for them to cross each other's boundary. They are of the same nature and hence they do not interfere with each other's affairs. Nanda has been entrusted the duty of caring for the child, but her own reclusive nature does not permit her to cross into the line drawn by her great granddaughter.

Only once during the whole period of her stay there is Raka is fascinated by her great grandmother's stories. Nanda narrates imaginary stories about her own childhood days in order to hold the child's interest and to win her attention. Truly speaking, these imaginary stories enable Nanda herself to gain some kind of satisfaction that she has missed in her bygone days. She also wants to escape the emptiness, resulting from the lack of care and love she either expects from Raka, or fails to provide the child, even when they live under the same roof. Nanda is craving for recognition and affection all her life, and, according to Bande, she is rightly presented "not like a specifically care giver to Raka but a human seeker of affection" (Bande 95). Raka influences Nanda in her perfect alienation from human society and her own family. With jealous admiration to Raka, Nanda once exclaims in a fit of confusion: "Would she own it herself one day, Carignano?" (*FOM* 80). Moreover, she knows that only Raka can understand Carignano and she alone values that. It is the first time that Nanda Kaul happens to think of making a will. But even that single thought is distasteful to her. It means asking the lawyer over and she wishes no one to come there. But at the same time, "she wishes no one to go either – certainly not Raka" (*FOM* 80).

Thus, she finds herself slowly getting involved in Raka's world, and is overcome by a strange desire to hold on to the child. This gives a personal appeal to her fantastic stories, and she is gratified when Raka listens to her attentively. An objective analysis of the stories fabricated by Nanda gives us an impression that she determines to act against her initial decision, that is, 'to be alone', at Carignano. In one of her last utterances before death, the author observes that her fictitious stories had a tranquillizing' effect on her: "All those graces and glories with which she had tried to captivate Raka were only a fabrication: they helped her to sleep at night, they were tranquillizers, pills" (*FOM* 145). Nanda is gratifying her unfulfilled wishes by fantasizing about a glorious past.

The real tension arises when the great grandmother's reveries are unbearable to Raka, who wants to be alienated, only to make an adventurous journey to the hill (cf. *FOM* 94-95). Even though Raka is fascinated by the stories of Nanda in the beginning, gradually she decides never to enslave herself to the same. After a while, Raka cannot understand the intention of that new talkativeness of her great grandmother's, "who had preferred till lately, not to talk to her at all, nor had wanted to be talked to. Now she was unable to stop" (*FOM* 97). We find Raka ensnared in this profusion of memory unable to shy away from the traps spread by the old lady: "She would have to break out into freedom again. She could not bear to be confined to the old lady's fantasy world when the reality outside appealed so strongly" (*FOM* 100). She feels that the most significant thing is to give more importance to make acquaintance with the new place than to listen to those boring stories. She is invited by the call of nature in the form of the sounds of wind among the pine trees and cuckoos. Here we are brought face to face with the real emotions and agonies of Nanda, who eagerly desires to be in the company of a loving and caring person. In her article, "Immeasurable Emptiness" Usha Bande asserts this by describing the nature of Nanda Kaul:

"Maternal love and her basic nature weaken Nanda's self imposed detachment" (Bande 98).

Raka displays a very tough character, and Nanda is left helpless before this inflexible and headstrong child. Moreover, neither affection nor understanding grows between them. The child presents herself to be a very independent person, far away from the requirements of any sort of socialization or human company. She very cautiously resents any such intrusion of outside world into her 'ivory tower of privacy.' This sort of jealous aloneness characterizes her furtive afternoon expeditions, as the novelist herself observes: "Secrecy was to have been the essence of it, she relished it so – Raka had all jealous, guarded instincts of an explorer, a discoverer, she hated her great grand mother intently watching her ascent, clenching her hands with tension when the goats nearly knocked her feet or when she slipped on those loose pebbles" (*FOM* 61). The child is a true progeny of nature; she is confident and self-sufficient in this wild ambience and even holds her to be above "the eagles, higher than Kasauli and Sanawar and all the other hills" (*FOM* 61). She has searched out hundreds of escape routes for herself in these unwieldy hills, which her great grand -mother would never trace out. The child is in another sense attracted by the hill, as if that is her home. Even when she learns from Nanda that her own mother is once again sick, there is a strong magnetic pull from the part of the dry and unattractive hill, with a force to keep Raka as its own child.

The hill becomes appealing to the child for its ability to stand destruction and devastation. The forest fire and its power to devour the whole greenness in no time and to leave the entire area in debris, allures her "with the strength of a sea current—pulling, dragging" (*FOM* 90). The imagery of 'sea current' becomes so natural to her, because Raka had envisioned her period of stay at Carignano as a kind of shipwreck: "I am ship wrecked, Raka exulted, I am ship wrecked and alone. She clung to a rock

– my boat, alone in my boat on the sea, she sang" (*FOM* 61-62). The forest fire also gives her a similar excitement, as she would watch a firework. Raka is more attracted by such wreckage than the innocence of the "nurseries or bedrooms of her infancy. The novelist observes that "[t]he scene of devastation and failure somehow drew her, inspired her" (*FOM* 90). She even felt that this "was the best of places she'd lived in ever" (*FOM* 91). She presents Raka inside out in her following observation: "It was the ravaged, destroyed and barren spaces in Kasauli that drew her: the ravine where yellow snakes slept under grey rocks and agaves growing out of the dust and rubble, the skeletal pines that rattled in the wind, the wind-levelled hill-tops and the seared remains of safe, cosy, civilized world in which Raka had no part and to which she owed no attachment" (*FOM* 91). Raka's yearning for annihilation is very clear from these lines. Her desire 'to be alone' finds expression in her love for nothingness—an expression of nihilism. This is in some sense a 'death-wish,' which enjoys the devastation of the live world. She gratifies her craving for aloneness by annihilating everything existing. When she declares, "'Look, Nani, I have set the forest on fire. Look, Nani —the forest is on fire" (*FOM* 145), she finally achieves her purpose in her life—to exterminate everything outside her and embrace nothingness.

Works Cited

Bande, Usha. *The Novels of Anita Desai: A Study in Character and Conflict*. New Delhi: Prestige, 1988.

Chellappan, K. "Being and Becoming in Anita Desai's *Where Shall We Go This Summer?*" *Subjects Worthy of Fame: Essays on Commonwealth Literature: In Honour of H. H. Anniah Gowda*. Ed. Chellappan. 10-16. *CLC* 97: 172-174.

Dengel-Janic, Ellen. "Exile as a Gendered Space in Anita Desai's *Fire on the Mountain*." *Journal of Literature and Aesthetics* 4.1-2 (2004): 117-124.

Desai, Anita. *Fire on the Mountain*. New Delhi: Allied, 1977.

24

Woman Imaging Nation: Buchi Emecheta's *Destination Biafra*

Sujarani Mathew

> As women put it: 'So far we have been the crutches of the legs the developed world has been standing on. Time has come to strengthen our own legs. . . . They don't say women hold up half the sky for nothing.'
>
> —Fatma Alloo

Woman writing from modern Africa sets new paradigms for the self of African womanhood as distinct from earlier images of the mules of the world or romanticized pictures of the super woman. Writers of the new era like Ama Ata Aidoo, Buchi Emecheta and Bessie Head accentuate the racial and gender discrimination confronted by the African women in the contemporary world.

Emecheta's heroines present a wide-ranging spectrum from the untamed and free willed native woman to migrant diasporic citizens who form a new tribe. Her *Destination Biafra* uniquely set in the thick of the Civil War following independence of Nigeria, depicts a heroine who is a modern woman determined to play her own specific part in the formation of the nation. The work falling under the category of war novels that were published in the wake of the momentous experience in African consciousness expounds the neocolonial conditions and the experience of women in the war—the by-products of colonization of Africa by the British.

The heroine Debbie exemplifies the educated indigenous elite who has a vision of her own added to her innate African woman power and is capable of defending herself and even the nation against aggressive forces.

The novel castigates the corruption and nepotism rampant in African politics of the postcolonial times, with a plot built around Debbie, the daughter of a rich and corrupt father. The protagonist defies the conservative role of marriage and motherhood offered to the African woman and dons military trousers and machine gun to undertake a mission of reconciling the two warring forces into overcoming the feuds fanned by colonialism. She is the epitome of the modern woman whose mind bears the imprint of modern feminist thought, she having received the education due to her status thereby setting heself apart from the ordinary run of African heroines. Katherine Frank calls her "the most compelling example we have of the New Woman of Africa. She embodies a liberating potentiality, of a rich, active and fulfilling future for the African woman, and she embraces a future without men" (qtd. in Biswas 85). Debbie can be considered Emecheta's mouthpiece in her political convictions.

As a war novel by a woman writer, *Destination Biafra* records the experiences of the woman in the war, and the rising consciousness of the African woman in her lot. Therefore the title of the novel gains in significance: if Emecheta describes the journey of Debbie to the Eastern land of Biafra, a place where justice will reign supreme to all men and women. "An ideal place where righteousness would rule, where there would be no bribery, was to be created, and that place would be Biafra" (Emecheta 223). Debbie Ogedemgbe realizes that her fight as well as that of the Civil war was against corruption born of class and ethnic inequalities—a positive indicator of neo-colonialism. She defies her parents and throws off the comfort offered by their position in order to help the country regain its feet from oppressive corruption. In due course of it she has to fight with her father

Samuel Ogedemgbe and her English lover Alan Grey. She soon finds out that the great military leaders are not better-even Ạbosi—the 'symbol of Biafra' turns out to be a betrayer.

Debbie also finds herself coming up against identity crisis in the novel due to her privileged life as indigenous elite. Her ambiguous position as an African woman who has assimilated western values due to her education is reflected in Alan Grey's musings about her: "intelligent, nice to be with, but independent. She was too English for his liking. ...The way he saw it, people like Debbie were building themselves big identity problems." (Emecheta 36). This is later felt by Debbie herself when she tramps across the country in the company of her less fortunate sisters. When she finds that she could not share her early life experiences with them, "Debbie really felt lonely surrounded as she was by other women. Her education, the imported discussion of class, still stood in the way....These women would only accept her if they did not know her real background, so she had to keep silent about her store of past experiences" (Emecheta 202).

The multifaceted figure of oppression converging on gender race and class that connived to bring down the African nation as a colonized state and the woman as a doubly colonized figure finds expression in the novel. The nation and the men are portrayed as an emasculated set, whereas the women take up active roles traditionally reserved for the masculine gender. The emasculation of the culture also led to the Africans being extremely dependent on the ex-powers so that the nation becomes a site of neocolonisation after independence. The ex-colonies though independent technically were still dependent on the colonial powers and the new superpowers.

Neocolonialism also refers to the new elite, brought up by Western education who exploit their own people and thus act as indirect agents of their former masters. This state of affairs has led to class distinctions and subsequent troubles in the country. African political scene, immediately after colonization sank deep in corruption. Debbie, the heroine in the novel, is introduced initially as the 'dutiful daughter' of the corrupt politician Ogedembge, "I had no choice . . . I thought things have changed. But no, even though the crowd today came in their best clothes, I saw that three quarters of them had no proper shoes, while my father bought a car costing ten thousand pounds just to drive through that crowd" (Emecheta 39). But this money helps her acquire the Oxford education and her discriminating views on her father's greed. After the federal coup, which kills her father, she decides to join the Federal army itself in building up the nation. As part of her official agenda, she becomes a peace emissary between Momoh and Abosi, the two leaders of the warring factions. But war spreads like wildfire when the class problem turns to ethnic differences. Debbie the only one in the novel with a clear vision amid a nation rife with ethnic tensions is bemused: "[W]hat was her position in all this mess? She was neither Igbo, nor Yoruba nor was she a Hausa, but a Nigerian" (Emecheta 121).

Though feminization of culture is a negative corollary of colonization, the education they impart invests the Africa mind with new outlook and modernity. The educated colonized behave and talk like the Englishman, ultimately bringing on a threat to the colonizer which questions the basic founding principles of colonialism, by making the subjects of the inferior race "more English than the English". This results in the psychological dilemma in the colonized termed 'dislocation' whereby the colonized find themselves in an in-between space neither accepted as pure native nor acknowledged by the colonial masters as part of them. This ambivalence that also generates fear in the colonizers at this new subjectivity of the people they have dominated is seen in Alan Grey`s attitude to Debbie in *Destination Biafra*. Acquiring the much-coveted foreign education, Debbie is the African woman who has assimilated the Western ideas of feminine emancipation and equality of the sexes. Her sojourn at Oxford University causes a psychological dislocation in her:

> She wanted to do something more than child bearing and rearing and being a good passive wife to a man whose ego she must boost all her days, while making sure to submerge every impulse that made her a full human . . . Yes, she would join the army . . . she was going to help the Nigerian army not as a cook or nurse but as a true officer!
>
> (Emecheta 44)

The critic Stratton defends Emecheta on examining the dilemma of the African woman caught between the traditional and modern settings (Buchi 124). The girls of the younger generation symbolized in Debbie and Babs who take up army as their career represent modernity as against the traditional life represented by their mothers. They refuse to be tied down to the old mode of living and strike out to make a new life of their own which would help realize their individuality.

Debbie is the symbol of the new woman of Africa whose liberation colluded with that of "Mother Africa". A criticism raised about the process of national liberation from colonial powers is that the records were extremely male-dominated. The written history of most postcolonial countries has erased out the part played by women. The 'violent act of decolonisation' is mostly pictured as a male-centred act, and the contribution of countless females in these colonies has been casually overlooked. Carol Boyce Davies says in her work *Black Women, Writing and Identity*, "[N]ationalism thus far seems to exist primarily as a male activity with women left out or peripheralised...the feminine was deployed at the symbolic level as in 'Mother Africa' or 'Mother India'" (72). In spite of such sexual politics of the dominant male history the distinctly active cast of the women in the nationalistic struggle will be evident by examining the short story collection by Nwapa (*Wives at War*) and Achebe (*Girls at War*).

But in most cases women during the war were treated as nothing but sexual objects. In *Destination Biafra* both the patriarchal male and the imperial masters use Debbie as a sexy tool. Debbie in spite of being a well-educated and influential female does not escape being categorized exclusively as female. Abosi declines to lend her his ear when she brings him the peace message from Momoh: "What good could you have done, just you, little you?" that taunts her to question him, "Tell me, if I were a man...would you have dismissed my mission?" (Emecheta 227). In the male perception, the national subject is by definition male and Debbie remains inescapably female despite her attempt to lay claim to the status of national object (Stratton 124). The fact that Debbie is used both by the African male and the European power in the same manner makes her position as a doubly colonized citizen pitiably exposed. Veteran writer, Ama Ata Aidoo, says, "Ours have been a double quarrel, "Not only as Africans, but also as women. Colonized by the colonizer, then by our own men, with their new power . . . " (qtd. in Iyer 123).

Kate Millet's *Sexual Politics* is an important feminist text in that it lays open literature to feminist criticism, by proving that the written word is the "record of the collective consciousness of patriarchy" (Humm 33). She speaks of the role of women as sexual objects, used as means of pleasure—forcefully or otherwise. Andrea Dworkin's *History of Rape* also deals with this aspect of male-female relationship. Rape as a potent weapon of the dominant to establish and proclaim their power over the powerless is dealt with by Emecheta in this realistic rendering of the Civil War. This record by Emecheta breaks the conspiracy of silence that was bolstered even by his-story and discourse, which promoted the male interests.

Since Debbie chooses to enter the male terrain of army officership the other male soldiers make her excruciatingly aware of transgression into masculine bastions. She is gang raped by the officers of her own army who refuse to believe her credentials. In yet another episode an officer, Lawal Salihu, also decides to show her that she is "nothing but a woman, an ordinary woman" (Emecheta 167). Rape is the sexual weapon used by the soldiers to establish their victory over the rival power and also as a way of settling scores with women who try to be equal to men. Colonization that gave the women new ideals and reminded them of their fair share of privilege and duties also upset the patriarchal status quo of the African male/female frame of balance, which led to the atrocities against women during the Biafran war. Emecheta records:

> In the distant past in that part of Africa women were treated almost as equal to men, but with the arrival of colonialism their frail claim to equality had been taken away. Now, with the coming of the independence, young women like them were determined to play their part in the new nation; and this in turn was making the army boys more brutal to unlucky women caught in any helpless situation. (113)

Rape is considered the male privilege in war situations where 'men lose their self-control.' Biafran war is no exception and cases of assault on women are considered part and parcel of the story.

Debbie is only one woman, in the thousand who lose their honor and whose life is blackened by the atrocities of the colonial and male-authored war conditions. The rape of Debbie, the protagonist symbolizes the rape of the nation. The war is an "allegory if the imperishable rape of Africa and her continuing trauma and humiliation at the hands of the African rulers" (Stratton 113). This is echoed in the words of Lawal Salihu who taunts her relationship with the English man, "To the Bature you are just a whore, to be used and discarded, just as they are doing to our country" (Emecheta 120). The real condition of the Biafran war and the trauma undergone by the women is given in minute and horrifying details by Emecheta in the novel. "War becomes a theatre not for male heroics, but for female endurance" (Driesen 7).

Being the progressive daughter of Africa, Debbie is able to reason out her life on her own. Though initially she had rejected marriage since she considered it a matter of 'breeding', her experiences during the journey to Biafra reawakens in her the basic quality of African womanhood: hiding in the bushes along with the other women to escape from the Federal soldiers; foraging for food to feed the children with them; the poignant event of the orphan baby 'Biafra' whom they had adopted dying, were incidents that invoke in her the value of motherhood. Her decision to bring up some children orphaned in the war, as a single mother, is a means of serving Africa as part of the womanist nature in her.

The bloody civil war comes to an end, opening the eyes of the people to the reality of colonialism. The capacity of the colonizers for exploitation and manipulation of the native land is clearly depicted in this historical novel. Alan Grey arranges mercenaries from Britain to help Momoh in his attack of Biafra. Later he comes to the aid of the Biafrans, to show the world-conscience that they are against the war and stand for peace. As Abosi says: "Alan Grey... he is England in this war. He arranges mercenaries and arms to be sent to Momoh, then comes to Red Cross our people. He wants to fatten us up for the slaughter. . . . Some people have not conscience. This war is Britain's greatest shame" (Emecheta 217).

In giving her vituperative denouncements of the English exploitation, Emecheta does not lose sight of the negative aspects of her own country. If the English is able to manipulate them, it is mostly because of the corruption built into their system. Neo-colonialism following colonisation sounded the death knell of peaceful existence of the African tribes, pushing the nation into civil war. Thus Africa was degraded in the hands of the colonialists like Grey and later by the neocolonial powers such as Abosi who finally abandons his army and makes his escape. Debbie tells Alan Grey in the end, "I see now that Abosi and his like are still colonised. They need to be decolonised. I am not like him, a black white man; I am a woman and a woman of Africa. I am a daughter of Africa, and if she is in shame, I shall stay and mourn her in her shame" (Emecheta 245). Her rejection of her colonial male oppressor in strident terms forms the anti-colonial feminist statement in the novel. "No, I am not ready yet to become the wife of an exploiter of my nation. . . . I didn't mind you being my male concubine, but Africa will never again stoop to being your wife; to meet you on an equal basis, yes, but never again to be your slave" (Emecheta 245).

Debbie's defiance of the colonial oppressor completes the process of her emergence as a new woman, who carves out a niche for herself in the man's world. Debbie is the true feminist who flouts the conventions and patriarchal prejudices and brings out the androgynous character underlying every woman. She embodies the rebellious reawakening of the 'superwoman' of Africa. A striking transformation is to be seen even in Debbie in the course of the plot. Being close to the major historical moments taking place in the country, Debbie comes across as an extension of the nationalistic image: the women characters in *Destination Biafra*, crystallized in Debbie signify the changing flux of time in African history. Colonized by the English, Nigeria—the African nation loses its integrity as their cultural values were questioned and denigrated. Missionary zeal educating the native people brought on a new wave of acculturation and assimilation of ideas into the colonized land. Though Debbie is seen voicing the Western values of feminism vigorously, in the end, surprisingly she holds up the major tenet in African womanhood—that of mothering. The African woman may have lost sight of her ideals under the fog of novel and enchanting ideas, but finally she seeks her way into a rational reunion of both the values. Women, the traditional repositories of culture, function as founts of change in the new milieu. The return of the native to a hybridized national outlook introduces new paradigms and identity to the African continent.

Works Cited

Biswas, Chandrani. *Women and War*. New Delhi: Book Plus, 1998. Print.

Davies, Carole Boyce. *Black Women, Writing and Identity: Migrations of the Subject.* London and New York: Routledge, 1994. Print.

Drisen, Cynthia Vanden. "Doughty Slave Girls and Slavish—Career Girls: Representations of the West African Ibo Females in Selected Works of Buchi Emecheta and Ba." Web. 28 Apr. 2009.

Emecheta Buchi. *Destination Biafra.* London: Heinemann, 1989. Print.

Humm, Maggie. *Feminist Criticism: Women as Contemporary Critics.* Harvester Press, 1986. Print.

Iyer, Lisa H. "The Second Sex Three Times Oppressed: Cultural Colonisation and Coll(i)(u)sion in Buchi Emecheta's Women." *Writing a Nation: Self and Country in Postcolonial Imagination.* Ed. John C. Hawley. Critical Studies Ser. 7. Amsterdam: Rodopi, 1996. Print.

Stratton, Florence. *Contemporary African Literature and the Politics of Gender.* London and New York: Routledge, 1994. Print.

25

The Dilemmas of Human Relationships in the Novels of Shashi Deshpande

Taniya Chakraborty & Joydeep Banerjee

Throughout the fictional career of nearly three decades Shashi Deshpande has been dealing with the dilemmas of human relationships. In one of her novels she has shown that since the dawn of civilization human beings have been suffering from this dilemma. This is one of the major causes of human sufferings. She quotes from the *Rig Veda* in the epigraph of her novel *Small Remedies* where the psalm begins as:

> Father of the earth, protect us; Father of the sky, protect us; Father of the great and shining waters, protect us, —To which God shall we offer our worship?
>
> (Rig Veda, Mandala X, Song 121)

This prayer from the *Rig Veda* speaks of the eternal human dilemma which leaves an overwhelming effect on human psyche. People often puzzle how to act in certain circumstances which lead them to take wrong decisions. Be it a man or a woman, situation rules over both of them when he or she is overpowered by the demands of the society as well as of themselves and is bound to take wrong decisions in life. A man, being a member of patriarchy, though gets some advantages; a woman becomes the worst victim of the social pressure.

Shashi Deshpande tries to give an emancipation of the long-suppressed voice of a woman. Being a woman herself she is more competent to describe a woman's psyche, woman's predicament more convincingly than a male writer. She feels comfortable in writing about women and so, her characters "happen to be women". But, she provides her male characters an equal space along with her female characters.

The focal point of Deshpande's novels is women and their struggles for existence in the rigid Indian society. Her protagonists are educated women hailed from the middle- class backdrop. With the social and cultural change in post- independent India these women sometimes find themselves in a cul-de-sac. The consciousness of changed time and value on one hand, and the given role which society inflicts upon them on the other hand make their situation tormenting. Caught between these two aspects of the society they want to define their "selves", their place in society and their relationships with their surroundings. Their conflicts, their psychological and moral dilemmas, their predicaments—all these are the subjects of Shashi Deshpande. She is conscious about 'feminism', but, her idea of feminism is unique. Her concept is totally different from what we know about the western concept of feminism. She thinks that the Western thought of feminism is not applicable to the women of our country, especially to the women from the middle class society which constitute the largest part of Indian population. In a broader aspect, the word "feminism" somehow delivers the idea that it is "a Western concept, rejecting the family and home, hating men and waging a war against them." (Deshpande 1)

Shashi Deshpande emphasizes that feminism does not at all indulge in any of these actions – neither any of these actions is possible in India where women are supposed to be the home-maker. She even does not portray her male and female characters on the basis of master and servant relationship. In this matter her view is clear: "My idea of feminism is simple. It means that I see men and women as two halves of a whole. In every way, we have been created to complement each other, and together we can fulfil our roles in life. But the main thing is that we are both human" (Harish 28). She rather views "feminism" as an approach to make the world a better locale for both men and women where both can communicate with each other with a more cordial and mutually respectful approach. She opines: "... how can feminism be anti- men when it is really working for a better, a more meaningful and companionable relationship between men and women instead of the uneasy relationship between tyrant and oppressed?" (Deshpande 2)

Deshpande always gives emphasis on relationships. It is one of the very prominent themes of her novels. She conveys the fact that the fundamental and mutually dependent criteria of maintaining a relationship are communication and cooperation with each other. In every relation these two qualities are mandatory. If a person fails to communicate with another, he would not be able to co-operate. In all the novels by Deshpande people suffer because they fail to communicate with the other and a consequently each of them becomes a separate island.

Shashi Deshpande provides an open space where the activities of both man and woman be judged with equal measures. She tries to delve deep in human psychology to seek the cause of the dismal conditions that occur in the lives of human beings, both men and women. She inculcates the doctrine of Hindu mythology where booth man and woman have been treated with equal importance and legacy and it has been stated that the entire universe is created through the ultimate amalgamation of the divine "Purusha" and "Prakriti". But, in practical world, women are suppressed by some hackneyed ideologies and concepts of society and consciously or unconsciously try to fit themselves according to the convention.

A woman wants to be an ideal daughter when she is in custody of her parents; an ideal wife when she is married and after all, an ideal mother when she becomes a mother herself. The most interesting thing is that, she has never a choice of her own in any of these phases of her life. In every phase, she is taught to sacrifice for the benefit of others, to compromise with the situation and to tolerate almost all the ill-treatments showered upon her either by her relatives or by society. Sacrifice, compromise and tolerance—these are the three basic things an Indian woman is taught during her journey from girlhood to womanhood. But, the inevitable question which arises in our mind is, why this discrepancy between a boy-child and a girl child? Shashi Deshpande has tried to seek the answer.

The most tangible answer to this much debated and clichéd question is, the sense of insecurity which prevails upon the human mind. It is not that the girl-child is less beloved to her parents, but, in most cases, as it is rooted in Indian culture, a boy-child is preferred to a girl-child, because, in Indian concept, a girl is not supposed to take care of her parents after her marriage. On the other hand, parents rely on a boy for their future. Deshpande quotes from Upanishad in one of her novels to convey the fact that it is stated in Hindu mythology that a boy would save his parents from being doomed. It is not by a daughter, but, by a son that a generation continues. Deshpande quotes in her novel *The Dark Holds no Terrors:*

> Whatever wrong has been done by him, His son frees him from it all; Therefore he is called a son. By his Son a father stands firm in this world.
>
> (*Brhadaranyaka Upanishad* 1.5-1.7. 91)

So, it is the intrinsic Hindu belief that makes Indian parents to covet a boy-child. And the mothers are more biased than fathers with a boy. It is because she has a psychological conviction that she has to remain under the umbrage of her son in time of her husband's absence. In Indian society each woman is supposed to depend on a man for her living, both for money and for shelter. Therefore, the mother, consciously or unconsciously tries to appease her son by taking his side in all the needs. This activity of the boy's favor goes against the girl-child and consequently she becomes furious against her mother's selfishness. But, this kind of selfishness is rooted in human psyche; it is not an individual complex. Shashi Deshpande portrays this psychological conflict in almost all her novels. In all her novels, the mother-daughter relationship is antagonistic. The daughter finds her own mother hostile towards her, on the other hand, the mother feels threatened by her daughter's aggressive nature. This conflict is most prominent in *Dark Holds No Terrors* where the protagonist Sarita accuses her dead mother for her unsuccessful marriage with Manohar. She expresses her grievances against her: "If you hadn't fought me so bitterly, if you hadn't been so against him, perhaps I would not have married him" (144).

It is evident that Sarita marries Manohar in order to take revenge against her mother. Her mother, on the other hand, is angry with her decision of pursuing a career of a medical practitioner. Her mother says:

> Yes, but they're girls whose fathers have lots of money. You don't belong to that class. And don't forget medicine or no medicine, doctor or no doctor, you still have to get her married, spend money on her wedding. Can you do both? Make yourself a pauper, and will she look after you in your old age? ...Let her go for a B.Sc...you can get her married in two years and our responsibility will be over. (96)

This is the difference between a boy and a girl according to Indian society. A boy is always a big support, a broad shoulder, upon which his parents can rest their heads in times of need, but, a girl is always supposed to be the responsibility of a family. Mothers have always a sense of insecurity regarding girls, because, physically, conventionally and financially they are much weaker in comparison to boys. So, parents can't depend on their daughters in times of their needs. Besides, there is a huge generation gap between the mothers and the daughters.

Mothers try to present the world as they have experienced through her life, but, the daughter opposes the fact because, education has made her enlightened and she has her own aspirations of life. So, the gap is often unbridgeable. Father does not involve himself actively in this conflict and he remains an onlooker. Though he has sympathy for his daughter, he can't transgress the limits which society imposes on him as a father, as a husband and above all, as a member of patriarchy. In all her novels Shashi Deshpande has tried to show, how deeply men and women in society are cocooned in their respective roles. Sometimes, they struggle to emancipate themselves; yet, they can't cross the limits which are provided to them.

Another very controversial relation that Deshpande has brought forth recurrently is man-woman relationship within marriage. Deshpande opines that marriage is the most expected and desired fate of almost all Indian women. In Indian culture, it is said that women does not marry, but, their marriages are organized by their relatives. In all the novels by Deshpande, the protagonists marry the persons of their own choice with their full consents. All the protagonists consider marriage as an escape from the restrictions and obligations of their parental homes. It is for the supposed 'misdemeanours' of their mothers particularly that they leave their parental homes. They marry the person by their own choice, and often, the marriages take place against their parents' approvals. But, in each case, the marriage has to confront a tough situation and the wife has to return to her parental home which she had left a long-time back.

Deshpande emphasizes upon the interesting aspect of human psychology that every human being wants to be loved and cared by someone and this is true in case of both man and woman. So, when the daughter feels neglected and deprived of her mother's love, she seeks the love and dependence elsewhere, preferably in a man whom she finds dependable and caring. Her expectations rise high as she marries him, but, in course of time when she finds her husband demanding and the situation is against her favour, she gets threatened and tries to withdraw herself.

Though many romantic thoughts are related with marriage, the scene changes with the advancement of time when husband and wife become familiar with each other. In most cases, it appears as a mere ritual, or rather, a legal permission of society to live together. Deshpande has delivered the practical truth of married life through her characters. Jaya, in *That long Silence* thinks marriage means a claustrophobic situation where "Two bullocks yoked together…it is more comfortable for them to move in the same direction. To go in different directions would be painful" (11-12).

In another context Urmi finds marriage as a 'closed room' where two people are locked in and they 'can't get out'. For the parents, to marry a girl to a suitable groom means the completion of their responsibilities towards their daughter. If a marriage becomes unsuccessful, all the discredit goes to the daughter and no one accuses the groom, as it is supposed that the girl will try her best to continue the relation even at the cost of her self-respect. Mira, in *The Binding Vines* expresses the situation when her mother teaches her how to behave in her in-laws, house, through one of her poems:

> Don't tread paths barred to you obey, never utter a 'no'; submit
> and your life will be a paradise, she said and blessed me. (83)

The married daughter finds her life extremely exhausted and suffocating and tries to retreat. So, again she goes in search of the lost maidenhood and lost 'self' in her parental home. She suffers most when after marriage society tries to omit her "self" in her in-laws house. It is as if her entire personality has to be changed after marriage.

The fear of losing the 'self' makes a woman bound to return to her parental home in search of her identity. She withdraws herself from the given role of a wife and a mother for the time being and a perpetual brooding of her overall condition makes her able to confront the reality. She partly compromises with the situation and that too, for her children and her own self. Shashi

Deshpande conveys the fact that relations have utter importance in everyone's life. One can't discard his relations, if he does so, his own identity would be in crisis. One makes his social identity in respect of another person. Thus, how far a person can neglect the existence of others in his life? If, a person escapes each relation, he will be no where because there will be none to restore his identity. So, escape is not a solution of any problem, however severe it is; rather, one should face the situation courageously and should assert his 'self' among all these complex conditions.

Shashi Deshpande displays the fact that all human beings are comprised of both virtues and vices and if anybody is to be responsible of all the mishaps, then it is our rigid society and our culture. The problems Shashi Deshpande deals with are not 'new'. She brings forth the problems cast upon women since the dawn of civilization. Women are the worst sufferers as they are supposed to be weaker. The problem she has discussed in *A Matter of Time* where Gopal walks out of her family and he simultaneously leaves his innocent wife Sumi, who falls in distress but never appeals to her husband to come back. Deshpande traces a similar incident from the ancient Hindu mythology where Yajnavalkya informed Maittreyi, his wife, that he would take renunciation from his family and would take "sanyas". Deshpande quotes in the beginning of her novel:

> 'Maitreyi', said Yajnavalkya, 'verily I Am about to go forth from this State (of householder)'.
>
> (*Brhadaranyaka Upanishad* II. 4.1. 1)

Yajnavalkya wished to provide some property to her wife so that she could earn her livelihood from that property. Maitreyi was an enormously learned woman and she was the seeker after self-knowledge or Atman. She disagreed to take any property and instead, wanted to have "Atma-gnanam" or self-knowledge. Sumitra in *A Matter of Time* also does not take any help from her husband. Neither she persuades her husband, nor does she follow her husband. Rather, she takes a practical approach towards life and starts a new struggle to establish herself in the society and be a support for her three daughters. Here, Deshpande rewrites history. She takes the point of view of a liberal humanist.

Every human being is different, so is his point of view. Marriage is such a bond where two human beings should live side by side, hand in hand in every situation. If anyone doesn't want to be with the other, none should compel the other one. Sumitra is definitely hurt by her husband's sudden apathy regarding his responsibilities towards his family, but, her self-respect makes her strong. Everyone should have such respect for his own self, be it a man or a woman. Shashi Deshpande conveys the fact that women like Sumitra are not rare in Indian history. It is not that the Indian women became conscious about their 'selves' after the western propaganda of 'feminism'. The image of Indian woman not only devoted by Sita and Savitri, there are also women like Maitreyi, Gargi, Lopamudra who are revered for their knowledge and wisdom.

The most pathetic scenario of a married couple in Indian society is that even if both of the husband and the wife are suffering in a tottering marital bond, marriage has to continue to exist. A marriage is supposed to be an institution for mutual convenience. Moreover, children are one of the most important issues. Generally children become the bridge between the father and the mother. In *Small Remedies*, we find, though Som and Madhu became separated for some different reason, one of the causes of their reunion was their only son's premature death. The relation exists even in the hardest and cruelest of situations as, the human beings let the relations to exist. These relations are the most valuable umbrage in which everyone finds solace in times of utter distress.

Shashi Deshpande provides 'space' to every character of her novels. None is judged by his faults. She gives most emphasis on the situations because it is the situation that makes a person vulnerable enough to act in a particular time and in a particular moment. That is why, a sensitive artistic self of Manu (Manohar), in *Dark Holds No Terrors,* turns into a sadist overnight. The racial instinct of domination was obviously inherent in his psyche, but, the question by a journalist makes him immensely hurt. She asks: "How does it feel when your wife earns not only the butter but most of the bread as well?" (200). This question directly attacks Manohar's dormant ego. Had she not asked the question, the situation would not have been worst.

Manohar is also a victim of the social structure that has made the concept that women are always men's responsibilities and the man who is not capable of taking responsibilities of his family, is considered to be a eunuch by his fellow men. His grudge is not against his wife Sarita, but it is a grudge against his economic impotence. Sarita is a successful doctor, where as his career as a promising writer is already doomed. This is also an unconscious threat to his psyche. When he is not able to dominate his wife economically and socially, he unconsciously tries to dominate her physically. It is the only way through which he can show his power. Deshpande provides the 'space' for Manohar and treats his psychological disorder with a very sensitive mind. It is not that, always women suffer, men's sufferings are not discussed because a man cannot express them as he has a more prominent and dominant ego. This is a very unique nature of Deshpande that she never gets biased with any particular race.

After reading the novels by Deshpande a question may arise: What is the purpose of marriage, if there are so many problems in marital life? Deshpande has dealt with this question also. In her recent novel, *In the Country of Deceit* she herself has raised this question repeatedly. It is a very relevant question in Indian subcontinent where marriages happen after negotiations. In consequence, two people actually compromise with each other because once the marriage is done, there is no option.

Divorce is supposed to be a menace in Indian culture, so is the live-together concept. In the novel, Devayani falls in love with a married person. But, both of them realize after some time that "Love is not enough" (237). One cannot do whatever he wishes to do as many other relations exist simultaneously and he can't ignore his responsibilities towards them. What happens if Devayani continues her secret love-affair with Ashok, both of them being mature enough to take the decisions of their own lives? But, Devayani can't, because, she is bound to be loyal to her other relations. Deshpande tries to convey the fact that a person can be highly qualified, he may have higher degrees, but he cannot ignore the cultural heritage which he inherits unconsciously with his upbringing.

The traditionally Indian psyche of Devayani unconsciously finds herself guilty for the fact that being engaged in a relationship which society has made tabooed, she is committing a sin and her other relationships are suffering for it. Ashok and she could never continue with the clandestine affair because in that case she would have been considered as a mistress or "the other woman". Besides, she could not depend upon a person who is already preoccupied with his own responsibilities. He can ignore the duty of a devoted husband, but he is passionate about his daughter. He says: "'I'm sorry, Divya, I'm sorry. I can't lose my daughter, I can't let her lose me'" (254). Devayani also realizes that if she marries Ashok, then his daughter's life may change forever and Devayani might be hated till the end of her life by Ashok's wife because, it is for Devayani that she will lose her husband as well as her family.

In Indian culture both an unmarried woman and a divorced wife are considered as "pariah." The social status for both of them is the same. First one is castigated because she has failed to acquire a husband, and the later is failed to restore a husband, who is nothing but, a sheltering tree.

Shashi Deshpande's characters are taken from our day-to-day surroundings. Her characters seem very close to us because, in a camouflage she presents our own lives with our own dreams and sorrows, our own aspirations and disappointments to ourselves. Her protagonists may talk about Betty Friedan and Virginia Woolf, but, at the core of their hearts they are the traditional Indian women who try to reconcile with their predicament not for their own selves, but, for the benefit of their family as well as their children. Deshpande is a liberal humanist who wants to put her feminist ideas not to keep the woman race distinct from the entire humanity, but, to provide the women their due respect and recognition for the betterment of humanity. At the end of the discussion, we may humbly put her words which the author herself quoted from Simone de Beauvoir as her concept of "feminism": ". . . that fact that we are human, is much more important than our being men and women" (Gangadharan 254). The ultimate realization which her novels provide is the emergence of a new consciousness that life comprises of the spontaneous cooperation of both man and woman and without the participation of one the other as well as the life are incomplete. So, life should be both the fusion and fruition of two independent, aesthetically vibrant and radiant selves of a man and a woman.

Works Cited

Deshpande, Shashi. *The Binding Vine.* New Delhi: Penguin Books India Pvt. Ltd, 1993. Print.

_______. *The Dark Holds No Terrors.* New Delhi: Penguin Books India Pvt. Ltd, 1990. Print

_______. *In The Country of Deceit.* New Delhi: Penguin Books India Pvt. Ltd, 2008. Print.

_______. *A Matter of Time.* New Delhi: Penguin Books India Pvt. Ltd, 1996. Print.

_______. "No Man is an Island." *The Times of India* 23April 1992:1-3. Web. 26 June, 2008. *http://ch.8m.com/cgi-bin/framed/1220/island.htm*

_______. *That Long Silence.* New Delhi: Penguin Books India Pvt. Ltd, 1989. Print.

Gangadharan, Geetha. *Denying The Otherness.* New Delhi: Creative Books. Print.

Harish, Ranjana. "I See Men and Women as Two Halves of a Whole." An Interview with Shashi Deshpande." *Littcrit* 31.2 (Dec 2005): 23-32. Print.

26

From Homemakers to Emancipators: A Study of Shashi Deshpande's Women Characters

Trayee Sinha

> Woman must not accept; she must challenge. She must not be awed by that which has been built up around her; she must reverence that woman in her which struggles for expression.
>
> (Margaret Sanger)

The journey of a woman from the womb to the outer world is full of multiple layers of experience. Although woman herself is considered as a womb yet the story does not end here. The post-womb journey of a woman can create a history and this journey is able to change the mindset of a nation, a country—even the entire universe. But the question is, what is the necessity of changing the mindset of a nation or a country regarding the role of women? This question tries to focus on the topic of this article—that is, the changing role of women: the Flaming Spirit. How the role of women has been changing gradually and what role they play in changing the situation of a country, nation or a universe becomes a significant issue.

During the Vedic ages, recollecting history, the position of women was glorified enough so that we can remember it as the golden era. Apala, Ghosha, Vishwabara, Gargi and Maitreyi—these women enriched the educational, astronomical and astrological fields with their expertise. Not only were these fields enriched by the contributions of women but also women's expertise can be felt in almost every sphere of life. But history reverses the picture and the position of women gradually degraded. The status of women is always in a state of flux and that gives a researcher a chance to evaluate this changing role of women through the extensive literature survey. Beginning from the historic ages up to the post-modern era the position of women has gradually been changing and the nature of their work is also changing. The changing face of women in Indian fiction definitely explores the flaming spirit of those women.

Simone de Beauvoir, in her famous and revolutionary book, *The Second Sex,* has defined a woman as: "Woman? Very simple, say the fanciers of simple formulas: she is a womb, an ovary, she is a female- this word is sufficient to define her" (35).

To assess the changing face of women in Indian fiction we need to talk about a bit of their long journey. For the last three decades, the period in which Indian female writers have emerged in a large number as a potential voice, the critical response to every work of the 'woman novelists' have been centred, more or less round the theme of gender bias or gender distinction. The way the female writers explore the journey of a woman—from the problems to the possibilities, and empowerment of woman binds us to think over their changing roles. Analyzing the fictional women characters of contemporary female writers, it can amply be evident how their potentials have empowered them in such a manner that they can change the course of the entire world, beginning their journey from home.

The present paper aims to focus on the changing role of women as a flaming spirit—studies of women characters with empowerment to change the course of a family, society, nation, even the universe with the help of a fictional narrative. This paper tries to show the changing face of women in the present day society by analyzing one of the novels of Shashi Deshpande, *The Dark Holds No Terrors.* The summary of the novel is given below.

Sarita (usually known by the diminutive Saru) is the young protagonist of the novel. From her early childhood days she has been deprived of many things for being a girl. She had a brother named Dhruv. From the very beginning of the novel Saru is reminded of the misfortune of being a girl—a girl is a liability where as a boy is an asset. When she grows up gradually she is getting accustomed with the patriarchal norms of society, that is, a girl cannot go and play in the sun because her complexion will become dark. She must not touch anything 'pious' during the days when she is 'unclean'. She cannot pursue her career in terms of employment because a girl is supposed to take care of her complexion and beauty so that she can get a good husband. According to the traditional beliefs this should be the ultimate achievement of a girl.

In this setting Sarita grows up but there is always the sense of denial—she can never accept the conventional norms of being treated as a 'woman'—she breaks the boundary of the domestic sphere and manages to achieve a medical degree—she became a doctor—really a strong means of emancipation. She is empowered and established and her strong position in society creates a tension in her conjugal life—her husband whom she marries against her family becomes jealous and tortures her physically. Then she gave up her career. But through the journey of this novel it is to find out how she comes out of her husband's trap and re-establishes herself, her bold attempt works as a catalyst for everyone – it binds us to think it as the universalization of women. It also signifies how feminism's search for identity would bring a result that could even empower a universe.

The Dark Holds No Terrors is a psychological novel designed to portray and understand the essential nature of the terrific darkness that gets seated in the mind of the individual and blurs the perception. Darkness has been used in the novel both as a pervasive energy of the narrative which grows with it and a weakness of human mind which is overcome through self-discovery. This self discovery has widened its sphere in the form of emancipation which is once again a turning point both in Saritha's life as well as it is the fictional narrative of thousands of women like Saru (diminutive of Sarita). Emotions of anger, hatred, frustration, loveless ness etc. grow in and around this darkness and cause terror and despair to the victim, i.e. Saru. But at the end we discover that Saru re-discovers herself and becomes an embodiment of a universal, emancipated woman who is able to change the course of a family, nation, country, even the universe. At the end of the novel Saru discovers the heart of darkness and develops insight into the psychic realities of life. As a result, the darkness of mind disappears and she becomes the living symbol of thousands of women.

The novel presents an honest probing into a human condition. It begins in an atmosphere of despair and disappointment but ends on a strong note of hope. It portrays a life's journey from darkness to knowledge, from blockades to opening outs. The narrative have been woven into the heart of pain and agony, the terror of silence, the fear of isolation, the burden of guilt, the repetitive patterns of life, the aches of ignorance and the joy of discovery. It shows that emancipation is the last word. A woman's liberation is possible only when she is able to take part in the emancipation business—Saru's instance becomes the turning point. Readers, after reading Saru's narrative will be inspired to think how Saru's job gave her power to burn as a flaming spirit.

Saru, the central figure in the novel, is a hypersensitive character caught in the travails of a middle class life. She suffers in both her homes- her parental home having father, mother, brother and her marital home having husband, son and daughter. Friends, colleagues and strangers frequent both her homes and influence in their own ways and the different orbits of her relationship with individuals. The novels shows how Saru becomes a changed woman—from the mental pain and suffering in both her homes she manages to pursue her career and she gains financial freedom. But how this financial freedom becomes the issue of gender politics becomes one of the turning points in the novel.

In the Indian fiction the changing faces of women can be identified in several ways. A paradigmatic feminine self is constructed through the narration of a central domestic crisis. This self is a manifestation of desire- it is a desire for something more than mere material comforts. It is a desire for an imagined self and setting that allows escape from the mundane domestic routine of everyday life and from the usual alternative that a more public life (as working woman or as a socially committed public figure) would provide. It is a desire for a feminine/feminist self that will be a viable counter position to the gendered roles of daughter, mother and wife. It is also a desire for a place of feminine creativity where beauty, art and un fragmented universalisms can flourish unhampered by material realities and social relations.

The fictional narratives attempt to construct women who struggle to hold their shape outside of the vessels or containers provided by society. Hence, in a move that contradicts current feminist theory's close association of women of colour and the celebration of multiple subjectivities and fluid selfhood, the longed for ideal self in these narratives is a unified, solid entity which will not be splintered into fragments by the multiple demands made on these women. Women writers such as Anita Desai, Shashi Deshpande, and Nayantara Sahgal try to bring these self sufficient women into existence in their fiction, working with and against the resources available: a Romantic rhetoric and female role models constructed by religious, nationalist and feminist lore about "stree shakti". Ultimately the search for satisfying selfhood that these female protagonists undertake is frustratingly unspecific, invariably incomplete, and yet, always an un staunchable desire.

In *The Woman in Indian Fiction in English* Shanta Krishnaswamy documents the "one basic fact" that emerges from her study of women in the writing of six novelists:

> The woman, by occupying frequently the dominant or more significant role in the plot, proves to be a potent vehicle for an author who wishes to express himself forcefully and has the talent to do so. An author's interest in the woman leads to his involvement with the problems of human development within Indian society as he conceives them. Passive or assertive, traditional or modern, he reflects his own insecurity, isolation, fear, bewilderment and emotional vulnerability. Even when the author chooses to withdraw from Indian society and seeks escape abroad . . . the woman becomes a mirror image of the author's own predicament. (340-341)

Down through the ages most of the literary texts have cast women in sexually defined roles. A Woman's role was restricted only within the domain of household the outer world was an absolutely "no woman's land". The society did not permit women to take part in the activities which are purely "man's business". So there were certain works and roles assigned for men only. Women were not supposed to enter into that particular domain. We can remember what Tharu and Lalita said about the few aspects of womanhood: "Women are mothers, good submissive wives or bad dominating ones, seductresses, betrayers...the inspiration for male artists" (Tharu and Lalita 14). A woman's rôle as a good submissive wife or a mother was the ultimate requirement of the society. But if women were proved to be "unsuccessful" in fulfilling the demands and expectations of the society their life became miserable. Very few women had the language of protest. If they protest in self-defence they were labeled as the bad dominating women. Silence was the best policy for them.

Women can be seductresses, betrayers—it was the very familiar picture of a woman character portrayed in popular fiction. But for the last three-four decades the women novelists are trying to break this traditional concept. They have come forward to re-construct the identity of woman and in doing that they attempt to portray the changing face of women. Career orientation forms an integral part of the life of those women characters. They can balance both personal and professional life. So this is the turning point of the women characters in Indian fiction. The glorification of beauty is no more the only criteria for judging a woman. Re-thinking of one's own identity in terms of empowerment forms part and parcel of the recent trend of Indian English fiction.

The quest for the self is synonymous to what we call empowerment. When a woman is learned and worthy of doing a job, definitely she wants to prove herself. This is the journey of modern women from subjection to liberation—from ignorance to knowledge. They were made ignorant by the patriarchal society. But now the changing socio-cultural-economic set up has changed the status of women. They are no more the passive contributors to the society—now they have developed their decision-making capabilities

Saru is presented simultaneously as an individual and a female. Her journey from the female to an individual self who is empowered and is able to change the course of a family, country, nation—even a universe—this concept can be synonymous to engendering a nation or a universe. When even in the twenty-first century we have so many examples of bride burning, dowry, domestic violence, rape, molestation of women and it is surprising to find out that these social evils can also change the course of a family, nation, country but working as a negative indicator. So something, especially which gives woman a base to establish her definitely serves the purpose of a positive catalyst. Saru has hardly got any positive approach from her family, mainly by her mother—she imposed so many restrictions on her. Saru wanted to pursue her career and went to Bombay to study medicine in spite of her mother's opposition. Luckily for her, she was encouraged by her father. Her mother was not able to understand the importance of a girl's education. "But she is a girl … . And don't forget medicine or no medicine, doctor or no doctor, you still have to get her married, spend money on her wedding. Can you do both?" (144)

But it is Saru who manages to pursue her career as a doctor. She marries Manohar, against her mother's wishes because he is from a "lower caste." She is happy with him in the early years. At the time of their marriage Saru's study is not finished, she is still a student. The problem begins when the emancipated Saru starts earning more than Manohar and wants to move on to a better locality. As long as she is a student, Manu (diminutive for Manohar) has been the breadwinner. They have peace at house despite its filth and stench. But problems begin to slowly creep in the moment Saru is recognized as a doctor. Her economic independence makes Manu feel thoroughly insecure and this casts a shadow on their married life. Saru, young and dynamic, playing her role as a responsible doctor, is liked by all. She gets thrilled with the likings and as a result Manu feels himself neglected. She initially fails to see this change in him but later realizes that "... the esteem with which I was surrounded made me inches taller. But perhaps, the same things that made me inches taller made him inches shorter" (42).

In her new role as a career woman Saru is no longer happy in their shabby apartment and she prefers to move into something more decent and beautiful. So it is a step forward to the new women's dreams, dreams to fulfil by means of emancipation. But Manu could not take it with a broad mind. He becomes a sadist who brutally tortures his wife in order to get rid of the insult that she more established than him. His male ego could not accept her success because in comparison to her, he was underpaid and less successful. She cannot stand his brutal behaviour and also that she is prepared to sacrifice everything as long as he leaves her alone. But he disapproves of her idea of leaving the job. The study of post-colonial trend gives us the idea that the women in post colonial times started looking for jobs—and this is a way of one's emancipation. But on the other hand they were preparing themselves to get blows from their intimate ones in opposition to emancipation—the way Saru was dissuaded by her mother first and now by her husband.

When Saru is asked by Manu to leave her job then she thinks deeply. She finds that she has every reason to break away from her marriage of convenience, shorn of genuine love. She says to herself: "I have to orient myself; I have to be surer, more certain" (69).

Proper education and financial independence can definitely instil confidence in a woman. It is synonymous to an inner journey of discovery rather than a practical programme for social change. But very few women could manage to envision a different world, much less recognize the need for change in the situation. In Shobha De's *Socialite Evenings* Karuna is a model who is deserted by her husband. She has written and made ad films, done a script on Kalidasa's *Shakuntala*, and is currently working on a major television serial. She is looking forward to "the freedom to do what (she) wanted" (274). As a woman who is emancipated, established, she need not pine for the man who is unable to give her honour, love and value. So does Sarita. When she finds her identity is in danger she walks out of her husband's place. Karuna's satisfaction is expressed through the following words: ". . . I am earning as much as any man. I have a roof over my head. . . . I am at peace with myself. I am not answerable to anyone . . ." (276).

Karuna is not answerable to anyone because she can take her own responsibility. She earns her own money. So does Sarita. There are thousands of Saritas who really need to think about their lives in terms of empowerment. Otherwise the condition of the women of India (the focus of the essay is on Indian women in fiction) will never be changed.

Saru's self-orientation transforms her from a loving wife to an absolutely career minded woman. She establishes herself as a successful doctor and her profession satisfies her ego. Her predicament is contrary to the assertion of most feminist that financial independence brings security to woman. Saru begins to think of her mother's generation. Women like Saru's mother are nothing but puppets in the hands of their husbands because they were not strong enough to raise their voice and their only alternative is to keep silent. But we find Saru as the representative of the changing phase. So novelists like Shashi Deshpande cannot restrict Saru within the household. She helps her to cross the threshold and to taste the flavour of life according to her wishes—the "bitter pill" with a "sugar coating."

Saru's way of thinking is conditioned by the era she lives in. She is capable enough to earn her livelihood and support her family financially. Emancipation is something which enables all human beings to support themselves. When it becomes the question of a woman the issue gets more importance because it is very difficult for a woman to establish her position in a man-made hierarchy. Saru has initially been a lovable object and child-producing machine to Manu but later he becomes a cruel person and starts: "Monstrous onslaught on her person and personality. He attacked like an animal that night. I was sleeping and I woke up and there was this…this man hurting me. With his hands, his teeth, his whole body" (201).

Saru finds a kind of hegemony when she considers the works of men, women and children—men go to office, children go to school but women stay at home and wash, scrub, bear children, beaten by their husband in spite of managing everything properly—that becomes the destiny of thousands of women. To think about the women in the third world the word 'emancipation' adds extra value. When the fictional narratives represent woman as an emancipated being, especially a woman from the third world country (the novel *The Dark Holds No Terrors* is based in the Indian set up and India being a third world country) it is the great and bold job done by the novelist to present the changing face of her heroine—to begin a journey from the "home" to the "world" and this journey is possible only because Deshpande has made her women characters emancipated. She may have several barriers but finally she manages to overcome every difficulty by means of emancipation.

In a richly textured introduction to *Third World Women and the Politics of Feminism,* Chandra Mohanty stresses the need to move beyond the notion that "simply being a woman, or being poor or black or Latino, is sufficient ground to assume a politicized oppositional identity" (33). While she draws our attention to the fact that "not all feminist struggles can be understood within the framework of organized movements", she also notes that she does challenge the notion "I am, therefore I resist". So, apart from the organized movements, fictional narratives can also be an integral part as a means of resistance.

Our present study of Deshpande's novel shows how Saru, in spite of not being a part of organized movements, resists the patriarchal domination and paves the way of the liberation of the self by means of emancipation. She is oppressed by her husband repeatedly but that cannot extinguish her inflammable spirit. So it is seen that: "Women's oppression and inferior status combine in one to cause the most suffering to the victims, both qualitatively and quantitatively, although this suffering may often go unnoticed and unrecognized because of the sexist prejudices of both the oppressor and the victim" (Pandey 83-84).

Saru's suffering goes unnoticed even by her for a long time; she cannot recognize it for the sexist prejudices. Especially Indian women find it very difficult to narrate her own story because critics like Anees Jung have pointed out that not long ago a woman who spoke about herself was considered as a loose woman.

So when Deshpande focuses on Saru's fictional narrative, Saru may be considered as a loose woman because she makes her speak of her problems, but, very soon, through the linear progression of the narrative Deshpande focuses on the much more concrete part of Saru's character—her journey from subjection to liberation—she feels liberated when she is empowered—her journey compels the readers to think how she becomes the flaming spirit which is the embodiment of "stree shakti."

Down through the ages women have proved their potential in different ways. The quest for self has always been a very significant issue. Our present topic of discussion is to focus on the changing faces of Indian women through the fictional narratives. The Indian context under the discourse analysis of power structured relationships—how the power of man is imposed on woman and works as a tremendous means of domination. The idea that in masculinist culture woman is positioned as the object of man's subjectivity is one of the central, perhaps the most ubiquitous themes of feminist cultural criticism. This idea is evident in varied but compatible development in feminist writing from Simone de Beauvoir to Laura Mulvey.

The Indo-Anglian literature reveals a chain of women liking up with each other as the country is gradually approaching from tradition towards modernity. In such a transitional period women have been playing an important role as an agent of change. Indo-Anglian literature spans such a rich variety of themes- from the theme of a conventional woman to that of the new women, reflecting in the progress the changes that have been going on in society. Saru represents that changing woman. At the outset of the novel she was performing her role as a conventional woman but Deshpande, through a gradual, linear progression of her story, prompts Saru to change—she becomes a new woman with her new thoughts and ideas. But this new ideas could develop only because she has the potential—she can earn.

The empowerment of women through Indo-Anglian literature has undergone changes in keeping with the changing social image of women in India. Whether written by men or women, today it presents women, whose identity is absolutely different from that in the literature written during the earlier years because, for the empowered women implies changed society.

As Saru becomes a symbol of the empowered woman, Sonali becomes the representative of the same. She is portrayed by Nayantara Sahgal in her novel *Rich Like Us*. Sonali is an IAS officer. Although her marital life is not successful in that sense but she makes her career promising. The typical image of woman has been changing gradually. Indian fiction bears that significance. Not those women are portrayed as doctors, engineers, models and IAS officers in the current Indian fiction. In R.K Narayan's novel *The Guide* Rosie is a dancer. She has mastered the art of dancing and performs several stage shows—she is capable enough to earn her livelihood. As she is a dancer, Mohini is a singer in *Music for Mohini*. She climbs up the social scale with her innate qualities.

Our point of focus is Shashi Deshpande's heroine Sarita. But only one empowered Sarita cannot change the course of an entire society, nation or a universe. We need characters like Rosie, Karuna, Sonali to help thousands of women to come forward and think about their personal establishment by empowering themselves. In most of the societies the identity of a woman is always related to a man. Women need to break this androcentric structure of society. A woman is equally capable unlike a man.

Empowerment enables someone to develop a decision-making power. A woman need this more than a man because she has always been the "other" in the patriarchal societal structure. Her status is always secondary, she is destined to depend on someone else—whether "He" be the father, brother, husband or son, in other words, someone "male." Education brings emancipation and thousands of women like Saru to emancipate themselves by means of empowerment. When Saru happens to meet her two childhood friends, Smitha and Nalu, after a long time, she finds two of them in different situations. While Nalu is a spinster who teaches at a college, Smitha is a housewife. If Nalu moulds herself with a dignity and confidence, Smitha surrenders herself totally to her husband. Nalu has searched her own identity by means of empowerment. It is synonymous to the question of the self. At this juncture Anita Desai's concept about "the question of the self" is worthy to be mentioned: ". . . without this sense of dignity and sanctity of the self, existential awakening of the self remains vulnerable and the inner space can once again become contaminated" (13). Saru is focused upon in this paper as an empowered woman. Shashi Deshpande's other women characters like Jaya in *That Long Silence*, Indu in *Roots and Shadows*, Manjari in *Moving On*, Sumi in *A Matter of Time*, Urmi *in The Binding Vine*—all of them are empowered. If one could go through these characters they will find that Deshpande's women characters are strong enough to move on—from the point of subjugation to liberation. Their means of liberation is freedom—both mental and economic freedom.

So the above study of the changing face of women in Indian fiction focuses on some of the women characters in some fictional narratives portrayed by some women novelists. This study proves how the empowerment of women can change the course of a family, society, nation and the universe. There is a sea-change brought in the lives of women. The marginalization of women has not yet stopped but women have come forward to upgrade themselves. It is only possible though their attempt and the attempt of the novelists to bring women from the margin to the centre. Above all, a general awareness is needed among the people of the universe to engender the nation and the self.

Works Cited

Beauvoir, Simone de. *The Second Sex*. Translated and Edited by H. M. Parshley. London: Vintage Books, 2007. Print.

Chandra, Mohanty, "Cartographies of Struggle." *Third World Women and the Politics of Feminism*. Eds. Russo Mohany and Torres. Bloomington: Indiana University Press, 1991. 1-50. Print.

De, Shobha. *Socialite Evenings*. India: Penguin, 1989. Print.

Dalmia, Yasodhara. "An Interview with Anita Desai." *The Times of India*. 29 April 1979. 13. Print.

Deshpande, Shashi. *The Dark Holds No Terrors*. New Delhi: Penguin, 1990. Print.

Krishnaswamy, Shanta. *The Woman in Indian Fiction in English*. New Delhi: Ashis Publishers, 1984. Print.

Pandey, Rekha. *Women: From Subjection to Liberation*. Delhi: Mittal Publications, 1989. Print.

Susie Tharu and K. Lalita. *Women Writing in India: 600 B.C to the Early 20th Century*. New York: Feminist Press, 1991. Print.

Index